ST. MARY'S COLLEGE OF MARYLAND

W9-BWI-783

PUBLISHED ON THE FOUNDATION ESTABLISHED
IN MEMORY OF AMASA STONE MATHER OF THE
CLASS OF 1907 YALE COLLEGE

EDMUND BURKE

Romney's portrait, 1776. From the mezzotint by J. Jones, December 10, 1790. This copy is reproduced by permission of Timothy Dwight College, New Haven, Connecticut.

41064

Our Eminent Friend Edmund Burke

SIX ESSAYS

BY

Thomas W. Copeland

GREENWOOD PRESS, PUBLISHERS
WESTPORT, CONNECTICUT

Copyright 1949 by Yale University Press

Reprinted with the permission of Yale University Press

First Greenwood Reprinting 1970

Library of Congress Catalogue Card Number 76-104217

SBN 8371-3334-3

Printed in the United States of America

THE AMASA STONE MATHER MEMORIAL PUBLICATION FUND

The present volume is the twenty-fourth work published by the Yale University Press on the Amasa Stone Mather Memorial Publication Fund. This Foundation was established August 25, 1922, by a gift to Yale University from Samuel Mather, Esq., of Cleveland, Ohio, in pursuance of a pledge made in June, 1922, on the fifteenth anniversary of the graduation of his son, Amasa Stone Mather, who was born in Cleveland on August 20, 1884, and was graduated from Yale College in the Class of 1907. Subsequently, after traveling abroad, he returned to Cleveland, where he soon won a recognized position in the business life of the city and where he actively interested himself also in the work of many organizations devoted to the betterment of the community and to the welfare of the nation. His death from pneumonia on February 9, 1920, was undoubtedly hastened by his characteristic unwillingness ever to spare himself, even when ill, in the discharge of his duties or in his efforts to protect and further the interests committed to his care by his associates.

PREFACE

EACH of the essays in this volume concerns itself with some particular problem in Burke's biography; it is to be hoped that each will justify itself by the light it casts upon that problem. The group of essays taken collectively, however, tries to do slightly more than make random additions to our information. It attempts to focus attention upon a single central question: the question of why Burke is so inaccessible at the present time. This is a more complicated matter than one might at first suppose. I have attacked it in two different ways. In my first two essays, which are rather interrogative in character, my chief effort has been merely to suggest the complications and pose the enigma. How has Burke managed to elude our curiosity to the extent that he has? In the other four essays I have been more positive, if sometimes more laborious. I have chosen four representative mysteries, out of a good many Burke's career could offer, and striven to solve them. Perhaps these four essays will show by example what the first two show in other ways, namely, that Burke's life is very much more obscure to us than is generally thought. I am convinced that we must recognize the extent of our present ignorance before we can initiate the kind of thorough re-examination which Burke's career still needs.

My first essay, "Boswell's Portrait of Burke," is a considerably expanded version of a contribution made last year to *The Age of Johnson: Essays Presented to Chauncey Brewster Tinker*. The conditions of that volume made it impossible for me to treat the subject of Burke in the *Life of Johnson* there as fully as I can here, or to include the annotation which some readers may expect in this kind of a study. The present enlarged version I wish to dedicate anew to Professor Tinker. Any eighteenth-century studies of mine, past, present, or future, belong equally to him if they are worthy of his acceptance.

I should like to name and thank at least a few of those who have given me aid and criticism on individual essays, and who though never implicated in their deficiencies have contributed to them by interest and encouragement. Professors Frederick A. Pottle,

Frederick W. Hilles, James M. Osborn, René Wellek, Richard B. Sewall, and Charles H. Bennett of Yale, Professor Raymond W. Short of Hofstra College, and Mr. Robert A. Smith of New Haven are the chief of those I wish to name. I am also grateful for the very useful assistance, beyond the call of duty, which I have had from the staffs of the Yale University Library, the New York Public Library, the Pierpont Morgan Library, and the Library of Congress.

The works most frequently cited in my notes will be Burke's biographies. There are many of these, and some of them went through several successive editions varying widely from each other. As I shall be constantly quoting and comparing both the biographies and their differing editions, I have adopted the following short titles for those most often mentioned. These short titles will be used throughout the notes:

M'Cormick (1st ed.): Charles M'Cormick, *Memoirs of Edmund Burke* (1st ed. London, 1797)

M'Cormick (2d ed.): Charles M'Cormick, *Memoirs of Edmund Burke* (2d ed. London, 1798)

Bisset (1st ed.): Robert Bisset, *Life of Edmund Burke* (1st. ed. London, 1798)

Bisset (2d ed.): Robert Bisset, *Life of Edmund Burke* (2d ed. London, 1800). 2 vols.

Prior (1st ed.): James Prior, *Life of Edmund Burke* (1st ed. London, 1824)

Prior: James Prior, *Life of Edmund Burke* (2d ed. London, 1826). 2 vols. This is the indispensable edition of Prior's biography, much fuller than either the first edition or the revised fifth edition. When my citation is simply "Prior" this edition is meant.

Prior (5th ed.): James Prior, *Life of Edmund Burke* (5th ed. London, 1854)

Murray: Robert Murray, *Edmund Burke* (Oxford, 1931)

Magnus: Sir Philip Magnus, *Edmund Burke* (London, 1939)

There are a small number of other works which are used often enough perhaps to justify the use of arbitrary short titles:

Burke, *Works: The Works of Edmund Burke* (Boston, 1894). 12 vols.

Burke, *Correspondence: Correspondence of Edmund Burke*, ed. Charles William, Earl Fitzwilliam, and Sir Richard Bourke (London, 1844). 4 vols.

Life of Johnson: Boswell's Life of Johnson, ed. George Birkbeck Hill, rev. ed. L. F. Powell (Oxford, 1934). 4 vols. Where a reference to Volume V is made, this must at present refer to the earlier edition of this work (ed. George Birkbeck Hill [Oxford, 1887]). The pagination will not be changed when Mr. Powell brings out his own fifth volume.

Boswell Papers: Private Papers of James Boswell from Malahide Castle, in the Collection of Lt. Col. Ralph H. Isham, ed. Geoffrey Scott and Frederick Pottle (New York, 1928–34). 19 vols.

CONTENTS

ILLUSTRATIONS

INTRODUCTION

MANY readers of the *Life of Johnson* must have noticed a curious shyness of Boswell's in referring to Edmund Burke. In passages where we are almost certain from the context that Burke is being quoted or discussed, Boswell seems to take elaborate pains to avoid the use of his name. "An eminent friend of ours" takes part in the conversation, or Johnson gives his opinion of "an eminent publick character"; Boswell may ask discreetly, "Has not —— a great deal of wit?" or in a long report of conversation "E." may argue warmly for the value of a good speech in parliament.

Such passages need not confuse the reader, for Boswell's editors have long since added helpful footnotes explaining that "*Eminent* is the epithet Boswell generally applies to Burke," or "Burke almost certainly is here meant," or "Boswell commonly describes Burke as 'an eminent friend of ours.'" But although the explanations forestall any serious confusion, they do not extinguish a mild curiosity. Why was it necessary to disguise Burke in this manner? Johnson's other friends were not usually protected from identification (if that was Boswell's aim here); some of them thought their names were used a great deal too freely. Was there some special reason for Boswell's being so discreet in the case of Burke?

One scarcely asks the question, however, without discovering that there is a more important question relating to Boswell's treatment of Burke. We are accustomed to admiring the artistic skill with which Boswell drew the lesser figures who appear in the *Life of Johnson*. Almost every reader will remember Goldsmith in his bloom-colored coat, or Garrick mimicking Johnson, or Gibbon tapping the lid of his snuffbox, or some other sharp, vivid images of the men around Johnson. How many readers recall any such images relating to Edmund Burke? Burke is actually referred to in the *Life* as frequently as nearly any of Johnson's friends, and yet his portrait remains one of the dimmest Boswell ever drew. He is praised in extravagant terms by both

Boswell and Johnson, as "an extraordinary man," "the only man whose common conversation corresponds to the fame which he has in the world," "the first man everywhere." The praises only make more obvious the fact that we have no vivid picture of him. Most readers will not be able to recall a single detail of Burke's appearance, or a single specimen of his extraordinary conversational powers.

This would be worth noting if only as a comment on the *Life of Johnson*. Unfortunately for the reader interested in Burke, the same observation must be made about a much wider field. It is not only in the pages of Boswell that Burke has been left a dim, unillumined figure. In the whole area of research which has grown up around the Johnsonian circle he is almost equally obscure. In the last century and a half, but more particularly in the sixty-odd years since Birkbeck Hill's edition of the *Life of Johnson*, most of the prominent figures of the late eighteenth century have been very fully studied. Scholars outside this field may sometimes have wondered at the vast labors expended on Boswell, Horace Walpole, Fanny Burney, Mrs. Montagu, Mrs. Thrale, and many less significant figures. It might be imagined that in the general illumination of the period Burke would have had a large share of attention. Actually, Burke has been very little studied. There have been of course scattered works dealing with his career, or with particular aspects of it, but if the whole mass of them were put in the scale with, say, the works devoted to Boswell or Walpole, they would be ridiculously unimpressive in bulk; with three or four honorable exceptions they would be even more unimpressive in quality. At the end of a great period of eighteenth-century research the man whom Johnson called the "first man everywhere" has received less attention than at least a dozen of his contemporaries. There is not now a definitive biography of Burke; the edition of his works completed in 1827 has never been superseded, though it is hopelessly inadequate by modern standards; there is no edition of his letters which contains more than a fifth of those known to be extant; there is no full bibliography of his writings; there is only the lightest sprinkling of reliable monographs relating to him.

Perhaps many readers if they were asked to explain the neglect of Burke would give a very simple answer. The industrious scholarship which has done so much to illumine the late eighteenth century has been primarily a literary scholarship, and it has tended to pass over Burke because he is not essentially a literary man. He is a statesman, an orator, a political philosopher; it is the business of scholars in these other fields to deal with his career.

This answer would have a certain plausibility if one were not acquainted with the actual practices of literary scholars. But it is no use pretending at this date that these gentlemen carefully refrain from raiding the fields of their neighbors. Quite the contrary is the case. A mere glance at the literary shelves of a modern library will show us impressive studies of such figures as John Wilkes, David Hume, Edward Gibbon, Lord Chesterfield, Bishop Percy, Sir Joshua Reynolds, Joseph Ritson, not to mention Robert Dodsley, Edmund Curll, and many similar figures. A strict guardian of the boundary lines between scholarly fields would long since have grown frantic over the literary scholars' reckless disregard of limits.

As a matter of fact it is quite futile to attempt to draw a clear line between literary and all other research, and no such line has actually ever existed. The sensible critic only asks that literary scholars justify their choice of subjects by the rather vague test of "relevance." Does a particular figure, such a critic says, have a genuine interest for the literary public? If he has this interest, it is unimportant that he is not technically a literary figure. Boswell is primarily a biographer, Gibbon primarily a historian, but if the best judges and the public decide that Boswell and Gibbon have artistic powers which distinguish them from other writers in their fields, then there can hardly be a question that they should attract the attention of literary scholars.

But this is the very reason that it is so difficult to explain the degree to which Burke has been neglected. Burke is, of course, a "mixed author," whose claims are only partly literary. But the quality of his literary talent has been fully recognized. It may even have been overpraised. When John Morley wrote the volume on Burke in the English Men of Letters series in 1879, he of course attempted to give an estimate of Burke's position among classic English authors. It was framed as a cautious agreement with the dicta of two other critics. "We feel no emotion of revolt," said Morley, ". . . when Mackintosh speaks of Shakespeare and Burke in the same breath as being both of them above mere talent. And we do not dissent when Macaulay, after reading Burke's works over again, exclaims, 'How admirable! The greatest man since Milton.' "

Some modern readers would express astonishment to find Edmund Burke in such company. Actually Morley was not attempting to astonish. He was stating cautiously, as his manner was, the received opinion of his day. In the first two thirds of the nineteenth century the leading critics had reached a virtual unanimity as to the literary position of Burke. Hazlitt had said, "If there are greater prose writers than Burke, they either lie out of my course of study, or are beyond my sphere of comprehension." De Quincey had said, "All hail to Edmund Burke, the supreme writer of his century, the man of largest and finest understanding." Coleridge had said, "I cannot conceive of a time or a state of things in which the writings of Burke will not have the highest value." Arnold, not very long before the time of Morley's biography, called Burke "our greatest English prose-writer." Leslie Stephen said, "Considered simply as a master of English prose, Burke has not, in my judgment, been surpassed in any period of our literature." Hazlitt, De Quincey, Coleridge, Arnold, and Stephen were surely the leading literary critics of their century, and with the exception of Coleridge each made it perfectly clear that his judgment of Burke was on a literary standard.

As one might guess by this time, there are more specific causes for the neglect of Burke than mere mental reservations about his status as "pure" author. One is the curious fate which overtook Burke's private papers. For one reason or another the great body of these was withheld from the public for nearly a hundred and fifty years. At first this was the result of unlucky accidents. The two men whom Burke appointed as his literary executors started out with the idea of producing a definitive biography, as well as an edition of Burke's writings; very naturally they held on to the papers which had been left in their care, as well as the letters which they obtained from Burke's correspondents shortly after his death. Unfortunately both men were far too busy to make ideal biographers or editors; one of them, Dr. French Laurence, was an active lawyer and Member of Parliament; the other, Dr. Walker King, a bishop. The former, who first undertook the responsibility of a biography, died about twelve years after Burke, having scarcely begun the enterprise—though to be sure he had made some headway toward completing the edition of the works. His successor unluckily had very weak eyesight, so that although he labored on over the papers until he was almost totally blind, he too died, nearly thirty-one years after Burke, without having done more than complete the edition of the works. No biography was based upon the papers, which nonetheless had been withheld from other scholars during a period of thirty-one years. But a worse disaster followed. Before the death of the second executor, Mrs. Burke had appointed two more guardians of her husband's papers, the survivor of whom, Earl Fitzwilliam, took over the full body of Burke material at the demise of the blind bishop, and continued to withhold it from the use of scholars. At his death it passed to the members of his family, who from that time forward kept the papers from being examined, even by such a semiofficial organization as the Historical Manuscripts Commission. The natural result was that thorough scholars, since they knew they could not speak with authority about innumerable details of Burke's career, or indeed even about the texts of his writings, were discouraged from making him the subject of serious research.

This was the scholarly obstacle in the way of any major work upon Burke. There was a critical obstacle which may have been almost as forbidding. We have said that Burke was a "mixed author," not completely within the literary fold. That is an understatement. Though he has certainly the right to be called a man of letters, Burke ranged into more semirelated and downright nonliterary fields than perhaps any single man of letters who ever wrote in English. He was an orator, a pamphleteer, a political philosopher, an aesthetician, a historian, and a journalist—if we go no farther. Naturally such multifariousness increases the difficulty of passing judgments upon him. Unless the critic is as protean as Burke, he will find it impossible to judge in all fields at once; if on the other hand he attempts to disentangle and examine a piece of Burke's work in some single department, he will surely find that his judgment is blurred and confused by the co-existence of all the other departments. There is no easy evasion of this difficulty, and whether critics admit it or not it is the kind of difficulty that "puts them off" the study of an author. Lord Byron said rather airily, "One hates an author that's *all author*," but the practicing critic has reasons for finding himself more comfortable with that kind. Grappling with the author who is part statesman, part orator, part philosopher, and the rest, has some analogies with the classic feat of wrestling with the Hydra.

Nonetheless it would be a great cultural misfortune if the undoubted obstacles in the way of the serious student should altogether discourage those whose business it is to know Burke and to interpret him for modern readers. Matthew Arnold, lamenting the tendency of the British to neglect their prose classics, once said: ". . . to lose Swift and Burke out of our mind's circle of acquaintance is a loss indeed, and a loss for which no conversance with contemporary prose literature can make up, any more than a conversance with contemporary poetry could make up for an unacquaintance with Shakespeare and Milton." The British and American publics are today in much greater danger than they were in Arnold's day of losing Burke out of their "mind's circle of acquaintance." At a time when a humane and enlarged view of politics could hardly be more needed in the world, our greatest political writer is still very difficult of access.

The scholars who in recent years have done most to correct this state of things and to revive a healthy interest in Burke have worked under the handicaps we have been considering. It is not surprising that none of them has produced a definitive major study. Even Sir Philip Magnus is scarcely an exception here. His *Edmund Burke*, although written after he had been granted access to the Fitzwilliam collections, was not planned as an exhaustive and final biography. It adds more to our knowledge of Burke than any biography since James Prior's, but it is essentially an interpretation of Burke's personality rather than an attempt to handle thoroughly all the available facts. Robert Murray's *Edmund Burke* was written without access to the Fitzwilliam materials. Dixon Wecter's *Edmund Burke and His Kinsmen* made use of the Fitzwilliam materials but was of course designed as a rather restricted monograph. It may be that in the present state of Burke scholarship studies definitely limited in scope have a better chance of being successful than more comprehensive works. Certainly the majority of the best recent studies are of this limited sort. Besides Wecter's, such studies as A. P. I. Samuels' *Early Life, Correspondence and Writings of Edmund Burke*, Alfred Cobban's *Edmund Burke and the Revolt against the Eighteenth Century*, Donald C. Bryant's *Edmund Burke and His Literary Friends*, and Ernest Barker's *Burke and Bristol* are those which come readily to mind.

The literary side of Burke seems to have been rather neglected by recent students. His historical and political achievements have been (at least relatively) well recognized. He was the most eloquent British advocate of the cause of the American colonies; he was the stubborn Whig opponent of George III and the "King's friends"; he managed the great Impeachment of Warren Hastings for imperialist crimes in India; he championed his native Ireland against oppression; he was the first public man to warn England of the dangers of the French Revolution. Without denying the importance of any of these actions on the historical stage, one may nonetheless feel that they have been allowed to overshadow other essential—and perhaps the most essential—aspects of his greatness. Burke was a great man of mind, never a great man of practical action. Though he exerted power in a good many political situations, it was not usually by any personal ascendancy he had among the Whigs, or any adroitness in handling the levers which move Parliament or the electorate. He was, as we should now say, an intellectual in politics, and his weapons were those of the intellectual—his tongue and his pen.

It is to be remembered, too, that Burke's life did not begin and end within the four walls of the House of Commons. He had had a literary and journalistic career of about ten years' duration before, at the age of thirty-seven, he entered Parliament; it was in this early period that the *Sublime and Beautiful* and the *Vindication of Natural Society* were written and Dodsley's *Annual Register* launched. But what is more easily overlooked, he had another literary and journalistic career in the last years of his life. Nearly the whole of the campaign against the French Revolution was waged in the popular press. The *Reflections on the Revolution in France*, the *Letter to a Noble Lord*, the *Letters on a Regicide Peace*, were the triumphs of a resourceful writer, not of a great politician. In the 1790's Burke had already lost most of his earlier influence upon either the House of Commons or the councils of his own party; he used his pamphlets to appeal over the heads of his parliamentary colleagues to the Common Reader of his day.

The moment we center our attention upon Burke's literary and journalistic roles, we discover of course a new set of mysteries surrounding what ought to be the simplest matter-of-fact affairs. Why are we uninformed concerning Burke's work on the *Annual Register*, of which he was apparently editor for over thirty years? Why do we know so little of some of his most significant personal relationships, such as that with Tom Paine, his greatest opponent in controversy? Why is there such a secret about the origin of the *Reflections*, the most famous of his writings? There are no answers to such questions, except the general answer that our ignorance of Burke extends into every field and has been favored in its growth by a century and a half of neglect.

Fortunately one of the principal causes of that neglect has now been removed. Within the last year the present head of the Fitz-william family has ended the long period during which the main body of Burke's papers was withheld from the free use of scholars. The materials formerly shut up at Wentworth Woodhouse, the Yorkshire seat of the family, are now being made accessible in the Public Library of the City of Sheffield. This means that we are entering upon a period in which Burke will be more actively studied than he has been in at least a century. Whether this will immediately give us the great definitive works which we still need is, however, a question. I am myself of the opinion that neither the ultimate full biography nor the very desirable fresh edition of the *Works* is likely to be achieved in less than another fifteen years. Too many preliminary tasks lie in our way. The unpublished letters of Burke are extremely numerous, and by no means all of them were at Wentworth Woodhouse. Scholars must collect and study those which can be found, and put many of them into print. When this has been done, specialists in particular fields must relate the new facts revealed to other recent findings in historical and literary research. Burke's connections with America, with India, with France, with Ireland, will all need to be reconsidered. His personal relationships with scores of his contemporaries will demand fresh examination. Only when many such limited studies have supplied the materials should we expect the great summary works to be produced.

The essays in this volume are an extremely modest contribution to the present needs of Burke scholarship. They were all completed before I was able to consult any of the materials now at Sheffield. I am pleased to say, however, that a fairly full subsequent survey of those materials has not forced me to alter substantially any of my conclusions. It has rather convinced me that the appearance of these essays at the present moment may have a value which I did not fully anticipate when they were being written. It is now of peculiar importance that both historical and literary scholars should realize how much uncertainty still hovers around the figure of Burke. If I have contributed only a little to our knowledge, I have given a rather full account of the nature of our ignorance.

I

BOSWELL'S PORTRAIT OF BURKE

IN THE period when Boswell's artistic powers were regarded as scarcely more than mechanical, one could give a very simple account of the lesser figures in the *Life of Johnson*. They were men who, being close to Johnson, had come within the range of Boswell's recording lens. As it was a most efficient lens, they were recorded vividly. Apparently all equally vividly. Therefore the modern reader might expect to find in Boswell's book not only a picture of Johnson but a kind of group picture of his whole circle. When we reach the last page, as Macaulay said, ". . . the clubroom is before us, and the table on which stands the omelet for Nugent, and the lemons for Johnson. There are assembled those heads which live forever on the canvas of Reynolds. There are the spectacles of Burke and the tall, thin form of Langton, the courtly sneer of Beauclerk, and the beaming smile of Garrick, Gibbon tapping his snuff box and Sir Joshua with his trumpet in his ear." [1]

This is an attractive description of what Boswell achieved, but we hardly need Macaulay's reputation to make us suspect that it is not wholly realistic. Every reader of the *Life of Johnson* has marveled at the vividness of particular scenes; but Boswell would have had to be either a mere instrument like a camera or, what is hardly more credible, the greatest artist who ever lived to have drawn every scene with the uniform vividness apparently being ascribed to him. To tell the truth, the details of Nugent's omelet, Burke's spectacles, and Sir Joshua's ear trumpet did not come from the *Life of Johnson*. In order to represent that work as being equally graphic in all of its parts, Macaulay had to import them from elsewhere. If we pause to consider the question raised by the passage, we may actually prefer the exact opposite of what Macaulay seems willing to imply. The *lack* of uniformity on Bos-

1. Macaulay's essay "Boswell's Life of Johnson," in *Critical and Historical Essays, Thomas Babington Macaulay* (Boston, 1900), II, 361–362.

well's canvas is one of its notable characteristics. Certain of the lesser figures, such as Goldsmith and Garrick, are, to be sure, almost always picturesque. But what of other figures such as Burke and Reynolds? It was not an accident that these two had to be supplied with their "properties" of spectacles and ear trumpet; Boswell never sharpened either figure with a single physical detail.

The twentieth century has been willing to recognize that Boswell was an artist, and of a somewhat temperamental sort. There is nothing surprising in the fact that he had different manners of treating different subjects, or that he responded more eagerly to some of his material than to other. Those who have analyzed his portrait of Johnson have accustomed us to look for such variations. Certain traits of the older man had special interest for Boswell, either because they were traits his own nature needed—such as strength of will or moral clarity—or on the other hand because they corresponded to parts of his own nature he wished to understand—such as a disposition to melancholia. In treating such traits Boswell's art never failed him. But other aspects of Johnson, such as his softer, more playful moods, seem to have been less important to Boswell, and we find them better recorded by other writers than they are in the *Life*.

Analysis of the artistic success of "Boswell's Johnson," and also of "Boswell's Boswell," has been carried out with the greatest subtlety. We may ask, however, whether comparable analysis of Boswell's emotional and artistic relationships to his other principal characters has not been neglected. What psychological or other factors are involved in the success of the portrait of Goldsmith? Why do Garrick and Gibbon, in different ways, lend themselves so well to Boswell's art, and appear (when they do appear) in such sharp outlines? On the other hand, why does the luminous canvas so often fade into dark, blurred patches when Boswell tries to record the features of his "eminent friend" Edmund Burke?

I

Coleridge once commented on Burke and Johnson as talkers, and offered his own account of the disparity of their reputations:

Dr. Johnson's fame now rests principally upon Boswell. It is impossible not to be amused by such a book. But his *bow-wow* manner must have had a good deal to do with the effect produced; for no one, I suppose, will set Johnson before Burke, and Burke was a great and universal talker; yet now we hear nothing of this, except by some chance remarks in Boswell. The fact is, Burke, like all men of genius who love to talk at all, was very discursive and continuous; hence he is not reported; he seldom said the sharp short things that Johnson almost always did, which produce a more decided effect at the moment, and which are so much more easy to carry off.[2]

The final remark is doubtless the proper beginning for any comparison of Burke and Johnson as talkers. They clearly had different styles, and it was easier to "carry off" what Johnson said. The dramatic explosions of wit, wisdom, and rudeness which Boswell recorded by the hundred a great many other people who knew Johnson could report with some success; they were already formed for circulation as anecdote. The Doctor *coined* his talk. Burke, if we can judge at all by his parliamentary eloquence, was at the opposite extreme. His virtues Johnson summed up as "copiousness and fertility of allusion; a power of diversifying his matter, by placing it in various relations." [3] He spoke very rapidly, with a marked Irish accent. Boswell himself commented on the trouble Burke must have given the parliamentary reporters: "Dempster described Cavendish taking down while Burke foamed like Niagara. 'Ay,' said I, 'Cavendish bottling up.' " [4] Perhaps Boswell's own experience gave him an idea of the inefficiencies of that kind of bottling.

From comments, if not reports, one can guess a few additional

2. "Table Talk" (July 4, 1833), in *The Complete Works of Samuel Taylor Coleridge*, ed. W. G. T. Shedd (New York, 1853), VI, 469.

3. Boswell's "Journal of a Tour to the Hebrides" (September 15, 1773), in *Life of Johnson*, V, 213.

4. *Boswell Papers*, VI, 132. The present essay draws very largely upon materials in these papers, and also upon materials in the *Life of Johnson*. As these works are magnificently indexed, it does not seem necessary to give references for facts and quotations taken from them, unless special circumstances require a comment. A thorough review of the relations of Burke and Boswell—based primarily upon the *Boswell Papers* and very full and accurate in its references—is in Donald C. Bryant's *Edmund Burke and His Literary Friends* (Washington University Studies, St. Louis, 1939), pp. 99-135.

qualities Burke's talk must have had.[5] It must have been, like Johnson's, gladiatorial. Burke had vigorous opinions on a wide range of topics, great confidence in his powers of expression, and exceptional experience in debate. One should not be deceived by the evidence that he sometimes showed a greater humility than Johnson, as in saying that it was enough for him to have "rung the bell to him"; he was undoubtedly the most persistent and assertive of the Doctor's conversational opponents. Indeed, if one can have an opinion at this distance, there is a likelihood that purely as a controversialist he was Johnson's superior. Johnson's strokes were more violent, but violence in controversy is not always the sign of victory. "Burke keeps to Johnson," someone said in Boswell's presence. "Yes," was the reply, "like a man fishing salmon with single hair: lets him flounce, then draws." Burke was a mental athlete par excellence; it is worth remembering, too, that he was about twenty years younger than Johnson, and a public life of strain and shock is a better conditioning for debate than the more self-indulgent life of a man with a pension. The Doctor sometimes groaned when he thought of the eternal readiness of his opponent: ". . . the pulse beat higher in Burke's tongue," he said, "at two o'clock in the morning than in that of any other man at 9 at night." [6]

Though he was energetic and persuasive, Burke never took "good talk" as seriously as Johnson did, or strove to make a high art out of his daily conversings. Burke was always in a hurry. The magnitude of his mind gave one kind of distinction to any of his extended utterances, but "distinction" in the sense of a carefully preserved superiority of expression he flouted on principle. He was much more likely to go to the opposite extreme. Johnson's strictures on the low quality of Burke's wit were amply provoked by Burke's habits of punning, playing with ideas, fooling and *letting himself down* in ways most able speakers try to avoid. It was hardly true that Burke "never once made a good

5. An excellent survey of contemporary comment on Burke's conversational powers is in Donald C. Bryant's essay "Edmund Burke's Conversation," in *Studies in Speech and Drama in Honor of Alexander M. Drummond* (Ithaca, 1944), pp. 354–368.

6. *Queeney Letters*, ed. Marquis of Lansdowne (London, 1934), p. 255.

joke," but he certainly made hundreds of poor ones. As a man who cared deeply about the art of conversation, Johnson had some right to indignation. He must also have reflected that in wit, an important attribute of good talk, Burke was simply putting himself out of any "serious" competition.

The eighteenth century valued one element in conversation far more than we usually value it today. This was the element of sheer information. A talker was admired by his hearers for being ready to instruct them extempore in subjects with which he was acquainted; as the phrase was, he "diffused knowledge" through his conversation. In the power to diffuse knowledge, much as in the aptitude for debate, it is possible to believe that Burke might have excelled Johnson; his printed *Works* range over a wider variety of subjects, and his active involvement in every department of affairs was even more astonishing. It is understandable that men like Malone [7] and Reynolds,[8] who among the Johnsonian circle were perhaps those most soberly bent on self-improvement, were the ones who in comparing Johnson and Burke inclined to give the palm to Burke. Boswell, caring less for knowledge but a better judge of wit and dramatic qualities, naturally preferred Johnson.

As is obvious, every one of the main characteristics we attribute to Burke's conversation tended to make him hard to record. The range of his information, the "copiousness and fertility of allusion," the style of his debating, the style of his wit, all strengthen Coleridge's supposition that a great deal of his power was foredoomed to elude posterity.

II

Boswell tells us that he was a law student at Glasgow when he

7. William Shakespeare, *Plays and Poems*, ed. Edmond Malone (London, 1790), I, xviii.

8. James Northcote, *Life of Sir Joshua Reynolds* (2d ed. London, 1819), II, 211. Goldsmith may also have been inclined to Burke's side. At least he argued against Boswell's eager praise of Johnson: "Is he like Burke, who winds into a subject like a serpent?" Fanny Burney thought she could compromise the dispute: ". . . I think Dr. Johnson the first Discourser, and Mr. Burke the first Converser, of the British empire." *Memoirs of Dr. Burney* (London, 1832), II, 237–238.

first "contemplated the character of Mr. Burke . . . and viewed him like a Planet in the heavens." The two men did not actually become acquainted till they met at the table of Sir Joshua Reynolds about twelve years later. If we can judge from Boswell's enthusiastic record, the first meeting was an auspicious one; it certainly had one kind of animation. Burke was in a very unexalted mood for a planet in the heavens: punning and disporting himself carelessly. When Boswell made some remark about "Liberty and necessity to be tried by law," Burke said *he* would be for necessity, as necessity has no law. When Goldsmith, commenting on international affairs, said the French were "licking their sores," Burke rejoined, "I hope we shall lick their sores"—which presumably was a feeble effort at a pun. When Goldsmith remarked that at great folks' tables one was uncomfortable "as in an ice house," Burke cried, "What! a NICE house." [9] Boswell was enchanted.

But though it began so very happily, the acquaintance of the two men did not develop at once. Indeed, Boswell in the *Life of Johnson* appeared to forget this first meeting altogether. Referring to their second meeting, the following year, on the night of his own election to the Club, he spoke of "Mr. Edmund Burke, whom I then saw for the first time." The phrase is doubly inaccurate, for besides the meeting at Sir Joshua's Boswell had before this seen Burke in the House of Commons, and recorded, again with enthusiasm, his impressions of him:

It was a great feast to me, who had never heard him before. It was astonishing how all kinds of figures of speech crowded upon him. He was like a man in an Orchard where boughs loaded with fruit hung around him, and he pulled apples as fast as he pleased and pelted the ministry. It seemed to me however that his Oratory rather tended to distinguish himself than to assist his cause. There was amusement instead of persuasion. It was like the exhibition of a favourite Actor. But I would have been exceedingly happy to be him.

Perhaps one reason the acquaintance did not progress more rapidly was that although Boswell was much impressed by Burke

---

9. In the text of the *Boswell Papers* (X, 263) these two last puns are printed as Boswell's. Professor Pottle tells me that he now believes they should both be assigned to Burke.

and eager to cultivate his friendship, Burke was not able to feel equally serious about Boswell. He granted that Boswell was entirely good natured, but insisted that that was no more credit to a man than having a strong constitution; when Johnson proposed Boswell for election to the Club, Burke doubted that he was "fit for it." Once he was elected Burke, like the other members, enjoyed his company fully, but he perhaps never much changed his opinion of Boswell's intellectual capacities.

On Boswell's side there was an exactly opposite failure in the relationship. Boswell cared too much about attaching himself to Burke. Nothing is clearer after reading his journal than the degree to which Boswell distrusted his own moral and psychological strength and struggled to appropriate the strength of famous and powerful people. If the word tufthunter, which has sometimes been applied to him, means a person who has only frivolous or external reasons for seeking out the great, it is unfair to apply the term to Boswell, for his pursuit of strength in the men about him was anything but frivolous: it had the seriousness of an instinctive drive. But Boswell did stalk the great, for serious reasons if not for light ones; there was an unpleasant rigidity about his manner of approaching any man who carried a Name. An acquaintanceship begun with unadmirable motives—as that of Boswell and Johnson no doubt was, too—may grow into something much better, but it starts at a disadvantage.

One of the uses to which Boswell put his great Names when he had them was that of serving as models of rectitude, or of worldly poise and easiness, for the incessant self-judgments of the journal. Burke was admirably qualified for such a use. Boswell adopted him as a kind of symbol for happiness of a public kind. "I was in such a frame as to think myself an Edmund Burke," he would write, ". . . a man who united pleasantry in conversation with abilities in business and powers as an Oratour." Or, "I was in fine cheerful spirits tonight, spoke a good deal, fancied myself like Burke, and drank moderately of claret." If he chose to condemn himself: "I felt my own emptiness sadly while I heard him talk a variety of knowledge, ten times more than I have recollected."

This purely private manner of using a friendship may have had psychological dangers of its own, but it was scarcely so embarrassing to the relations of the two men as the open efforts Boswell soon began to make to win Burke's political patronage. Burke, in spite of Boswell's idealized image of him, was never in so comfortable a political situation that he had many favors to bestow; and though he found Boswell a congenial companion, he may well have doubted that he was a public servant worth a strenuous recommendation. Boswell himself was diffident of his claims and slow to come to a request. The first letter he wrote to Burke explained most awkwardly that he would have written at an earlier date, but Burke's party had seemed about to come into power, and he was afraid his cordiality would be misconstrued by Burke as the activity of a placehunter. Nothing could be farther from his thoughts. He felt free to write now, however, since it was at last clear that Burke's party was not coming in just yet . . .[10] What Burke thought of the art of this letter we do not know; he seems not to have answered it. Boswell wrote two more letters within the next year; the one which survives was to inform Burke of the political situation in Edinburgh, which was hostile to a bill Burke was championing.[11] Burke's reply was light and mocking, making a joke of the whole matter, and speaking of a happy meeting he had had with Johnson in London when no politics was discussed; [12] one can't help wondering whether a hint to Boswell was not intended. So far as we know, Boswell did not write to Burke again until three years later, at a time when Burke's party finally had come to power. This letter is a lightly disguised request for a place. Boswell said he could move to London, as he had long thought of doing, if he could only increase his income by £600 a year. Did Burke have any ideas on that subject? "When I was last in London," Boswell said, "you asked me on one of our pleasant evenings over your homebrewed, 'how I *could* live in Edinburgh?' I answered 'Like a cat in an air-pump.' " [13] Before Burke had responded to these hints, Boswell heard of a specific post in Scotland which he thought he might get if he were properly

10. Burke, *Correspondence*, II, 207–209.
11. Printed in Dixon Wecter's article "Four Unpublished Letters from Boswell to Burke," *Modern Philology*, XXXVI, 48–49.
12. *Catalogue of Papers found at Fettercairn House*, ed. C. C. Abbott (Oxford, 1936), p. 25.
13. Wecter, *loc. cit.*, pp. 50–53.

recommended. He wrote to Burke again asking him to use his influence.[14] Burke wrote at once to the proper official in Boswell's behalf.[15] His letter, though Boswell later spoke of it as very precious to him because the recommendations were so strong, did not secure the post.

Nonetheless Boswell had not completely wasted his Boswellian blandishments. His efforts had got him onto intimate terms with Burke and with the members of Burke's family—had formed just the kind of attachment dearest to his heart. Henceforth whenever he was in London he called regularly at the house on Charles Street: for tea, for dinner, for a social evening, for a family breakfast, or while Burke was shaving . . . He was a constant and apparently always a welcome visitor. As usual with him, he improved his opportunities and tightened the bonds of friendship by asking for a great deal of advice as to all the affairs of life. What was Burke's serious opinion as to the prudence of his plan of moving to London? Would Burke mind putting his thoughts on the matter into writing? What were Burke's deeper feelings on religion? How would Burke counsel a young man who was inclined to sexual incontinence? If he were the father of such a young man, how did he think that he would feel about it? How should a father treat his son in matters involving money?

Luckily Burke was almost as fond of giving advice as Boswell was of asking it. He entered readily into the game. He advised Boswell fully on the matter of moving to London—though we have no evidence that he thought it necessary to put his opinion into written form. In a long evening (one of Boswell's triumphs) he entered fully into religious matters. On several occasions he took up the sexual problem. He wouldn't agree with Boswell's hope that sexual incontinence could be cured by carrying it to greater extremes: "If you had the inclination it would not easily be cured," he said. As to the problem of how he would feel as a father, "I should think of a son's licentiousness," he said, "as of my own, with tenderness and regret." He only joked a little over the question of money. He discussed marriage, and gave his opinion that it was a certain sign of corruption when husband and

14. *Boswell Papers*, XV, 74.
15. *Fettercairn Catalogue*, p. 228.

wife occupied separate beds. "A Woman in that case never went to bed to her husband but with a gross purpose; whereas if she slept with him constantly, that might happen or not, as inclination prompted."

Boswell eagerly recorded Burke's wisdom, along with an extraordinary number of his bad puns and quite a little other relaxed conversation, in the pages of the journal. Occasionally, not often, he also recorded some question of fact related to Burke's career. Burke said that the *Account of European Settlements in America,* which had been attributed to him, was not actually his; he knew the author, however, and had revised the book and perhaps written a little of it. Burke himself had published his two most famous speeches on America; the better-known one on Conciliation he could not have recalled without Cavendish's notes, as he wrote it out long after he gave it.

The great interest of Boswell's record, however, is not in the opinions nor in the information which eager questioning was able to elicit from Burke. It is in the careful day-to-day recording of the progress of one of Boswell's friendships—or one is tempted to say, one of Boswell's courtships. Burke is important, as the prize of a quest, and we follow the stages of Boswell's approach to the prize: the early meetings, Boswell's cautious overtures, Burke's first signs of reciprocating interest, the first visits, the increasing intimacy, the establishment of a genuine bond . . .

The climax of Boswell's social romance came on the day when he was finally invited to come and visit the Burke family at "Gregories," their country estate near Beaconsfield. The entries in the journal record a fever of excitement over the event:

(MONDAY, 21 APRIL, 1783) EASTER MONDAY. Away in Coach. Be powdered near Gregory's. Mem: You're going to enjoy as much as can be had on earth perhaps. Write to Grange and Wife while there. Learn farming. Write Memorial on choice of life as well as you can. Write to Sir W. Forbes. Learn farming. Be sober.

The trip from London to Beaconsfield was not wholly spent in this state of virtuous resolution; Boswell chanced to encounter in the coach a pretty young lady's maid, and had a few thoughts below the level of Burke's instructive conversation. But after reaching

Beaconsfield, bidding a sentimental farewell to the girl, and paying his visit to a barber, he finally arrived at Burke's establishment, which he found vastly impressive at first view:

> The place looked most beautiful. He was at the window with a scratchwig, and let me in. His hall was admirable; contained many busts . . . I was affected with wonder by seeing a suite of rooms hung with valuable pictures in rich-gilded frames: seven Landscapes of Poussin which Sir Joshua values at £700, a fine Titian, a ——; in short a great many.

Boswell investigated the question of how Burke, who was by no means wealthy, had happened to acquire this impressive collection:

> . . . he got house, Busts, pictures, and furniture all at once, for ——. He has done a good deal to the place himself. . . . The soil here is gravelly and bears a beautiful verdure; and the ground is formed into swells and hollows as if in a Mould by an exquisite Artist. He begins his husbandry course by dunging his land well . . .

The rest of this entry suggests that Boswell was really serious about his resolution to "learn farming" during this visit.

We do not have the whole story of the visit. The page or so devoted to it is one of the most tantalizing passages in the journal. A kinsman of Boswell was wounded in a duel in London, which forced Boswell to return to town. The story of Beaconsfield and the Burke family was left incomplete.

III

There was more than the accident of Boswell's kinsman, however, to interfere with the smooth course of the friendship of Boswell and Burke. One whole aspect of the friendship—its political aspect—threatened difficulties almost from the start, and with the passage of time it became not less but more embarrassing.

It is not easy to see why this was so. The mere fact that Burke was a Whig and Boswell a Tory should not in itself have been any cause for worry to either. They knew very well how to skirt contentious topics and make the most of their field of agreement.

In the period when Burke was the great champion of the American colonists, Boswell also happened to sympathize with them, and could emphasize the fact in dealing with Burke. Later on when the French Revolution had aroused all of Burke's conservative instincts, Boswell could claim, as he did, that Burke was showing himself essentially a Tory. Neither had to be taken in by these convenient compromises, but both could make them socially useful. A conversation Boswell recorded in 1790 summarizes pretty well the extent of their real agreement:

BURKE. "This revolution in France would almost make me adopt your Tory principles." I. "Nay, you are one of us. We will not part with you." BURKE. "You have the art of reconciling contradictions beyond any man I know." I. "Yes, I was a Tory and an American." BURKE. "You were not always an American." (This was an unjust suspicion of time serving on my part.). . . . He (indelicately, I thought) mentioned Mr. Hastings. I could not but say, "I am on the other side there, I know not how." He was irishly savage a little, but full and flowing.

On these terms or something like them there is no reason that the two men could not have got on forever without serious friction —even when, as on the Hastings Impeachment, they had directly opposite opinions. Indeed, there is no reason that their mere difference of party should have discouraged Burke from trying to assist Boswell's political career. The eighteenth century was exceptionally tolerant of purely personal motives in politics; if Burke had had the influence to dispose of a place, he could have disposed of it to a Tory friend without scandal.

Unfortunately there was more to the situation than any mere conflict of Whig and Tory principles. Another conflict was involved, of a more fundamental kind. Boswell's attitude toward Burke was much entangled with his attitude toward his own political ambitions, which gave him a great deal of the unhappiness of his life. Like most men of his period, Boswell regarded prominence in public affairs as the crown of human felicity. It was his dream to be an impressive parliamentary figure. But being abnormally self-critical he naturally was also more or less conscious that he was not really suited to the role. Boswell never resolved this dilemma. He couldn't make up his mind either to fore-swear political ambitions (certainly the prudent course, consider-ing his temperament) or to muster the truly desperate courage he would have needed to vanquish his difficulties. His permanent state of indecision was both the cause and the consequence of a great many of those violent fluctuations of spirits to which he was always subject. The journal is full of dark passages recording his miseries:

(April 14, 1782) Took physick. Lay in bed all day and read . . . Was in miserable Hypochondria. Saw my ambitious views in London all madness. Vexed at being neglected by Burke. Thought I'd indulge a proud distance and just be an old Scottish Baron and Tory. A Slumber in the afternoon produced shocking Melancholy. Up to tea. A LITTLE better. Thought myself unworthy of valuable Spouse. Was quite sunk. To bed without supper.

It is fairly easy to see how the whole relationship with Burke could be touched by these private anxieties. On the one hand Burke was, as we have seen, a shining image of the felicity Boswell dreamed of, but on the other hand he was the potential savior who never actually came to Boswell's rescue. It was thus possible for Boswell at almost the same moment to admire Burke extravagantly and expect every worldly good to come from him, and yet to blame him for some of the most painful disappointments of his life.

Not long after his father's death in August, 1782, Boswell made an unusually resolute effort to launch himself into politics, and by way of assisting his candidacy for a Tory seat in Parliament wrote a pamphlet opposing Fox's East India Bill. He did not win his seat, but from this time on he was haunted by the idea that the pamphlet had given offense to Burke, who therefore would not use his influence on Boswell's behalf. It is not likely that Burke paid any serious attention to the pamphlet. After all, half of po-litical Britain was up in arms against the India Bill; Burke would have been paralyzed indeed if he had allowed himself to feel bitter at all the pamphlets written in the campaign of 1784!

Boswell did not seem capable of taking this cheerful view of things. His whole attitude toward Burke was strained by the inci-dent. Formerly he had been exceptionally relaxed and cheerful when in Burke's company; now he began to act perpetually ill at ease. But he was ill at ease too when he did not see Burke for a time; he was afraid Burke was consciously avoiding him. He complained of Burke's "coldness" on what seems very slight provocation. When in 1784 Burke went to Glasgow to be installed in the honorary post of Lord Rector of the University, he may have been a very little late in giving Boswell notice of his arrival in Scotland. Boswell's manner of responding to the "slight" gives us an idea of the insecurity he now felt in their whole relationship. As soon as he heard of Burke's arrival he set off in wild haste for Glasgow, where he appeared at Burke's inn before breakfast on the day of the installation. But he decided not to speak to Burke personally, or even let him know that he was in the house, until he had prepared the ground with a letter. Two drafts survive of the letter he wrote. The sentiments are extraordinary. He admitted that Burke might have been offended by his Tory zeal and hence have intentionally neglected him. But, he pleaded, could they not be friends again—especially since it was a season of forgiveness: the week before Easter? However, if Burke thought they could not, ". . . if in this cursed strife you 'have ought against me,' and will not be fully 'reconciled' with me even in *this week,* pray tell me frankly." Before Boswell had made up his mind to send the letter in to Burke, Burke's servant chanced to see Boswell on the stairs, recognized him, and asked him if he wished to see Burke at once. Boswell declined, but asked the servant to deliver the letter to Burke, which he accordingly did. Likely enough Burke was puzzled when he read it; nonetheless he came immediately to the parlor where Boswell was waiting. They "embraced complacently." Boswell again said something about his fears of an estrangement. Said Burke, "What has made you go so mad of late? As to quarreling with you, that cannot happen; for as you observe as to Langton . . . ;" "in short," the journal breaks off, "he conveyed a compliment that my pleasantry was such that one would be a loser by quarreling with me." Burke explained his delay. "As to telling you when I should come to Scotland, I did not know myself till we were dismissed. Deus nobis haec otia." He invited Boswell to breakfast at once.

This was not the end of Boswell's suspicions, however; they

continued to find their way into the pages of the journal. "I was sorry to perceive Burke shy to me," he was still saying four years after the fatal pamphlet. "But my loyal zeal against the India Bill was a *lethalis arundo* in his side." Whether Burke really was "shy" at all it would be hard to establish from any of the entries in the journal; if he was, it was hardly because of the India pamphlet. But as time went on much slighter circumstances seemed to be enough to convince Boswell that he and Burke were at odds:

I walked out with Courtenay. We overtook Burke in Pall-mall, going to the House. He talked of secret influence and bad government, and I felt aukwardly at being so conspicuously on the other side. It was unpleasant. I parted from them as soon as I decently could. I lamented that politicks made a cold separation between us which could never be got over.

Ordinary social intercourse could be equally poisoned:

Went to Drury Lane. I sat in Mrs. Burke's box, where was Edmund. It was aukward and uneasy to be cold with people with whom I had once been on the easiest footing. I was not enough entertained with the Play, though some passages struck me. I thought of the shortness and uncertainty of life.

The buoyant spirits of Burke's brother Richard did nothing to cheer Boswell up. The journal notes after a meeting:

Dick Burke was too rough and wild in his manner today, and I could perceive either liked me worse than his brother did, or had less art to conceal his dislike—on account of politicks.

When Edmund at about this time accepted an invitation to dinner at Boswell's, his nervous host sent him two separate letters reminding him not to neglect the engagement. Burke did not, and "seemed quite easy and polite" while talking with Boswell's family. He did not succeed in disarming everybody. This time it was Mrs. Boswell who had the suspicions. According to the journal:

She said he must be a very perfect politician who could conceal the resentment he must entertain against me for having so keenly opposed his party, but that she believed he would shew it whenever he had the opportunity.

Poor Burke's efforts to maintain an atmosphere of good will were finally so little trusted that it was a matter for comment and astonishment if he did *not* produce a feeling of discomfort. In the latter part of 1790 Boswell described a social occasion to Malone:

Burke was admirable company all that day . . . easy with me as in *days of old*. I *do* upon my honor *admire* and *love* him. Would that he had never seen Lord Rockingham, but had "ever walked in a perfect way." [16]

This is by far the most reassuring reference to relations between Boswell and Burke during any part of the period when the *Life of Johnson* was being written.

IV

The unprecedented minuteness with which Boswell recorded the details of Johnson's life disturbed a good many of his friends, some on general critical grounds, others for more personal reasons. Today it may be more difficult to understand the former disturbance: that on general critical grounds. We are accustomed to admiring Boswell almost without qualification for the very extremes of minuteness which his contemporaries regarded as misguided and inartistic. How incomparably vivid, we say, is an author who tells us everything, without fearing to be too trivial! It is fascinating that we should know the condition of Johnson's second-best wig, burned in front by his habit of reading at night and leaning too close to the candle! This kind of detail was exactly what disturbed the eighteenth-century critic. *Should* a biographer record such petty matters? Wasn't it beneath the dignity of his art and of a subject like Johnson? Contemporaries spoke with scorn of the attempt to preserve "the colour of Dr. Johnson's coat, his oaken staff, his inordinate love of tea, and his flatulencies." [17] Boswell, Mrs. Piozzi, and several others had aban-

16. *Letters of James Boswell*, ed. Chauncey B. Tinker (Oxford, 1924), II, 408.
17. Richard Graves, *Recollections of William Shenstone* (London, 1788),

doned all "propriety," and deserved not praise but censure. When Boswell on the publication of the *Journal of a Tour to the Hebrides* let it be known that this was a sample of the style the *Life of Johnson* would have, some of the best critical voices rose in lament. Jack Wilkes is said to have told him that "he had wounded Johnson with his pocket pistol & was about to dispatch him with his blunderbuss, when it should be let off." [18]

The personal objections to Boswell's practices are less puzzling to us than the critical. It was known that Boswell had no idea of restricting himself to details which concerned Johnson alone; his "method" made it inescapable that Johnson's friends should be recorded with an almost equal particularity. After all, if meetings were described, the persons present could not be ignored; if conversations were preserved, they had to have two sides. Names made the record more authentic, and Boswell was quite frank in admitting that he had a partiality for names of eminence. When Bishop Percy expressed the hope that his name might be suppressed in one passage of the *Life*, Boswell explained that this was quite impossible:

As to suppressing your Lordship's name when relating the very few anecdotes of Johnson with which you have favoured me, I will do anything to oblige your Lordship but that very thing. I owe to the authenticity of my work, to its respectability, and to the credit of my illustrious friend, to introduce as many names of eminent persons as I can. It is comparatively a very small portion which is sanctioned by that of your Lordship, and there is nothing even bordering on impropriety. Believe me, my Lord, you are not the only bishop in the number of great men with which my pages are graced. I am quite resolute as to this matter. [19]

---

p. vii. The full quotation reads: "But a rage for anecdotes of every kind seems to distinguish the present age: and the colour of Dr. Johnson's coat, his oaken staff, his inordinate love of tea, and his flatulencies, are listened to with patience and complacency." Donald K. Stauffer's *Art of Biography in the Eighteenth Century* (Princeton, 1941), cites other contemporary writers who shared Graves' views.

18. Quoted in James Clifford's *Hester Lynch Piozzi* (Oxford, 1941), p. 259. Professor Clifford has an excellent brief treatment of contemporary disapproval of Boswell's minuteness.

19. Boswell, *Letters*, II, 394.

It was a form of resoluteness which Bishop Percy and several other of Boswell's friends found rather uncomfortable for themselves. People in active life, when struggling for preferments, battling with determined enemies, or merely making the normal effort to protect their reputations, have a reasonable fear of publicity, from knowing the ways in which it can be used against them. Such people had cause to dread Boswell's strange zeal for minute recording. Some acted as Horace Walpole says he did, when he once thought he was sitting next to Boswell in company: "I sewed up my mouth." [20] It is said that Charles James Fox made a rule not to talk freely when he met Johnson at the Club, because "all his conversations were recorded for publication." [21]

Naturally, fear of Boswell's recordings was at its highest pitch in the period between the publication of the *Journal of a Tour to the Hebrides* and the ultimate appearance of the *Life of Johnson*. No one knew how many of his own words, which he had repented or forgotten, might presently be given the embarrassing immortality of print. Some few were able to prevail upon Boswell to spare them particular revelations. Bishop Percy secured the cancellation of one page (though he wanted more).[22] Sir Joshua secured as much.[23] William G. Hamilton, according to Boswell, sent an agent and guaranteed a payment of money to make sure of one change. Boswell wrote Malone about three months before the *Life* was published: ". . . I shall have more cancels. That *nervous* mortal W. G. H. is not satisfied with my report of some particulars *which I wrote down from his own mouth*, and is so much agitated

20. Horace Walpole, *Letters*, ed. Mrs. Paget Toynbee (Oxford, 1904), XIII, 272. Actually the person Walpole was sitting next to was Burke's brother Richard. The anecdote is worth quoting fully to make clear what happened. Walpole says:

". . . t'other night I was sitting with Mrs. Vesey; there was very little light; arrived Sir Joshua Reynolds, and a person whom I took for Mr. Boswell. I sewed up my mouth, and, though he addressed me two or three times, I answered nothing but yes or no. Just as he was going away, I found out that it was Mr. Richard Burke, and endeavoured to repair my causticity."

21. Hill questions in a footnote (*Life of Johnson*, IV, 167 n.) whether Fox could have believed that *all* Johnson's conversations were recorded. He agrees, however, that "when Boswell was by, he [Fox] had reason for his silence."

22. See Professor Tinker's Introduction in the Oxford Standard edition of the *Life of Johnson* (New York, 1933), I, vii.

23. Boswell, *Letters*, II, 417.

that Courtenay has persuaded me to allow a *new edition* of them by H. himself to be made at H's expense." [24]

One would like to know whether in that period of general nervousness Edmund Burke was one of those who cowered at the thought of the Boswellian notebooks. On the face of it he had more reason to cower than Fox or Hamilton or Percy or Reynolds. He was far more vulnerable than they. His enemies and their agents, the paid scandalmongers of the newspapers, were fully practiced in turning every shred of knowledge they got of him to malicious and libelous uses. Nothing could be more helpful to such enemies than Boswell's extraordinary power of accurately reporting conversation.

We have hints at least as to Burke's response to the publication of the *Journal of a Tour to the Hebrides*. He was one of those who thought its particularity was beyond "propriety." Apparently this was on general critical grounds. Hannah More recorded his remark on the excessive minuteness of the early Johnsonians: "How many maggots have crawled out of that great body!" [25] We are not told whether he made any such remarks in Boswell's presence, or applied them directly to the *Tour;* we do hear, though, that he "fell hard upon him for the absurdities in that performance." [26]

Very likely Burke made no issue of it, but there was one of the "absurdities" of the *Tour* in which he was very much involved. Boswell when he published the work had not been willing to suppress Johnson's low opinion of Burke's wit, but in preparing the second edition either Boswell himself or Malone had been worried at the offence which might have been given to Burke. It was decided to make amends, not by suppressing Johnson's opinion, but by rebutting it. Since Boswell and Malone could think of no better way of doing this than by constructing a monumental footnote in which they *argued* that Burke was quite witty (citing a list of his jests, chiefly puns, to clinch the matter), any normally irritable reader was left more certain than he ever had been that Johnson was entirely right. No one can be argued into

24. *Idem*, p. 424.
25. William Roberts, *Memoirs of Hannah More* (London, 1834), II, 101.
26. Unpublished letter of Michael Lort, quoted by Clifford, *op. cit.*, p. 259.

laughing at wit. Even Boswell probably realized that the footnote had its silly side. When he sent Burke a copy of his second edition, he assured him in an accompanying letter that Malone had supplied the footnote, though he didn't choose to acknowledge it.[27] Burke replied with remarkable restraint that he was very grateful to both Malone and Boswell, but for himself, he was willing to accept Johnson's original judgment.[28]

It is pretty clear, however, that although he could be good humored when he had to, Burke saw the danger to himself of Boswell's habit of exposing his friends. It is even clear that he made one or two efforts to remonstrate with Boswell about it. One entry in the journal in the early part of 1786 describes what may have been a genuine quarrel. Boswell is speaking of a conversation at Burke's lodgings in Pall Mall: ". . . I imprudently touched upon a calumny against Mr. Burke, in order to be enabled to refute it. We parted on sad terms. I was very uneasy." It was hardly a major break in the relations of the two men, though it was not cleared up before five letters had passed between them. Boswell insisted that he had never intended to "chronicle" the matter they had discussed.[29] Burke in reply admitted that this time he had been really angry, but was prepared to make it up; he assured Boswell privately that the calumny was false, but added that he did not want it to be denied by his friends; denial would do more harm than good.[30]

Boswell, as the entry in the journal itself tells us, knew that he had been imprudent in questioning Burke. He also knew, long before the *Life* was completed, that Burke was made uneasy by his habit of recording conversations. Malone expressly warned Boswell, in a letter of September, 1787, that the habit of recording was the cause of "B----'s coldness." According to Malone, B---- felt that it was a "restraint on convivial ease and negligence."[31]

We can only speculate as to whether at the last moment Burke grew uncomfortable enough, like Percy, Reynolds, and Hamilton,

27. *Fettercairn Catalogue*, p. 171.
28. *Ibid.*, p. 25.
29. *Ibid.*, p. 171.
30. *Ibid.*, pp. 25–26.
31. *Ibid.*, p. 87.

to remonstrate openly with Boswell. It would be easy to suppose that he did. Describing events in the latter part of 1790, Boswell's editor says: "On 4 December the second volume of the *Life* was at page 216. On the 7th Boswell reported that he and Burke were on easier terms again." [32] The easier terms were by no means free of an element of nervousness. In early March, 1791, Boswell was defending himself hotly against a charge he thought Burke might bring against him. He assured Burke that he had *not* written an epigram which had appeared over his name in the *Oracle*, and which was disrespectful to Burke; he was as indignant with the author of it as Burke himself could be! [33] Burke replied that he had never seen the epigram but was sure that Boswell would do nothing unworthy of his character. [34]

The *Life of Johnson* was published on May 16, 1791.

V

Boswell's practice of disguising Burke under such phrases as "an eminent public character" and "an eminent friend of ours" is only one of several puzzling characteristics of the portrait of Burke in the *Life of Johnson*. Indeed, this practice itself is not quite a simple phenomenon—never being carried out quite consistently: after Boswell has protected Burke's name in a dozen contexts not particularly compromising, he will name him in a passage which strikes us as far more likely to be dangerous.

Many of Boswell's references to Burke are extravagantly admiring. It is a curious fact, however, that they are not usually very convincing in their admiration. The reader hears of "Mr. Burke . . . whose splendid talents," "Mr. Burke, whose orderly and amiable domestic habits . . . ," "Mr. Burke, who while he is equal to the greatest things, can adorn the least;" very frequently the effect of these fulsome phrases is only to arouse disbelief. Johnson once warned Boswell about a lamentable perversity in human nature which biographers especially ought to study. Boswell recorded the warning but did not always heed it:

32. *Boswell Papers*, XVIII, 100.
33. *Fettercairn Catalogue*, p. 172.
34. *Ibid.*, p. 26.

Upon the subject of exaggerated praise I took the liberty to say, that I thought there might be very high praise given to a known character which deserved it, and therefore it would not be exaggerated. Thus, one might say of Mr. Edmund Burke, He is a very wonderful man. JOHNSON. "No, Sir, you would not be safe if another man had a mind perversely to contradict. He might answer, 'Where is all the wonder? Burke is, to be sure, a man of uncommon abilities, with a great quantity of matter in his mind, and a great fluency of language in his mouth. But we are not to be stunned and astonished by him.' So you see, Sir, even Burke would suffer, not from any fault of his own, but from your folly."

It is an odd fact, of course, that the many splendid tributes Johnson himself paid to Burke seem almost invariably to have flouted this very principle. They praise Burke to the skies; yet on the whole they do not sound unconvincing. "Yes, Sir, if a man were to go by chance at the same time with Burke under a shed to shun a shower, he would say— 'This is an extraordinary man.' If Burke should go into a stable to have his horse dressed, the hostler would say—'we have had an extraordinary man here.' " Or, "Burke's talk is the ebullition of his mind; he does not talk from a desire of distinction, but because his mind is full." Or, "I can live very well with Burke; I love his knowledge, his diffusion, and affluence of conversation; but I would not talk to him of the Rockingham party." Or, "Yes, Burke *is* an extraordinary man. His stream of mind is perpetual." Why such unrestrained praise from Johnson seems to ring true and from Boswell seems to ring false, one would like to understand.

Still we must not insist too strongly upon Boswell's relative failure with Burke. Among many irregularities, his treatment of him is at least capable of rising to his best dramatic manner. The *Life of Johnson* offers one splendid instance. It is in the record of conversation at the Club on April 3, 1778. This particular day's record, quite aside from Burke's part in it, is one of the high points of the *Life;* perhaps purely as a piece of dramatic recording it is the highest point. In a kind of tour de force of his art Boswell presents no less than eight people taking part in a general conversation. Unhappily he does not name them all, so that the passage has to be read with a key, but we now have Boswell's own key. The speaker identified as "E." is Burke, "R." is Richard Sheridan, "P." is Sir Joshua Reynolds, "J." is Gibbon, and so on. Johnson and Boswell are named.

Burke, who in the rest of the *Life of Johnson* seldom speaks at all and almost never makes two speeches consecutively, on this one day enters the conversation seventeen times in all. His range of topics includes the value of a good speech in Parliament, the effects of emigration on population, the relationships of primitive languages, the goodness to be expected from human nature, and two or three facetious matters on which he waxes witty.

It would be pleasant to quote the entire passage—which deserves it too; it is almost the only good record we have of Burke's much-praised conversation. But the treatment of one topic may serve as a sample. Young Richard Sheridan—not yet committed to the field of politics; he was to enter it as a member of Burke's party within two years—addressed a leading question to Burke:

R. "Mr. E., I don't mean to flatter, but when posterity reads one of your speeches in Parliament, it will be difficult to believe that you took so much pains, knowing with certainty that it could produce no effect, that not one vote would be gained by it." E. "Waving your compliment to me, I shall say in general, that it is very well worth while for a man to take pains to speak well in Parliament. A man, who has vanity, speaks to display his talents; and if a man speaks well, he gradually establishes a certain reputation and consequence in general opinion, which sooner or later will have its political reward. Besides, though not one vote is gained, a good speech has its effect. Though an act which has been ably opposed passes into a law, yet in its progress it is modelled, it is softened in such a manner, that we see plainly the Minister has been told, that the members attached to him are so sensible of its injustice or absurdity from what they have heard, that it must be altered." JOHNSON. "And, Sir, there is a gratification of pride. Though we cannot out-vote them we will out-argue them. They shall not do wrong without its being shown both to themselves and to the world." E. "The House of Commons is a mixed body. (I except the Minority, which I hold to be pure, [smiling] but I take the whole House.) It is a mass by no means pure;

but neither is it wholly corrupt, though there is a large proportion of corruption in it. There are many members who generally go with the Minister, who will not go all lengths. There are many honest well-meaning country gentlemen who are in parliament only to keep up the consequence of their families. Upon most of these a good speech will have influence." JOHNSON. "We are all more or less governed by interest. But interest will not make us do every thing. In a case which admits of doubt, we try to think on the side which is for our interest, and generally bring ourselves to act accordingly. But the subject must admit of diversity of colouring; it must receive a colour on that side. In the House of Commons there are members enough who will not vote what is grossly unjust or absurd. No, Sir, there must always be right enough, or appearance of right, to keep wrong in countenance." BOSWELL. "There is surely always a majority in parliament who have places, or who want to have them, and who therefore will be generally ready to support government without requiring any pretext." E. "True, Sir; that majority will always follow

'Quo clamor vocat et turba faventium.' "

BOSWELL. "Well now, let us take the common phrase, Placehunters. I thought they had hunted without regard to any thing, just as their huntsman, the Minister, leads, looking only to the prey." J. "But taking your metaphor, you know that in hunting there are few so desperately keen as to follow without reserve. Some do not choose to leap ditches and hedges and risk their necks, or gallop over steeps, or even to dirty themselves in bogs and mire." BOSWELL. "I am glad there are some good, quiet, moderate political hunters." E. "I believe in any body of men in England I should have been in the Minority; I have always been in the Minority." P. "The House of Commons resembles a private company. How seldom is any man convinced by another's argument; passion and pride rise against it." R. "What would be the consequence, if a Minister, sure of a majority in the House of Commons, should resolve that there should be no speaking at all upon his side?" E. "He must soon go out. That has been tried; but it was found it would not do."

Such a passage is enough by itself to convince us that Boswell was *able* to record Burke's conversation. It merely makes it a more puzzling fact that, having the ability, he chose to demonstrate it fully only once in the *Life of Johnson*.

There is another reason why any one interested in Burke will pay particular attention to that record of April 3, 1778. It is our best specimen of Burke's conversation, but it is very likely also our best specimen of general conversation at the Club. One cannot help guessing that it tells us something about Burke's position in the group. He hardly appears on that evening to be a dim or a subordinate figure. The current of the talk centers around seven main topics. Of these Burke introduces four, and a fifth—that we have quoted—rises out of a flattering question Sheridan addressed to Burke.

Such a record may help to restore to proportion our group picture of the Johnsonian circle.

II

THE LITTLE DOGS AND ALL

BURKE'S unworldly Quaker friend Richard Shackleton once attempted to do him a service. It was very shortly after Burke's spectacular first appearance in the House of Commons, when there was still a great deal of unsatisfied curiosity about him, which had provoked a number of misleading rumors. Shackleton, who had been Burke's schoolmate and closest friend in Ireland, was of course in a position to correct errors and slanders, and give an accurate account of his friend. When he received a letter from someone in England asking for information about Burke, he at once responded with a most informative and unreserved communication. It described Burke's family, their circumstances, Burke's religious affiliations, the early evidences of his genius, a few facts concerning his marriage and his wife's religion, and many proofs of his having a good heart.[1]

Poor Shackleton, who undoubtedly intended the letter as an assistance to his friend's fame, must have been horrified at Burke's response to its contents. Instead of being pleased and flattered, Burke concluded at once that the letter would do him serious harm, and indeed that it had been elicited with that intention by his political enemies. He wrote to Shackleton:

Their purpose was, since they were not able to find wherewithal to except to my character for the series of years since I appeared in England, to pursue me into the closest recesses of my life, and to hunt even to my cradle in hope of finding some blot against me. It was on this principle they set on foot this enquiry. I have traced it as far as Mr. Strettel, who refuses to let me know from whom in England he received his commission.[2]

1. This account is reprinted in an appendix of A. P. I. Samuels' *Early Life, Correspondence and Writings of Edmund Burke* (Cambridge, 1923), pp. 402–404.

2. *Ibid.*, p. 396.

When four years afterward the letter was published in one of the London newspapers, Burke wrote again to Shackleton, in a tone of real bitterness:

I am used to the most gross and virulent abuse daily repeated in the papers—I ought indeed rather have said twice a day. But that abuse is loose and general invective. It affects very little either my own feelings or the opinions of others, because it is thrown out by those that are known to be hired to that office by my enemies. But this appears in the garb of professed apology and panegyric. It is evidently written by an intimate friend. It is full of anecdotes and particulars of my life. It therefore cuts deep. I am sure I have nothing in my family, my circumstances, or my conduct that an honest man ought to be ashamed of. But the more circumstances of all these that are brought out, the more materials are furnished for malice to work upon; and I assure you that it will manufacture them to the utmost. Hitherto, much as I have been abused, my table and my bed were left sacred; but since it has so unfortunately happened that my wife, a quiet woman, confined to her family cares and affections, has been dragged into a newspaper, I own I feel a little hurt. A rough public man may be proof against all sorts of buffets, and he has no business to be a public man if he be not so; but there is as natural and proper a delicacy in the other sex, which will not make it very pleasant to my wife to be the daily subject of Grub-street newspaper invectives; and at present, in truth, her health is little able to endure it.[3]

Poor Shackleton was reduced to apologizing miserably to both Burke and Mrs. Burke for what he had intended as an act of friendship. He allowed himself a mild protest, to be sure, at the excessive vehemence of Burke's second letter: "Thou art so used to lay about thee," he wrote, "and give and take no quarter with thy enemies, that it is unsafe for thy friends to be near thee."[4] Burke in his turn apologized humbly for having said more than he intended.[5]

There is one reason to be glad, however, that Burke was led

3. The full text of this letter is printed in *Leadbeater Papers* (London, 1862), II, 109–112. Samuels prints a slightly shortened form (pp. 398–399).

4. Samuels, *op. cit.*, p. 400.

5. *Ibid.*, p. 401.

into his bitter outburst against Shackleton. It made him declare in explicit terms what might otherwise have been a very difficult thing for posterity to be sure of. This is that Burke made it a conscious policy to conceal the facts of his private life. He was not ashamed of his conduct, his situation, or his personal connections; still, "the more circumstances of all these that are brought out, the more materials are furnished for malice to work upon." He deliberately withheld from the public even what would seem quite harmless details about himself.

This was not wholly the result of harsh experience in British political life. Burke was a schoolboy of sixteen in Ireland when he wrote in a letter to Shackleton: "We live in a world where everyone is on the catch, and the only way to be safe is to be silent— silent in any affair of consequence; and I think it would not be a bad rule for every man to keep within what he thinks of others, of himself, and of his own affairs." [6] It is an extraordinary sentiment for a boy of sixteen, and suggests that from the start Burke may have had a kind of temperamental predisposition toward the policy he later followed.

But the origins of the policy are of less interest than its effects upon Burke's mature life. These are of the greatest importance, and explain a great deal about both his relations with his contemporaries and the peculiar character of his reputation. Intrinsically Burke was far from possessing what would be called a mysterious personality; he was honest, positive, with few affinities for the half-lights or oblique shadows congenial to some retiring spirits. But his contemporaries—except for his most intimate friends—habitually thought of him as a questionable figure. Were they to believe the innumerable rumors which circulated about him? Was he a prolific anonymous writer as well as a politician? Was he, as was sometimes asserted, the editor of the *Annual Register?* Was he author of the "Junius" letters? Was he an unscrupulous speculator in stocks, using his parliamentary position to make money out of the East India Company? Was he a secret pensioner of the Crown? Did he draw a salary from Lord Rockingham? Was he concealing the fact that he had been educated as a Jesuit at St. Omer? Some of these rumors might well

6. *Ibid.*, p. 88.

have had elements of truth in them. Was the public to believe any part of them? Burke gave not the least assistance to the curious mind. Save in one or two exceptional instances he treated all rumors as "loose libels" to be met with nothing but silence and contempt. No one could say whether any given report was more authentic than another, or whether none, or all, were entirely false.

Even Burke's friends were puzzled and a little suspicious at his extraordinary reticence. They usually knew no more about the mysteries of his career than his enemies or than complete strangers. Johnson, after knowing Burke for fifteen years, was willing to believe him Junius, and only resigned his opinion when Burke broke his usual rule and denied it to him personally.[7] Baretti made the same not very flattering mistake as Johnson;[8] Malone at least gave Burke a "considerable share" of the responsibility.[9] Goldsmith, who had gone to school with Burke, long believed the reports about his being a Jesuit; "the assertions of a Newspaper are taken up insensibly," he explained later to Boswell.[10]

An effect of Burke's policy upon his political life was that he sometimes found himself being persecuted in causes which were not really his own. This was particularly true in regard to his supposed religion. We are now certain that Burke was not a Jesuit, or even a Catholic, though some of his close relations were Catholic, and though he had a strong sympathy for members of that faith when he felt they were being oppressed. But he was hounded all his life by anti-Catholic fanatics who believed—since he would not contradict them—that he was secretly a Papist. When Lord George Gordon in 1780 stirred up the Protestant Riots in London, Burke was one of his principal targets. The leaders of the mob proclaimed openly their intention of burning Burke's house, which doubtless they would have done if a body of soldiers had not been set guard upon it. When the disorders were at their height, Burke with characteristic boldness insisted upon walking the streets as usual and freely telling his name. He was

7. *Life of Johnson*, III, 376–377.
8. C. R. Leslie and T. Taylor, *Life of Sir Joshua Reynolds* (London, 1865), II, 113.
9. James Prior, *Life of Edmond Malone* (London, 1860), p. 419 *et seq.*
10. *Boswell Papers*, VI, 92.

surrounded at one point by rioters, who demanded that he change his vote on a question involving toleration. Burke refused emphatically and began drawing his sword to defend himself, but he was not maltreated.[11] The incident was a kind of symbol of the relations between Burke and his anti-Catholic enemies: he was not intimidated by their malice, yet neither would he make it clear to them that he did not belong to the group they were attacking. The perversity of his situation sometimes put a great strain on his temper. On one occasion, also in 1780, when he was casting his vote in a Westminster election, another excited mob became convinced that—being a Catholic—he would not dare to take the required oath. They crowded around him with eager cries of "Tip him the long oath! TIP HIM THE LONG OATH!" and presented him a Bible on which to swear. Burke was so angry that when he had kissed the book, he threw it at the crowd.[12]

The permanent effects of the policy of silence are of course far more important than any temporary vexations of this kind. Posterity, which has largely forgotten that Burke ever had such a policy, suffers what may actually be the most important single damage from it. We cannot get Burke or his career into a sharp focus. Too many of the facts are missing or are still conjectural. This is true of even the simplest and most elementary facts. For nearly a century and a half after his death the year of Burke's birth was not settled.[13] The day is still in dispute.[14] The date of his marriage was only discovered ten years ago.[15] Right now one could argue for an uncertainty as to the number of his offspring.[16]

11. J. Paul DeCastro, *The Gordon Riots* (London, 1926), p. 65; see also Prior, I, 262–263.

12. M'Cormick (1st ed.), p. 248.

13. Library of Congress catalogue cards still give Burke's dates as "1729?–1797." There is no longer any doubt that the year of birth was 1729.

14. Magnus (p. 1) gives the date as Jan. 1, 1729; Dixon Wecter ("Burke's Birthday," *Notes and Queries*, CLXXII, 441) argues for Jan. 12.

15. Magnus, pp. 13, 307.

16. I would not argue this as at all a serious matter; it is only another instance of the difficulty of being sure of facts about Burke. It is generally accepted that Burke had two sons: Richard, who was born in 1758 and died in 1794; Christopher, who was also born in 1758 and who died in infancy. See Burke, *Correspondence*, I, 34 n. Prior, however, after mentioning Richard's birth in 1758, says (I, 74): "Another son, Edmund, born about two years afterwards, died in

While such simple vital statistics have been lacking, it is small wonder that scholars have not managed to illumine the dark spots of either his political or his literary career.

One way of beginning the exploration of the many mysteries of Burke's life would seem to be to ask a few questions about his policy of silence. Why did he feel it necessary to pursue it to such extremes? What specific "enemies" was he attempting to evade? Had he really any reason to believe that he was open to more, or more invidious, misunderstandings than other politicians? If he did believe anything of the kind, how much was it because of an oversensitivity of his own nature, which led him to suffer more than was required by his situation?

I

One point should be made quite clear at the start. When Burke speaks in letters and elsewhere of his "enemies," or of those who are striving to "ruin" him, the ordinarily suspicious reader wonders whether these persons might be pure figments of an active imagination. Politicians—and private citizens too if they happen to suffer from paranoiac tendencies—often surround themselves with fancied assailants who help them dramatize their struggles and account for their failures. Could Burke's "enemies" be, perhaps, fictions of this convenient kind?

There is plenty of evidence that Burke's enemies were of the flesh and blood variety, and that at least in a political sense they really were striving to ruin him. Politics was a far rougher game in eighteenth-century England than it is in twentieth-century England or America, and a man in Burke's relatively unprotected position bore the full brunt of its violence. He was not surprised at being called vicious names, or threatened, slandered, even exposed to physical attack. Neither was there much redress for any injuries he might suffer, bodily or in reputation, unless he got a satisfaction out of inflicting the same sorts of injury on his opponents. As he said, a "rough public man" expected these bru-

---

infancy." Edmund *could* be a third son. We also know that Mrs. Burke lost a child in 1770 (Burke, *Correspondence*, I, 226), though we know nothing of the circumstances.

talities. Still, some attacks were more harassing than others. In the same month in which Shackleton's letter found its way into the London papers, Burke had been through a particularly crude onslaught of abuse in the House. An opponent, wanting to discredit a speech he had made two days earlier, raked up all the old stock of anti-Catholic epithets. He was a "Black Jesuit," "educated at St. Omer's," fit to be "secretary to an Inquisition for burning heretics," and so forth. Burke had the presence of mind to treat the affair lightly, and was certainly not hurt by the encounter.[17] But he was not always so lucky or so well controlled. About a month earlier he had got into a violent altercation—"very gross on both sides"—with a still more abusive opponent, who told the House that Burke was a "scoundrel, and had been kicked down stairs." Burke used slightly better language in retort but was no less vehement. The Speaker had trouble in restoring order.[18]

Of course it was not in the House that Burke had most reason to fear attacks. He could speak—and he could also call names— as well as any who assailed him there, and at worst he and an opponent could offer each other "satisfaction" as gentlemen.[19] Abuse in the newspapers was not so easily met.

In the eighteenth century the ethics of the press had scarcely been discovered, and those able to hire the venal pens of professional slanderers could print nearly what they chose about their political opponents, with virtual impunity. As Burke told Shackleton, the libelee's best protection was the cynicism of the public, which usually discounted newspaper vituperation. Sometimes the commercialized nature of the attacks was accidentally made obvious. Burke's biographer James Prior reports that on one occasion a printer hired by one of Burke's enemies got into a quarrel with his employer and ". . . disclosed a bill which excited some amusement when made public, the items regularly marked and charged running thus— 'Letters against Mr. Burke,' 'Strictures upon the Conduct of Mr. Burke,' 'Attacking Mr. Burke's veracity,' the latter being charged at five shillings . . ."[20] That was

17. *Parliamentary History*, XVI, 924.
18. Helen H. Robbins, *Our First Ambassador to China* (London, 1908), p. 74.
19. See Dixon Wecter's article "Burke's Prospective Duel," *Notes and Queries*, CLXXIV, 186–187.
20. Prior, I, 478.

(for Burke) a fortunate case, hardly a usual one. Most of the time the malice was not exposed, and the paragraphs did whatever harm such paragraphs can do. As Goldsmith said, "the assertions of a newspaper are taken up insensibly."

We know of only one case in which Burke felt that he was obliged to make a counterattack against a newspaper. In the year 1780, from the most admirable humanitarian motives, he had urged Parliament to alter the punishment of homosexual offenders. Two men convicted as homosexuals had been exposed in the pillory, where an angry mob had pelted both of them to death. It was typical of Burke to take up such a case wholly on his own initiative and attempt to have the law altered that prescribed the pillory for such an offense. Perhaps it was equally typical of Burke's enemies to take advantage of his zeal to imply that he was sympathetic with homosexual vice. This time he felt that slander had gone too far, and brought a suit against the printer of the *Public Advertiser*. He won his case, of course, though he was not able to prevent even so outrageous a slander from being revived when his enemies again had need of it.[21]

It would be foolish to review all the scurrilous attacks which were kept up against Burke throughout his career. They are of little interest except as examples of the license of the press in that period. One would of course like to know whether Burke suffered *more* of such abuse than his contemporaries in public life. That would be an exceptionally hard point to prove.

Burke himself believed, and apparently with no special feelings of bitterness, that in another, and more innocent, kind of abuse, that is, pictorial caricature, he was favored beyond any of his contemporaries: he was the most caricatured man of his day.[22] The caricatures of him which survive show a magnificent range of attack and ridicule. He is represented, almost normally, in a long clerical robe and immense headdress, of the kind supposedly proper to Jesuits. Sometimes he is praying to saints, sometimes

21. Magnus, pp. 148–150. One of Magnus' illustrations (p. 149) is a contemporary cartoon in which the charge of homosexuality is not too subtly suggested.
22. Prior, II, 164–165. Burke may have been wrong. Mary Dorothy George's *Catalogue of Political and Personal Satires Preserved in the Department of Prints and Drawings in the British Museum* (London, 1935–38) would suggest that Fox and Lord North and the King received considerably more attention.

flagellating himself, sometimes begging barefoot (the caricatures made much of Burke's poverty). He was almost always pictured in spectacles, with a long beaky nose. In one veritable masterpiece, *only* the spectacles and nose, but of enormous size, are shown boring their way into some affair Burke happened to be investigating. When he attacked the French Revolution and in a famous passage of his *Reflections* lamented that the Age of Chivalry was dead, it became common to caricature him in shining armor, usually in the role of Don Quixote.[23]

Much of the caricature and probably nearly all of the newspaper vilification must have been paid for by real individuals, whom it therefore seems just to set down as genuine "enemies" of Burke. From the volume of their expenditure they must have had respectable resources at their disposal. Prior asserts that the sum of £20,000 was spent in attacking Burke on the Hastings Impeachment alone.[24] The full extent of the enemies' activities will obviously never be known. What we have some hope of discovering is the direction, rather than the quantity, of their malice. Where did they discover his most vulnerable points? With what techniques of attack were they best able to harass him? What genuine facts of his career lent themselves most readily to their exaggerations and distortions?

Of course we recognize that among those who attacked Burke there were many well-intentioned citizens who were his "enemies" by pure misunderstanding. Their motives are even better worth examining than those of more interested parties. What did men of *no* settled malice find in Burke's career which made them suspect his character and give ear to his more venomous attackers?

II

To many of his contemporaries Edmund Burke was scarcely an individual. He was part of a collective entity called "the Burkes."

23. The Morgan Library in New York contains Sir Robert Peel's excellent collection of political caricatures from Burke's period. It is preserved in twelve folio volumes, one of which is entirely devoted to Burke.
24. Prior, I, 478.

Reproduced from an illustration in Peter Burke's *Life of Edmund Burke*, London, 1853.

Miss Laetitia Hawkins, the daughter of Sir John Hawkins, Johnson's friend and biographer, once had occasion to describe this entity—particularly as it appeared to British society in the early part of Edmund's career. " 'The Burkes,' " said she, "as the men of that family were called, were not then what they were afterwards considered, nor what the head of them deserved to be considered for his splendid talents: they were, as my father termed them, 'Irish Adventurers'; and came into this country with no good auguries, nor any very decided principles of action. They had to talk their way in the world that was to furnish their means of living . . ." [25]

One might suspect Miss Hawkins of a little ill nature; her father had once been signally humiliated when his quarrel with Edmund Burke had led to his, not Burke's, exclusion from the Literary Club. Actually, it would be hard to show that the lady's description was in any way very unfair. Edmund, his brother Richard, and their so-called "cousin" Will Burke had set out on their careers in the 1750's with very few advantages indeed besides their collective wits. They had leagued themselves closely together to make their fortunes in British society. They were eager for success, sanguine of the future, willing to take some desperately long chances to gain their ends. In the ordinary innocent sense of the term they were certainly "adventurers." Whether they were so in a more blameworthy sense was a great deal discussed at the time; it is now quite clear that both Richard and Will were on occasion dishonorable in their dealings. [26] Edmund, though he has never been proved to have been consciously dishonorable, was so closely associated with the other two that he was inevitably and quite properly given part of the blame for their acts.

25. Laetitia Matilda Hawkins, *Memoirs, Anecdotes, Facts and Opinions* (London, 1824), quoted in Bryant's *Edmund Burke and His Literary Friends*, p. 197. Sir John Hawkins in his *Life of Samuel Johnson* (London, 1787), p. 231, referred to Samuel Dyer's having contracted an intimacy with "some persons of desperate fortunes, who were dealers in India stock." Malone, commenting on the passage, said, "Mr. Burke is darkly alluded to, together with his cousin." (Prior, *Life of Malone*, p. 419.)

26. See Dixon Wecter's admirable monograph *Edmund Burke and His Kinsmen. A Study of the Statesman's Financial Integrity and Private Relationships* (University of Colorado Studies, Boulder, 1939). In the present section I have drawn heavily upon Professor Wecter's treatment of Richard and Will Burke.

Miss Hawkins it will be noted made her strictures on the *men* of the Burke family. Jane Burke, Edmund's wife and the family's only female member, seems to have had a rare art of disarming hostile criticism. Many of her acquaintances described her, but always in flattering terms: as "gentle," "soft-mannered," "amiable," "the perfect English wife." Except for the fact of her having been bred a Catholic, there was no point at which her social character was regarded as vulnerable.

Of those who surrounded Burke "Cousin Will" was undoubtedly the principal target for hostile criticism. He was an aggressive, not-over-scrupulous person, constantly at work in his own interests, and capable of arousing intense antagonisms in the people about him. In several ways he was an able man—particularly in political controversy, where his skill as a pamphleteer was respected and won him some rewards. Unfortunately he was reckless as to means, and when his first efforts in life ended in failure he gradually developed into a desperate gambler. His career falls into two parts. In the early part he made some reputation as a writer, won a seat in Parliament, and held two more or less responsible administrative positions in the government. This period came to an end when in 1773 he lost heavily on some speculations he was carrying on in India stock, and when—far worse—in 1774 he lost the seat in Parliament which had given him immunity from arrest for debt. He was forced to leave the country to escape his creditors. He went out to India, returned, went out again, tried several more-than-shady maneuvers to make himself suddenly rich, and finally returned to England and bankruptcy.

If it is asked, as it must be, why Edmund associated himself with such a person, there are several answers. One is that the association was made at a time when both men were very young, and the less creditable sides of Will's nature had not had a full chance to declare themselves. Edmund was twenty-one, Will twenty, when they first met; both were full of ambition, and along similar lines. Edmund was never, in any part of his career, without some intense friendship; he had left Shackleton behind him in Ireland, but soon formed an equally close intimacy with Will in England. The two studied together, went on vacations together, shared lodgings, had their friends in common;

soon they were collaborating on their literary productions, and eventually they both got into Parliament under the same patronage.

Will, if he was overreaching in his other dealings with the world, appears to have been ideally generous when it came to Edmund. When in 1765 his patron Lord Verney offered him a seat in Parliament, he was so certain that Edmund's abilities were superior to his own that he persuaded that very accommodating nobleman to transfer the seat to Edmund. Fortunately another seat was later found for himself, so that the two friends actually entered the House of Commons at the same session. Nor was this a solitary instance of Will's eagerness to be of service to Edmund. It was through Will that Edmund was introduced to his own patron, the Marquis of Rockingham. We are told—though it would be hard to know—that Jane Burke, before she became Edmund's wife, had been courted by Will, who however accepted her preference for Edmund as natural and inevitable, and was not less but more devoted to both of them after their marriage. Will lived under the same roof as Edmund as long as his creditors allowed him to live in England.

Edmund was not a man who could respond coldly to such a frank affection. His own personal feelings were strong and unguarded, and he admired intensely the sort of unworldly devotion of which he saw Will Burke was capable. He accepted and returned what he regarded as a noble and generous friendship. Unfortunately he was either unable or unwilling to see that the man who could be so magnanimous in dealing with him might not be equally so in all his other dealings. When it began to be rumored that Will was more than reckless—was definitely dishonest—in some of his financial operations, Edmund would not for a moment consider that the charge might be true. "Enemies" manufactured such charges! One of Burke's most respectable friends remonstrated strongly with him, pointing out how much he was injuring his own reputation by his trust in Will. The man was completely in earnest, and incidentally was a bishop. Edmund's reply to him was, in substance, that it was *impossible* that Will should be dishonest. "Mr. William Burke," he wrote, ". . . has had the closest and longest friendship for me; and has pursued it with such nobleness in all respects, as has no example in these times, and would have dignified the best periods of history. Whenever I was in question, he has been not only ready, but earnest even, to annihilate himself . . ." [27] As far as the statement went, it was perfectly true, but only in the logic of the emotions would it result that Will must therefore be a good man in every aspect of his life.

It was probably fortunate for Edmund's career that Will Burke fled to India when he did, and remained there for over fifteen years. Edmund could not wholly escape being injured by his friendship for a discredited man (it was said, for example, that all of his labors in the Hastings Impeachment must have been caused by a resentment at Hastings for having slighted Will); [28] but injuries at five thousand miles distance are considerably less disastrous than those inflicted by a housemate. Not to be cynical, one might suggest too that the comfortable belief in Will's being wholly innocent was much assisted by his being extremely remote. His "enemies," his "cruel and unprovoked persecutors" [29] sound none too real even in letters, but their unmixed badness is easier to conceive in Madras or Calcutta than near at hand in England. Geography helped Burke to maintain both his loyalty to Will and the illusions by which it was supported.

Richard Burke, Edmund's younger brother, was a very different sort of person from Will, but he constituted a rather similar embarrassment to Edmund's career. He was neither very able nor very aggressive, disadvantages partly balanced by the fact that he was handsome, lively, and generally liked. His limitations are fairly well summed up in the statement that he always needed help. He was the very type of a dependent younger brother. He did not have a university training, as Edmund did, and he was late—too late—in finding himself a useful profession. The small fortune of Burke's father descended to Edmund, so that "Dick" had a kind of right to expect some assistance. He came to live with Edmund and Jane in the late 1750's and continued living with them off and on till his death in 1794.

27. Burke, *Correspondence*, I, 317.
28. See the *Farington Diary*, ed. James Greig (London, 1922–28), I, 136.
29. Burke, *Correspondence*, II, 484.

Most people found Dick good company. He had adequate native abilities, warm affections, and high spirits of a slightly boisterous kind. He got on well with such good judges of society as David Garrick and Sir Joshua Reynolds. Unfortunately he also got on well with some devotees of deep drinking and deep play. On one sensational occasion he lost £14,970 in one evening —a serious matter, because it later appeared that he had only £2,000 to his name when he sat down.[30] In a less offensive manner than Will Burke, Dick gradually acquired the reputation of a cheat. People called him "Duck" Burke. He never became so desperate a plunger as Will, but he repeated a good many of Will's mistakes. He too tried his hand at speculation in India stock, with unhappy results. He too attempted to recoup his losses by elaborate financial schemes, which did not save him from insolvency. On at least one occasion he too found he had to flee the country to escape his creditors. In one period when he held a minor governmental post in the West Indies he managed to get his accounts out of balance to the amount of £2,185 in his own favor.

Naturally there were harsh comments on Dick from an unsympathetic world. The bishop who objected to Will also objected to Dick; indeed he referred to the Burke household as a "hole of adders."[31] Edmund—perhaps more justifiably than in Will's case—flamed into defense. He knew that his brother was a lovable, well-intentioned, sensitive man; he refused to admit that he might also be weak and prone to self-delusions. Edmund never underestimated the obligations members of a family owed to each other; unfortunately he never knew how to go halfway in any matter of personal feeling. Again he was better able to blind himself to the realities of the situation than abandon an intimate who loved him and whom he loved.

Neither Dick nor Will ever married, and as both continued to live in Edmund's household when they were in England, sharing a common purse with him and always merging their

30. Professor Wecter points out (*Edmund Burke and His Kinsmen*, p. 71) the interesting fact that the account on which this narrative is based was found among the private papers of Warren Hastings. Burke's great enemy apparently had a use for a story so discreditable to Richard.

31. Burke, *Correspondence*, I, 285.

interests with his, it is not extraordinary that British society thought of "the Burkes" as a unit. Neither is it very extraordinary that society had its suspicions about such a family. Edmund was not the only one of them who had secrets. Will too went to fantastic lengths to keep his private affairs from being known.[32] Both Will and Dick were anonymous journalists, many of whose writings were on occasion attributed to Edmund. All three took almost officious pleasure in fighting each other's battles. Scholars and biographers have sometimes felt that in public estimates of character a clearer distinction should have been made between the integrity of Edmund and the moral weakness of the other two. Yet it is easy to see why the distinction was not made. Edmund more than anyone else was resolved that the family should stand or fall as a unit; he paid in reputation for his belief in their solidarity.

The outward symbol of the family strength of the Burkes was the estate at Beaconsfield, which they purchased in 1768 and which was their common home for the rest of their lives. The acquisition of this florid establishment, for the immense sum of £20,000, has always been one of the stock puzzles to be discussed in biographies of Edmund. How did a man whose worldly resources were no greater than his ever make up his mind to such an outrageous extravagance? Scholars have estimated that the mere upkeep of the place should be put in the neighborhood of £2,500 a year. Could Burke, who had no income as Member of Parliament, and a very trifling inheritance, ever have imagined that he was going to be able to support these charges? Why should he have sacrificed so much of his peace of mind—he was deeply in debt for the rest of his life—merely for this facade of luxury?

The purchase is much easier to understand if we bear in mind

32. Prior (I, 194), among other matters relating to Samuel Dyer, mentions "the intrusion, as it is said, of Mr. William Burke into his lodgings after his death, and cutting up a great variety of papers into the smallest possible shreds (there being no fire at that season of the year to burn them), which were thickly strewed all over the room, to the great surprise of Sir Joshua Reynolds, one of the executors, who, entering soon after, and asking for an explanation, was informed, 'they were of great importance to him (Mr. Burke) but of none to any other person.' "

two facts. It was not Edmund alone, it was "the Burkes" who embarked on the extravagance. Moreover it was "the Burkes" at a particular moment in their history. In 1768 the family had been battling the indifference and hostility of British society for a period of over ten years, during most of which time they were certainly "Irish adventurers," of not even a very respectable grade. They had lived very humbly. After his marriage Edmund had moved to the house of his father-in-law, where it seems more than likely that he had lived largely at his father-in-law's expense. He had a wife and soon two children, and Will and Dick had also come to live with him. Edmund worked furiously, first at literature, then at politics, without gaining more than the slenderest monetary rewards. Will also worked hard, as a journalist and politician, with a little more success than Edmund, but nothing that could be called marked prosperity. Dick, the least trained and least laborious, left England for the West Indies with the idea of making his fortune; he injured his health permanently without much bettering his finances. The whole family was struggling and—at first—struggling in very poor luck.

Finally in the middle 'sixties the situation began to change. Will began to have a wonderful run of luck. He found a patron, Lord Verney, who was both wealthy and—to put it simply—a little soft. Will established an astonishing hold upon Lord Verney.[33] By this time Will had served his political apprenticeship and reached the eminence of a post as Undersecretary of State at £1,000 a year. He was ready to ask for a seat in Parliament, which Lord Verney was ready to give him. Will had also succeeded in introducing Edmund to Lord Rockingham, who offered him a post as his secretary. Lord Rockingham was Prime Minister at the time, so that Edmund too now had a political role of some importance, and he too was ready for a seat in Parliament. In the early part of 1766 both of the "kinsmen" entered the House.

The whole worldly position of "the Burkes" changed com-

---

33. A letter of Henry Fox (later Lord Holland) to Lord Sandwich, Nov. 12, 1763, said of William Burke: "He has as great a sway with Lord Verney, as I ever knew one man to have with another." L. B. Namier, *England in the Age of the American Revolution* (London, 1930), p. 214 n.

pletely. Edmund's speeches during his first session were brilliantly successful; it appeared more than likely that, as Dr. Johnson predicted, he would be "one of the first men in the country" in a comparatively short time. The financial situation brightened too. Lord Verney advanced capital to both Will and Dick, who began to have amazing success in their purchases of East India stock. For two or three years the family enjoyed a heady prosperity. It was in this period that Beaconsfield was bought.

Scholars have discussed at some length the question of how the transaction—or at least Edmund's part of it—must have been financed. By his father's death in 1765 Edmund had come into a small estate (variously estimated at between £2,000 and £6,000 in value) which presumably went into the purchase. It has often been suggested, but never proved, that the Marquis of Rockingham may have advanced part of the money.[34] Of course the estate itself was able to bear mortgages. All three of the Burkes, one might add, must have looked prosperous enough to have borrowed something on their personal credit.

They had scarcely assumed the various obligations connected with the purchase before it began to appear that they had stretched themselves too far. They had picked the one moment of their highest collective prosperity to take their chance. The moment was soon over. First, their principal mortgagor died, which meant that £6,000 worth of mortgages which they had expected to have years to clear fell due at once. They were paid, though with great difficulty. Then the stock holdings of Will and Dick suddenly dropped 60 per cent in value, completely ruining both men. The prospects of political advantage which Will and Edmund had had some right to trust in 1768 were slow in realizing themselves; ultimately they proved very disappointing. Will failed of re-election to Parliament within five years and never regained his seat. Edmund, though he was still to be in the House of Commons for over twenty-five years and to rise to the reputation of one of the half dozen great statesmen of his age, managed

34. Burke himself offers testimony on the point. Replying to Shackleton's misleading account of him, cited above, Burke wrote in a letter of April 19, 1770: "Nor have I had any advantage except my seat in Parliament from the patronage of any man. Whatever advantages I have had have been from friends on my own level . . ." Samuels, *op. cit.*, p. 399.

to miss the financial rewards which usually belonged to such a career; in his twenty-five remaining years in Parliament he held office for less than twelve months.

If Edmund could have foreseen his whole future, he might have wisely resold the Beaconsfield estate some time in the early 'seventies: from then on it was a burden which was always far beyond his means. But he was of a hopeful nature and continued to believe that the fortunes of his family, or of his party, would change for the better. Meantime he held on. The appearance of prosperity which the estate gave him had a kind of speculative value; it warranted his respectability by making him an owner of land, and doubtless it really bettered his chances of winning one of those permanent prizes of politics—a pension or a sinecure— which might have enabled him to keep it up. There were more solid reasons too that an estate was important to Burke's career. It is part of the business of a statesman to be in contact with men of all groups: to know their opinions, aims, and political characters. The hospitality of Beaconsfield was one of Burke's chief means of doing this. He saw far more of young Charles Fox, of the Duke of Portland or the Marquis of Rockingham, or of foreign visitors like young Metternich or the Comte de Mirabeau, than he could ever have hoped to do if he had not been in a position to entertain them generously.

One must bear in mind too that though Beaconsfield was the façade of a luxurious establishment and was used as such on great occasions, the day-to-day life of the Burkes was anything but luxurious. It was full of rustic economies. They rolled up to their front door in an impressive family coach with four black horses, but when the horses were taken out of harness they might be used the next day for the family plowing.[35] Beaconsfield was a farm, and only secondarily a country estate. Burke told his friend David Garrick that he had better come there on a visit only after he had grown tired of splendid establishments: "You first sate yourself with wit, jollity, and luxury, and afterwards retire hither to repose your person and your understanding in early hours, boiled mutton, drowsy conversation, and a little clabber milk." [36] In part this

35. Prior, I, 348.
36. David Garrick, *Private Correspondence* (London, 1831), I, 208–209.

was a conventional hostly humility, but only in part. Those who really expected luxurious living could be shocked by what they found at Beaconsfield. Mrs. Thrale, who once paid the Burkes a surprise visit when on a trip with her husband and Dr. Johnson, never got over what she saw: the dust and cobwebs in the corners, the crudity and disorder, the colored servant who brought in tea with a cut finger wrapped in rags. She later wrote a very censorious "character" of Burke with a few prefatory remarks about the time when ". . . I lived with him & his Lady at Beaconsfield among Dirt Cobwebs, Pictures and Statues that would not have disgraced the City of Paris itself: where Misery & Magnificence reign in all their Splendour, & in perfect Amity." [37] Mrs. Thrale may not have been altogether familiar with the problem of keeping up a showy country house on the uncertain income of a public servant.

The worst strains of Burke family economy did not fall upon Edmund but on his wife Jane, and in later years on his son Richard. It was quite typical of the self-sacrificing devotion of these two that they bore those strains and yet managed to conceal from Burke the worst of their difficulties. He had his own difficulties, in other fields, and scarcely realized until after his son's death how serious the economic straits of the family sometimes were. In a memorial of Richard which was left among his papers he recorded his belated realization of their true plight:

My affairs were always in a state of embarrassment and confusion; but he and his mother contrived that this should be rarely visible to the world. Everything about us bore the appearance of order. It is incredible with what skill, patience, and clearness he provided for them, by discreet delay, or by method and foresight and every species of skilful management, in concert with his admirable mother. What is equally wonderful is that they both kept from me, personally, everything that was fretful, teasing and disquieting, so that in truth, I had but a kind of loose general knowledge of several things which, if they had, during so many years of other contention and close application to Business come to my knowledge in detail, I am perfectly

37. *Thraliana*, ed. Katherine C. Balderston (Oxford, 1942), I, 475. Mrs. Thrale added a note to this: "Irish Roman Catholics are always like the Foreigners somehow: dirty & dressy, with their Clothes hanging as if upon a Peg."

sure I could never have borne up against them, much less have preserved that cheerfulness and animation, which it was visible I enjoyed, whilst everything was untoward enough, within and without.[38]

Burke gives rather too much the impression that he and the
general public had *no* knowledge of his financial stresses. This
would be claiming too much. On at least one occasion he personally was sued in chancery in connection with the large debts
of Will Burke, some of which were supposed to be secured by
the Beaconsfield estate. If Lord Verney, his assailant, had proved
his case, it is hard to see how the Burkes could have paid him without selling the property. Fortunately the plea was dismissed, on
Burke's sworn denial, and the family left in possession.[39] But
there was another even more agonizing occasion, when the death
of a mortgagor threatened them with immediate foreclosure, for
the second time in their career as householders. It was in the most
unhappy part of Burke's life, after the death of Richard. He wrote
frantically to his friend Walker King:

I send you the letter which I received this morning from the Executors of Lloyd. They will be put off no longer. . . . It is not for me to
point out to you the immediate consequences. They are now directly
upon me. Had I foreseen this, I might perhaps in America, Portugal,
or elsewhere, have found a refuge; and the sale of what I have might
have gone some way toward doing justice to my creditors. But time
will not be allowed to me to make my arrangements, and I confess
so much weakness, that though I had conceived that very few things
could affect me after what has happened, I cannot quite reconcile
my mind to prison with great fortitude.[40]

The crisis passed, as others had, and actually the estate remained
in the family until the death of the last survivor, Mrs. Burke, in
1812.

In some ways the long struggle to hold Beaconsfield was a fit
symbol of the other struggles of the Burkes to hold their unity
as a family and to keep their place in a world which was never

38. Magnus, pp. 52–53.
39. *Ibid.*, p. 146; see also Wecter, *Edmund Burke and His Kinsmen*, pp. 40–41.
40. Unpublished letter of Burke to Walker King, June 30, 1795, in the possession of Professor Frederick W. Hilles of Yale University.

very friendly to them. Others besides Edmund's friend the bishop would gladly have seen him rid himself of the encumbrance of Dick and Will. In merely worldly terms it would have been well for him if he could have done so. Actually he did exactly the opposite. As their lives declined into failure he held them ever closer to him, valued them more highly, perhaps by his very loyalty increased their helpless dependence upon him. He was repaid by their affection, if not in other ways. So far as we can learn from any source, the Burkes never went through a single family quarrel from the beginning to the end of their long career. Edmund said that, with all the trials he had in his life, "every care vanished the moment he entered under his own roof." [41]

Young Richard, as he grew to manhood, became even more devoted to his family than the other members were to each other. He was the idol of them all in return. He does not seem to have been equally admired by the rest of the world. He was a handsome, earnest, ambitious youth, who so far from being morally undependable like his uncles Dick and Will, was almost too challenging an example of virtue and rectitude. He embarrassed more relaxed individuals. No one would agree with his father, who insisted on thinking him one of the first political geniuses of the age, as well as a moral paragon. Yet it is not easy to decide, amid conflicting testimony, what the balance of his faults and virtues really was for the world outside his family. Fanny Burney was attracted by him. [42] Dr. Johnson at least once paid him a high compliment. [43] He was elected to the Literary Club, an honor his father had tried in vain to win for Dick or Will. True, the members seem to have given him the irreverent nickname of The Whelp . . . [44]

It is pretty clear that in a social sense Burke *carried* Richard,

41. Prior, I, 61.

42. *Diary and Letters of Madame d'Arblay*, ed. Charlotte Barrett (London, 1904–5), II, 159.

43. *Life of Johnson*, IV, 219. Boswell's account in the journal of Richard's encounter with Johnson (*Boswell Papers*, XV, 212) is slightly fuller: "Young Burke did exceedingly well. I just lay by and let him play the great Organ. The Doctor said to me afterwards, 'He did very well indeed. I have a mind to tell his Father.'"

44. *Johnsonian Miscellanies*, ed. George Birkbeck Hill (Oxford, 1897), II, 32 n.

as he did Dick and Will. Nor was even Richard the last of his social encumbrances. One must always include in Burke's entourage a few additional figures—usually of indigent Irish relatives. The Burkes believed in hospitality and, especially in the summer season, Beaconsfield usually had an assortment of miscellaneous guests who were making long visits. This could be no light hazard for those who extended social invitations to the family. Sir Joshua Reynolds' sister, who entertained for him, used to complain bitterly that ". . . whenever any of Burke's poor Irish relations came over, they were all poured in upon them . . ." [45] One can feel for the poor lady. Wasn't it enough to make up one's mind to entertain, say, Edmund, Jane, Dick, Will, and young Richard, without worrying about extras? And as if to make it worse, her hospitable brother "never took any notice, but bore it all with great patience and tranquility." [46] He didn't have to plan the arrangements.

The miracle is that with such embarrassments as they had, "the Burkes" survived at all in the upper circles of British society. Sir Gilbert Elliot, one of their aristocratic friends, once described the way they must have looked to many a host and hostess:

Burke has now got such a train after him as would sink anybody but himself:—his son, who is quite *nauseated* by all mankind; his brother, who is liked better than his son, but is rather oppressive with animal spirits and brogue, and his cousin Will Burke, who is just returned unexpectedly from India, as much ruined as when he went many years ago, and who is a fresh charge on any prospects of power Burke may ever have. Mrs. Burke has in her train Miss French, the most perfect *she Paddy* ever caught . . . [47]

Sir Gilbert was not sympathetic, but his account was only seriously inaccurate at one point. He should not have said, "Burke has *now* got such a train . . ." Burke was never without the train, from the beginning of his political career. He always marched at the head of a clan.

45. Hazlitt's "Conversations of Northcote," *The Complete Works of William Hazlitt*, ed. P. P. Howe (London, 1932), XI, 220.

46. *Idem*, p. 220.

47. *Life and Letters of Sir Gilbert Elliot*, ed. Countess of Minto (London, 1874), II, 136.

III

Among the various unlucky statements in Richard Shackleton's unlucky account of Burke, that about his receipt of patronage was very likely the most misleading. According to Shackleton Burke had had the great good fortune, shortly after his arrival in England, of being "introduced to the acquaintance of Men in power, who made him easy in his circumstances . . ." [48]

The one essential thing to understand about Burke's circumstances is that they were perpetually *uneasy*. On its economic side his life was fantastically unlucky. Not that this was always the fault of "men in power" who should have succored him. First and last Burke received a great deal of assistance from the Marquis of Rockingham, the Duke of Portland, Earl Fitzwilliam, and other of his friends in their class. He and his kinsmen also received large sums of public money, as the legitimate (or in two or three instances, the illegitimate) rewards of holding office. Edmund also borrowed heavily from private friends, usually with little hope of paying them back. In mere terms of supply—of amounts received—Burke was not badly cared for, as public servants go. It was in the control and predictability of his supply that he was completely unfortunate. He lived on loans, gifts, and windfalls. From the beginning to the end of his parliamentary labors—and he was perhaps as hardworking a statesman as England ever knew—he had no settled income on which he could lay out a rational plan for his own security.

In part this was merely the character of the career he had chosen. Politics is at all times an adventurous life, and it was at least as adventurous as usual in the eighteenth century. Burke's private fortune was scarcely worth mentioning, and mere service in the House of Commons then carried no remuneration. This meant that there were very limited ways in which he could support himself directly by politics; none of the ways, obviously, offered any certainties. If his party came into power he might get a well-paid government post. If he was attentive and lucky in the general scramble for preferment he might win a pension or sinecure or other settled income from public funds. If things

48. Samuels, *op. cit.*, p. 403.

went well enough, and he attracted the right kind of notice, he might be raised to a peerage—perhaps at the end of his active career. But on the other hand if none of these chances should happen to turn out right, he might live and die as a meritorious public servant without ever becoming acquainted with a reliable means of support.

The opening of Burke's career in the House of Commons probably gave him far too rosy an opinion of his worldly prospects. His debut was exceptionally brilliant. Dr. Johnson, no giddy optimist, thought that he had "gained more reputation than perhaps any man at his [first] appearance ever gained before," [49] and agreed with the fairly general opinion that he would soon profit by it in a material way. "Burke is a great man by nature," he said, "and is expected soon to attain civil greatness." [50] When Sir John Hawkins was unfriendly enough to express wonder at so sudden a rise into prominence, Johnson's reply was, "Now we who know Burke, know, that he will be one of the first men in this country." [51]

The real question was how soon such splendid prospects would be fulfilled. At first there must have seemed to be no serious cause for worry. Burke's party was in power; he rapidly attained the fame of being their ablest speaker; he was discussed even by his opponents as "the readiest man upon all points perhaps in the whole House." [52] That he had a strong influence over Lord Rockingham was common knowledge; the political gossips referred to "Mr. Bourk, descended from a garret to the head of our administration." [53] It could not have seemed that it would take much time for so amazing a political paragon either to be placed in office or to be given a respectable share of party spoils.

Burke had been five months in the House when the Rockingham ministry was dismissed and entered upon a period in opposi-

49. *Life of Johnson*, II, 16.
50. *Idem*, pp. 16–17.
51. *Idem*, p. 450.
52. Letter of the Duke of Grafton to the Earl of Chatham, Oct. 16, 1766, *Correspondence of William Pitt, Earl of Chatham*, ed. William Stanhope Taylor and Captain John Henry Pringle (London, 1839), III, 110.
53. Unpublished letter of Lord Buckinghamshire preserved in the British Museum (Add. Mss. 22358, f. 35), cited by Murray, p. 132.

tion which was to last just short of sixteen years. This was the first ill turn of a promising career. Probably at the start Burke could have avoided his fate; it was fairly generally thought that by separating himself from the party in the summer of 1766 he could have had a place in the new government Lord Chatham was then forming. Rockingham himself generously urged him to make the most of his chances. Burke refused, and cast in his lot with Rockingham and his friends.

For the next sixteen years it would be accurate to describe Burke as a man who was always just about to reach some kind of satisfactory position. His parliamentary fame rose steadily; he extended his acquaintance among the leading figures of the day; toward the end of the period he was recognized as the real, effective head of his party. The party on more than one occasion was nearly returned to power; but for the American war, which had the effect of consolidating the position of Lord North's government, it would almost certainly have reached a position in which Burke's magnificent party services could have been rewarded adequately. Meantime he lived on expectations. His friends, partly through generosity, but no doubt partly in the belief that his difficulties were merely temporary, helped the cause of his finances. David Garrick lent him money,[54] Sir Joshua Reynolds lent him money; [55] Lord Rockingham began making him periodic loans of £1,000, each secured by a separate bond.[56] When Lord Rockingham died in 1782 his will canceled the bonds outstanding, which by that time were supposed to have reached the sum of £30,000.[57]

It is almost laughable in relation to such figures, and to the expenses we know Burke was incurring in running Beaconsfield, that we can point to two items of Burke's income in this period which might be described as "his own" earnings, not derived from either gift or loan. Before he entered politics Burke had launched the *Annual Register* for Robert Dodsley and run it for several

54. Garrick, *Correspondence*, I, 353-354.
55. Magnus, p. 231.
56. *Farington Diary*, I, 212.
57. Thomas Macknight, *The Life and Times of Edmund Burke* (London, 1858-60), II, 543. See also John Morley, *Burke* (English Men of Letters series, London, 1892), p. 51.

years at a salary of £100 a year. So far as we know, he was still its editor in the 'seventies and the early 'eighties.[58] He therefore had at least £100 a year in his own right at a time when his expenses were certainly in thousands. The second item was slightly more impressive, though the income lasted for a shorter period. The Assembly of the Colony of New York, having noted that Burke from the beginning of his parliamentary career championed the cause of America, in 1770 appointed him their London agent at a salary of £500 a year. This agency continued until the outbreak of the American war in 1775, and the salary was ultimately raised to £640 by the addition of a fund for expenses.[59]

In spite of Burke's excellent financial reasons for welcoming this latter employment, a pretty obvious objection could be raised to it. Had Burke the right, while he remained a Member of Parliament, and supposedly allowed nothing to prejudice his judgment of the issues of empire—had he the right to draw a salary from a single group such as the New York Assembly? As a man of strict conscience, which he tried to be, Burke must have examined this question carefully before he accepted the position. We can guess some of the arguments by which he rationalized his decision. He had established his general opinions regarding American policy long before the New York group employed him; he was not being bribed into sympathy with a cause that was alien to his beliefs. Moreover, most of his duties as agent were of a routine, and hence innocent, kind. He had to write letters of information to his colonial employers, and at the other end had to transmit their reports and petitions to the home government. He was in opposition, hence not in a position to exert much corrupting influence. Very likely, too, eighteenth-century legislators were less inclined to worry over matters of conscience than legislators today. There were other colonial agents in Parliament.

But one should not go to all lengths in defense of Burke's theoretical state of innocence. Even by eighteenth-century standards the American agency was a little questionable. Burke's enemies were still citing it as evidence of his venality seven years after he

---

58. See following essay, "A Career in Journalism."
59. See *Journal of the Votes and Proceedings of the General Assembly of the Colony of New York, from 1766–1776 inclusive* (Albany, 1820).

had ceased to hold it.[60] Even Dr. Johnson (facetiously, to be sure) spoke of the Americans putting "their vile agents in the house of parliament, there to sow the seeds of sedition, and propagate confusion, perplexity, and pain."[61] There is no reason to think that Burke's political conscience did not feel the equivocal nature, if not the vileness, of his position. If all his other resources had not been strained to the limit, very likely he would not have been tempted to earn £500 a year in so compromising a way.

Some men who began their political careers with no greater economic advantages than Burke had much greater success than he in catching those prizes—pensions, sinecures, and the like—which at the time were regarded as the quite legitimate rewards of public life. Isaac Barré, one of the Rockingham Whigs, whose claims on the party were certainly not superior to Burke's, had been in Parliament twenty years when in addition to an official salary of £4,000 he was granted a permanent pension of £3,000. John Dunning, on a shorter period of service, got a peerage and £4,000, and he had a sizable personal fortune to begin with. William Eden won his peerage twenty years after he came into the House.[62] These men were not thought at the time, any more than they have been since, Burke's superiors in political stature.

There were one or two special reasons for Burke's ill success. One was the generous vice we have already noted: his loyalty to his brother and Will Burke. By the early 'seventies, that is, before Burke's career in Parliament had run a decade, both of those had lost the ability to support themselves independently; if Edmund wished to keep them afloat, he could do it only by a dissipation of his own political resources. Richard's land speculations in the West Indies were the most unpromising kind of risk, yet Edmund exhausted himself attempting—vainly—to make them succeed. Will Burke had many enemies in India; Edmund, when he could gain the ear of power, fought Will's battles for him on the

60. *Parliamentary History*, XXII, 1134.
61. Mrs. Piozzi's *Anecdotes of Samuel Johnson*, ed. S. C. Roberts (Cambridge, 1932), p. 30.
62. Burke himself cited these three examples in a paper he drew up in defense of his own claims, when his pension was under consideration in 1794. See H. V. F. Somerset's article entitled "Some Papers of Edmund Burke on His Pension," *English Historical Review*, XIV, 110–114.

home ground. When the Rockingham Whigs enjoyed their brief moments of power, Edmund made reckless efforts to provide for the other two—always at the expense of his own credit.

In the later period of his career there was another reason that Edmund's share in the monetary spoils of office never nearly matched his deserts. In the early 'eighties he took a leading part in a very important movement for reform of government offices, which involved the suppression of many of the pensions and sinecure appointments which had been directly under the control of the Crown. The chief reason this reform was desired by the Rockingham Whigs was that these grants had been systematically by George III as means of buying an undue influence over Parliament. It was actually no part of the Whigs' intention to abolish them entirely, for they, like most of the rest of the public, regarded them as often the legitimate rewards of political services to the nation.

Of course the position was open to misunderstanding. Though Burke in his famous Speech on Economical Reform made a specific declaration of his own belief that many of the grants certainly should not be abolished, because they served a useful purpose, that was no more than a side remark, a qualification of his main argument; his principal aim was the elimination of many of the grants because of their corrupting influence. It was therefore easy for his opponents later to pretend that his position had been much simpler than it was, and that he was utterly inconsistent—hence himself a venal corruptionist—if he supposed that his own political services deserved any such reward. Horace Walpole, whose receipts from various types of preferment totaled around £250,000 in a well-protected lifetime,[63] once remarked sharply on some efforts of Burke to get the Clerkship of the Pells for a member of his family. The Clerkship of the Pells was the second largest preferment in the gift of the Crown. "Can one but smile," Walpole wrote in his Journal, "at a reformer of abuses reserving the second greatest abuse for himself?" [64] (Burke did not, of course, succeed in getting the Clerkship of the Pells.)

63. G. M. Trevelyan, *Early History of Charles James Fox* (new impression, London, 1928), p. 96.
64. Horace Walpole, *Memoirs of the Reign of King George the Third, 1771-1783* (London, 1859), II, 556.

When at the end of their sixteen years of waiting the Rocking-ham Whigs finally came into power, Burke's financial profit by the arrangement seemed likely to be very considerable. He be-came Paymaster of Forces with an official residence and a salary of £4,000. His dependents were gloriously provided for. Young Richard, aged twenty-four, was made a deputy paymaster to his father at a salary of £500 a year; Will Burke was made a deputy paymaster in India at £5 a day; Dick Burke had £3,000 as Secre-tary to the Treasury; even Edmund's sister in Ireland was re-membered with a small pension which was in the gift of the Ministry. If so satisfactory a set of arrangements had only endured for a time, the Burkes might have emerged from the desperate financial condition in which they had lived for so long.

Unfortunately the Marquis of Rockingham died three months after taking office, and the government fell. For the Burkes it was a cruel blow of Fate. Still, it was not absolutely irretrievable. After a series of maneuvers, not altogether creditable, Burke and Fox succeeded in making an arrangement with Lord North— their erstwhile bitterest enemy—which restored them all to power in a coalition government, and restored Burke and his re-lations to their preferments. This time Burke made a still further improvement in the financial status of the family. When Dick Burke had had a minor government post in the West Indies many years before, he had managed public funds so incompetently as to come under a serious charge of embezzlement. By such influ-ence as he possessed, Edmund had been staving off Dick's "ene-mies"—those who believed the charge justified—for several years. He now took advantage of his position in office to get the whole matter quashed—which made Dick an "honest man," but of course provoked a few comments upon Edmund. All might yet have gone well with the finances of the Burke family. Unfortunately the coalition ministry, like its predecessor, was doomed to a very short life. It collapsed after eight months. This was the last time during Edmund's parliamentary career that his party was in power: hence the last time that the Burkes could have been restored to solvency by receipt of the spoils of office.

Unsuccessful as they were, Edmund's efforts in behalf of his family were bitterly resented by his political opponents, who of course knew very well how to make the most of their discreditable aspects. It would be futile to attempt to defend them. The most that can be said on Burke's side is that the amounts of money involved—and they were by no means contemptible—were hardly beyond what would at the time have been thought a decent return for Burke's services to the nation. In the early 'eighties Burke stood at the pinnacle of his parliamentary fame. He had served the nation brilliantly, devotedly, and with infinite industry for nearly two decades, and at that moment he was even enjoying an unwonted popularity. He was also at just that point in his career when it was customary that "something should be done for" a successful politician. It would not have surprised many people if at the accession of Rockingham's government either a large pension or a peerage had been conferred upon him; there was widespread surprise that he was not given a more important post than that of paymaster. Actually Burke ought to be criticized far more for the impracticality than for the viciousness of the course he had followed. Why had he not taken what he could certainly have got—a large single reward for himself? The nation would have seen the justice of that, and he himself would then have been in a position to distribute largess to his kinsmen. By following the opposite course, of distributing his patronage over half a dozen members of so vulnerable a group, he did everything possible to invite attack, and to make it conspicuous that sometimes he had to think of his own, and not exclusively of the public, interests.

But the mistake was made, the harm done to his reputation, and never during Burke's period in Parliament was there a chance to do better in another trial. Once in 1789 the party came very close to returning to power, and the Duke of Portland, who was in charge of arrangements, evidently tried hard to help Burke. Sir Gilbert Elliot was present when plans were being discussed, and lets us know what would have been done if chance had permitted:

The Duke of Portland has the veneration for Burke that Windham, Pelham, myself, and a few more have, and he thinks it impossible to do too much for him. He considers the reward to be given to Burke as a credit and honour to the nation, and he considers the neglect of him and his embarrassed situation as having been long a reproach to the country. The unjust prejudice and clamour which has prevailed against him and his family only determine the Duke the more to do him justice. The question was how? First, his brother Richard, who was Secretary to the Treasury before, will have the same office now, but the Duke intends to give him one of the first offices which falls vacant of about £1000 a year for life in the Customs, and he will then resign the Secretary to the Treasury, which, however, in the meanwhile, is worth £3000 a year. Edmund Burke is to have the Pay Office, £4000 a year; but as that is precarious, and he can leave no provision for his son, it would, in fact, be doing little or nothing of any real or substantial value unless some *permanent* provision is added to it. In this view the Duke is to grant him on the Irish Establishment a pension of £2000 a year *clear* for his own life, with the reversion of half of it to his son for life, and the other half to Mrs. Burke for her life. This will make Burke completely happy by leaving his wife and son safe from want after his death if they should survive him. The Duke's affectionate anxiety to accomplish this object, and his determination to set all clamour at defiance on this point of justice, was truly affecting, and increases my attachment for the Duke . . .

Sir Gilbert ends his account:

You may think it strange that to this moment Burke does not know a word of all this, and his family are indeed, I believe, suffering a little under the apprehension that he may be neglected in the general scramble.[65]

One can only hope that Burke never did know how close he had come again to a rescue. The party, which for three months at least was generally believed to be on the verge of coming to power, ultimately failed of it.

It was five or six years later than this, and after Burke's final retirement from Parliament, that the arrangements to relieve his financial distress were at last given effect. The manner of doing it was a little awkward and more than a little humiliating to Burke. First, in August, 1794, William Pitt wrote Burke a letter announcing that a Civil List pension of £1,200 had been granted

---

65. *Life and Letters of Sir Gilbert Elliot*, I, 262–263.

him on his own life and that of Mrs. Burke, but that as soon as
Parliament reconvened another larger annuity would be proposed
by the government, in the form of a parliamentary grant. Burke
on the credit of this letter borrowed £4,500, which he applied
at once on his most pressing debts. Meantime Pitt, when Parliament met, found that Burke's enemies were stronger than he
thought, and would make it hard for him to procure the grant
in the form he had proposed. He therefore abandoned his own idea
of a parliamentary grant, and instead got Burke two further annu-
ities—totaling £2,500—from the Crown. It was disappointing of
course to Burke that the grants should not be from Parliament,
but under the circumstances he could hardly refuse them.

Naturally Burke's enemies saw only one possible meaning in
the fact that the grants were from the Crown. It was the final
proof of his venality. After a lifetime of posing as the great liberal
statesman, he had seen his chance of selling out to the forces of
reaction. His stand against the French Revolution, which they
had always insisted was a direct reversal of all his earlier principles,
was now revealed as having been bought. Thirty-seven hundred
pounds was the public price. (It was hinted of course that further
secret pensions were in the background; Burke had long been
accused of secret pensions, even by sincere men like Tom
Paine.[66])

As posterity well knows, two of the gentlemen who joined the
hue-and-cry against Burke's venality would have been much more
prudent if they had stayed out of the whole matter. The young
Duke of Bedford and the Earl of Lauderdale, strangely forgetting
that their own incomes were originally from the Crown, attacked
Burke publicly for having enriched himself by the sacrifice of
his principles. Burke's reply, the famous *Letter to a Noble Lord*,
was both a vindication of himself and a counterassault on these
assailants:

I claim, not the letter, but the spirit of the old English law,—that
is, to be tried by my peers. I decline his Grace's jurisdiction as a judge.
I challenge the Duke of Bedford as a juror to pass on the value of my
services. Whatever his natural parts may be, I cannot recognize in

66. Thomas Paine, "Rights of Man," *The Complete Writings of Thomas
Paine*, ed. Philip Foner (New York, 1945), II, 501, 508.

his few and idle years the competence to judge of my long and laborious life.[67]

Burke reviewed his own political services, as he himself saw them, at the end of his career. This autobiographical portion of the work is perhaps now its most interesting passage and tells us facts about Burke's life which we do not know from any other source:

> I did not come into Parliament to con my lesson. I had earned my pension before I set foot in St. Stephen's chapel. I was prepared and disciplined to this political warfare. The first session I sat in Parliament, I found it necessary to analyze the whole commercial, financial, constitutional, and foreign interests of Great Britain and its empire. A great deal was then done; and more, far more, would have been done, if more had been permitted by events. Then, in the vigor of my manhood, my constitution sank under my labor. Had I then died, (and I seemed to myself very near death,) I had then earned for those who belonged to me more than the Duke of Bedford's ideas of service are of power to estimate.[68]

Though careful to be elaborately respectful to the actual grantors of his pension, the King and the Ministry, Burke made it clear that he did not feel that his services had been overrewarded—nor perhaps rewarded nearly enough:

> I was not, like his Grace of Bedford, swaddled and rocked and dandled into a legislator: *"Nitor in adversum"* is the motto for a man like me. I possessed not one of the qualities nor cultivated one of the arts that recommend men to the favor and protection of the great. I was not made for a minion or a tool. As little did I follow the trade of winning the hearts by imposing on the understandings of the people. At every step of my progress in life, (for in every step was I traversed and opposed,) and at every turnpike I met, I was obliged to show my passport, and again and again to prove my sole title to the honor of being useful to my country, by a proof that I was not wholly unacquainted with its laws and the whole system of its interests both abroad and at home. Otherwise, no rank, no toleration even, for me. I had no arts but manly arts. On them I have stood, and, please God,

67. "Letter to a Noble Lord" in Burke, *Works*, V, 178.
68. *Idem*, pp. 191–192.

in spite of the Duke of Bedford and the Earl of Lauderdale, to the last gasp will I stand.[69]

The tone of these autobiographical portions of the *Letter* is not entirely a pleasant one. It is too nearly the tone of a man who is complaining of injustices to himself—and injustices of a more serious nature than were the merely temporary carpings of the Duke of Bedford or the Earl of Lauderdale. Burke could review his public services with pride. He was scarcely exaggerating when in one passage he spoke of his "life spent with unexampled toil in the service of my country": it was perhaps literally true that his critics could not have found one man in Britain's history who had outdone Burke in sheer laborious application to public business. Did not such efforts deserve a recompense—and a rather different one from the state of agonized insecurity in which Burke had lived out his life? Men may be wronged at every level of society, even at much higher ones than Burke ever reached, if their hopes are perpetually defeated, their best efforts ignored and misconstrued, if they are subjected to an eternal barrage of malicious and unintelligent criticism and not least if an ungrateful public chooses to pretend that it has no obligation to compensate great public services at something like their true value.

IV

One of the passages in Boswell's journal which was not used in the *Life of Johnson* is a discussion Boswell once had with Johnson about Burke's conduct in the House of Commons:

"But," said I, "they represent him as actually mad." "Sir," said he, "if A Man will appear extravagant as he does, and cry, can he wonder that he is represented as Mad?" [70]

Boswell and Johnson were discussing one of the most painful incidents of the Fox-North coalition government, namely, a persecution Burke endured in relation to two fraudulent clerks in the Pay Office named Powell and Bembridge. Burke when he first became Paymaster General had undertaken strenuous reforms of the Pay

69. *Idem*, p. 193.
70. *Boswell Papers*, XV, 234.

Office, which had been up to that time one of the most thoroughly corrupt departments of the government. In carrying out the reforms he had been helped by Powell and Bembridge, who knew the routines of the office far better than he. Unfortunately Burke did not realize at first how deeply both men were themselves involved in the corruptions which they were helping to eradicate. This would not in itself have been a serious matter, for Burke had to have help from within the office, and Powell and Bembridge do not seem to have cheated him. But by two rapid shifts in the political situation Powell and Bembridge became seriously compromising helpers. First, there was the fall of the ministry at the death of Lord Rockingham, which of course meant that Burke lost his post as Paymaster. His successor became convinced that Powell and Bembridge were guilty of corruption, and having extracted—perhaps forced—confessions from both of them, dismissed them from their posts. But then with the establishment of the coalition Burke was restored to the office of Paymaster. As his own experience of Powell and Bembridge had been favorable, and as in spite of their confessions no charges against them had actually been proved, he restored them to their former positions.

It was the occasion for a violent parliamentary storm. Burke's party, which for so many years had been always in the position of an opposition attacking the ministry, was now itself the ministry, open to attack. Burke's action had offered the new opposition an almost perfect target. In the first place Powell and Bembridge *were* guilty, as even Burke was gradually forced to see. But in the second place Burke stubbornly refused to admit that he had been wrong in reinstating them. It was true that the men had not been *proved* guilty at the time of their dismissal; Burke was himself under obligations to them; as they had assisted in major reforms, Burke also felt that the general public owed them something. He felt he had been right to protect them from an arbitrary dismissal.

Though his position was not entirely unreasonable, Burke's manner of asserting it was foolish in the extreme. Taking himself to be in the right, he flew into a rage when the opposition assailed his integrity. Even the gray language of the parliamentary report suggests an explosive scene:

Mr. *Martin* said, that when he heard from the highest authority, that two considerable clerks in office had been dismissed for gross misbehavior, and that they were afterwards restored, he could not help looking upon their restoration as a gross and daring insult to the public.

Mr. *Burke*, rising in a violent fit of passion, exclaimed, "it is a gross and daring-------;" but he could proceed no farther, for Mr. Sheridan by this time had pulled him down on his seat, from a motive of friendship, lest his heat should betray him into some intemperate expressions that might offend the House.[71]

At the next debate on the subject Mr. Burke made an apology to the House for his rage. It was, however, the kind of apology which scarcely disarms attack, for he insisted on restating his position and showing clearly that he had not changed his mind:

. . . with respect to his conduct on that subject, he felt such a sunshine of content in his mind, that were the act undone, he was convinced that he should do it again. It had ever been, and it ever should be a maxim with him, to compassionate the unfortunate; and, if they happened to be connected with him, to protect them, as long as he found them nothing worse than unfortunate. He called Messrs. Powell and Bembridge two unfortunate men; and said they had been committed to his protection by the hand of Providence, and that he did no more than his duty in restoring them to their situations . . .[72]

Indeed Burke revealed that Messrs. Powell and Bembridge had themselves protested against being reinstated:

. . . it was even contrary to the prayers and entreaties of the very parties concerned, that he kept them in his office. He said, that one of them had been with him, and appeared almost distracted; he was absolutely afraid the poor man would lose his senses; this much he was sure of, that the sight of his grey hairs, and the distraction in which he had seen him, had so far affected and overcome him, that he was scarcely able to come down to the House. He then read his own letter to Mr. Powell, by which he signified to him his restoration to office; but at the same time stated, that he was aware that there

71. *Parliamentary History*, XXIII, 803.
72. *Idem*, XXIII, 902–903.

were charges of a very grave and weighty nature talked of against him, about which his mind was by no means made up; and he declared that if those charges should hereafter be proved, it would be utterly impossible for him to keep him in the situation that he then offered. He then read a letter from Mr. Powell, in which that gentleman implored him to permit him to resign, and entreated him to sacrifice him to public clamour rather than bring it on his own head.[73]

Mr. Powell, of course, had not felt it necessary to tell his superior that the charges were substantially true. Burke's generous defense of his subordinate ended in pure disaster. Powell committed suicide, which was taken as a clear acknowledgment of guilt. As might be imagined, Burke's attackers charged that he was directly responsible for the death.

The whole affair was an excellent instance both of Burke's weakness in certain parliamentary situations and of the techniques by which his opponents were able to discredit him. Burke had the defects of his qualities. He was courageous, persevering, full of imagination and fire, varied and brilliant in expression; but he could on occasion be violent and obstinate, and utterly indiscreet in his language. When he was excited by debate he was capable of almost any discourtesy to his opponents as well as any extravagance of statement. His opponents' task, which they gradually learned, was to take advantage of these weaknesses while evading his strength.

During more than half of Burke's parliamentary career—roughly the sixteen years his party was in opposition—circumstances tended to favor the exhibition of his virtues, and prevent his weaknesses from being prominent. An opposition leader, though he lacks power and various material advantages, has certain privileges from his position. Since he cannot act, he is allowed to talk fairly freely—both to show his own capacities, and to expose the weaknesses of the ministry. He is not envied if he shows himself more intelligent or better informed than his peers, since it is quite obvious that his intelligence and information have not won him any ultimate superiority. He is not much blamed for bad manners. He is respected for standing obstinately by his principles

73. *Idem*, XXIII, 903.

in spite of all defeats. He is not even censored for fighting his cause in rather wild and reckless language; since the House must hear him a good deal, a little variety and extravagance is better than mere sober insistence. Burke profited by all of these indulgences in the early part of his career.

Burke had also in the early part of his career a rather special advantage from his relation to the Marquis of Rockingham, and this had an important bearing on his position in the House of Commons. The Marquis of Rockingham was by hereditary wealth and influence one of the most powerful men in England—twice actually Prime Minister, and during most of his political life one of the leading competitors for that office. Yet he was not in reality a powerful statesman. He was a weak if well-intentioned man, very much in need of political advice and of moral support. Burke happened to be the strongest political mind with whom he had connection, and almost from the beginning of his career in politics the Marquis leaned heavily on Burke. This naturally had advantages for Burke; we have seen how indispensable an aid it was to his finances. The rumor of it was certainly of assistance to his parliamentary career. Long before he was well known in the country political analysts were speaking of "Mr. Bourk (I think that is the name not of Lord Rockingham's right hand but of both his hands) . . ." [74] The consequences of such a reputation are obvious. When Burke got up to speak in the House of Commons, he did not speak, to the more worldly members, merely in his own voice: he was the mouthpiece, and perhaps also the brain, of one of the wealthiest landowners under the crown. Such a man deserves attention. If he should have a few parliamentary weaknesses (as who has not?) they could be borne with patience and sympathy.

It is not easy to calculate the extent of the change in Burke's position brought about by Lord Rockingham's death. It appears to have been one of the crucial turning points of his career. Henceforth he was not supported, either in the House or in the councils of the party, by any one powerful influence. He had, of course,

74. Letter of Lord Buckinghamshire, previously cited. British Museum, Add. Mss. 22358, f. 35.

loyal friends with some resources. Charles Fox, who on the Marquis' death became the principal figure in the party, was devoted to Burke. But Fox did not *need* Burke as Rockingham had; Fox was a strong man, capable of directing his own course. Furthermore, if he had had the desire, he had little means of assisting Burke; his own affairs were in a fantastic state of confusion, and though he was immensely popular in Parliament he was not a respectable enough figure in the country to be the kind of defender Burke needed. Young Earl Fitzwilliam, Lord Rockingham's heir, was kindly disposed toward Burke, but not at first close enough to him or politically strong enough to be the indispensable patron. The Duke of Portland was full of good will, but no substitute for Rockingham.

Burke suddenly found that he was supported almost solely by his own abilities, and to a lesser extent by his own national reputation. He was still, doubtless, the best-informed and readiest speaker in the House. He could master the detail of a political problem, he could marshal his arguments in an extended speech, more expertly than any other Member. He had vast experience, and the wisdom of his experience. His reputation in the nation at large had grown steadily for a generation.

Unfortunately, in a political assembly mere intellectual power or mere public reputation cannot alone ensure success. In such incidents as the Powell-Bembridge affair Burke's opponents had learned that, giant as he was, Burke could be attacked with impunity by those who kept on his weaker side; he could be provoked into losing his temper and discrediting his own political wisdom. In the latter days of his parliamentary life Burke was constantly being baited by those who wanted this result. They found many ways to infuriate him. When he spoke, certain members were overwhelmed by frightful fits of coughing; others called him to order for his statements; some went out to dinner, or retired from the chamber for other reasons. If he spoke long, as he frequently did, he was treated as a hopeless bore; those who were themselves quite incapable of answering his arguments affected to despise his abilities. If he became vehement or extravagant, he was much more open to censure. On at least one occasion he was told to his face that he had better restrain himself if he did not want to be imprisoned as a madman.[75]

For a man of Burke's temper it was not easy to deal with attacks of this kind. A dignity that was an essential part of him was outraged and distracted by them, and he was without any adequate idea of an appropriate retort. He would have preferred to ignore the attackers entirely, as beneath his notice. Unfortunately this was not always possible when the chamber was noisy with coughing. Burke was much more likely to go to the opposite extreme and fly into useless anger, which was what his opponents had intended. Sometimes he was utterly nonplussed and reduced to mere silence. On one occasion when a country member treated him with unusual rudeness, Burke simply ran from the House to prevent himself from boiling into rage.[76]

The members of Burke's party might have been expected to give him some assistance against what was certainly an organized campaign to discredit him. Actually, many of the younger members of his own party were nearly as much out of sympathy with him as his most open opponents. They too thought he talked too often and too long, and should control himself better. Most of them thought he took political issues with too tragic a seriousness. Fox was the great idol and model of their set: Fox, with easy manners, all the attractive dissipations of a gentleman, infinite spirit and courage in debate, and (conveniently) a vast private fortune to throw away generously at the gaming tables. Burke's earnestness, his vast long speeches, his passion for detail, not to mention his graceless poverty, showed up meanly by the side of Fox. Young men a generation, or even two generations Burke's juniors found him far below their standard of a statesman; they joined the hue and cry against him.

Paradoxically, Burke offended the young men of the gayer social set by his opposition to the French Revolution. The Revolution was splendidly popular among the *jeunesse dorée*, partly because Fox was sympathetic with it, partly because it was new and daring, partly because the young men had not grasped the fact that its principles opposed their own existence. They all

75. *Parliamentary History*, XXVII, 1249.
76. Prior, I, 447.

thought Burke decidedly oppressive when he took it seriously and made speeches against it. There was no subject on which he was more certain to be coughed at or called to order.

The climax of the persecution Burke endured at the hands of his own party was in the famous debate of May 6, 1791, when, maddened by repeated attacks from Fox's younger followers, he finally renounced publicly his long friendship with Fox. It is a scene which has been described almost too often; it appealed to a somewhat florid eighteenth-century taste for great scenes in the Roman manner. Its peak of senatorial emotion—when Burke renounced his friendship of over twenty years in the name of the British Constitution, and Fox stood up to reply with tears streaming down his face—is slightly overdone to a modern taste. Yet it is a scene which tells us a great deal about what Burke had to endure in his later days in Parliament.[77]

Burke was well warned that what he wished to say in this debate would not be welcomed by Fox and his followers. He had prepared his speech as a formal answer to Fox. On a number of occasions in the session Fox had declared his general sympathy with the French Revolution; in a debate of April 15 he had reached the point of calling the new French Constitution "the most stupendous and glorious edifice of liberty which had been erected on the foundation of human integrity in any time or country." Burke had risen in great excitement to rebut opinions so opposite to his own but had been stopped by cries of "Question" from the House. He had, however, served notice that he would answer Fox and set forth his own opinions of the French Constitution at the earliest opportunity. This had been resisted; Fox privately asked him to defer his answer for an indefinite time; when he insisted upon setting his reply for the debate of May 6, Grey publicly warned him that if what he had to say wandered from the announced subject of debate—the framing of a bill for the government of the Province of Quebec—he would be called to order.

Burke accordingly rose on May 6 well aware that he faced the hostility of a large portion of his own party. He began his speech cautiously by giving his justifications for discussing the new French Constitution on this occasion. The principles for govern-

77. Magnus describes this scene very fully and vividly (pp. 213-220).

ment of a province were under discussion; the province contained
a large proportion of French; the new principles of the French
state were being widely applauded as superior to the principles of
the British Constitution. He, Burke, would not admit that they
were superior, and pointed out disastrous results they had already
had. There had been bloody insurrections in France's West Indian colonies when the new revolutionary principles had been
introduced there. In France itself the King, though supposedly a
free and consenting party to the Constitution, was virtually a
prisoner of the mob. Burke was going on to describe a riot in
which the French King was humiliated by the mob when he was
called to order by one of Fox's followers. Fox himself took a
part in the attack. He rose to say, ironically, that he did not think
Burke could be called out of order: ". . . this was a day of privi-
lege, when any gentleman might stand up, select his mark, and
abuse any government he pleased, whether it had any reference
or not to the point in question."

Burke had only begun to answer Fox when he was called to
order a second time. Again he undertook his self-defense with
considerable restraint, offering to leave it to the proper authority
in the House whether he was in order or not. While he was making
this proposal he was again called to order. He repeated his appeal
to authority, amid loud cries of "Order, order," and other cries
of "Go on, go on." Half distracted, he tried to go on, amid further
calls to order. After several more interruptions and a good deal of
confusion, a motion was made to the effect that a "dissertation on
the French Constitution" was not appropriate to a debate on the
Quebec Bill. Fox supported this motion in a speech of some
length. Burke again answered, again with amazing restraint. But
the restraint could not last forever. New provocations were used
against him. While he was speaking Fox rose to leave the chamber,
whereupon twenty or thirty of Fox's followers departed in a body.
Fox may not have intended that they should act as they did (he
himself returned presently), but Burke naturally took it as an
insult. He retorted with a reference to "well-disciplined troops
. . . obedient to the word of their commander," for which he
was immediately called to order.

By this time Burke was in a high rage, pouring out self-defense, counterattack, and abuse of the French Constitution at a white heat. He himself realized that the House was appalled at his state of excitement. After one burst of passion he turned to the bewildered Chairman to say "I am not mad, most noble Festus, but speak the words of truth and soberness." At another point when most harried by his assailants, he cried in the words of King Lear:

. . . the little dogs, and all,
Tray, Blanche, and Sweetheart. See, they bark at me!

The passions of that evening might have reminded a good many people of the extravagances of the theater. When Burke reached the point of declaring that he had to stand to his duty and his principles even at the loss of his friend, Fox leaned forward to whisper: "There was no loss of friends." He had not guessed how serious Burke was. "Yes, there was a loss of friends," Burke cried, "he knew the price of his conduct—he had done his duty at the price of his friend—their friendship was at an end." When Fox rose to answer this he was himself in such a state of agitation that it was a matter of minutes before he could force anything out. When he finally mastered himself and began to speak, tears were running down his cheeks as he tried to induce Burke to reconsider his words. It was too late; Burke had made his Spartan decision. He was never again willing to regard Fox as his personal friend; when years later he lay on his deathbed and Fox wanted to come to visit him, Burke refused his consent.

One wonders whether political struggles should ever be permitted to reach so terrible a seriousness. They are certainly important struggles—sometimes far more important than any of the participants realize—but the intensity with which Burke could take them was sometimes little short of obsessive. Burke's friend Therry, with whom he went home from the House on the night of May 6, afterward described the state of excitement in which the debate left Burke. Therry's son many years later gave the account to the public:

When the debate concluded, my father accompanied Mr. Burke home. In the carriage, Mr. Burke observed stern and inflexible silence; and after their arrival, he only replied to questions in harsh and abrupt monosyllables. Gradually a strong fit of passion came over him; he threw up the windows of the apartment, flung open his coat and waistcoat, and in a paroxism of passion, paced up and down the room, until nearly four o'clock in the morning. So vehement was the excitement under which he labored, that my father deemed it but consistent with his duty not to leave him until he became so composed that he was disposed to retire to rest.[78]

V

About a week after the session of May 6 the *Morning Chronicle*, which was regarded as Fox's organ, printed a short paragraph referring to Burke: "The great and firm body of the Whigs of England, true to their principles, have decided upon the dispute between Mr. Fox and Mr. Burke; and the former is declared to have maintained the pure doctrine by which they are bound together, and upon which they have invariable acted. The consequence is that Mr. Burke retires from Parliament." [79]

Burke was stung, as of course it was intended that he should

78. R. Therry, *A Letter to George Canning, to which are annexed Six Letters of Edmund Burke* (London, 1826), p. 60. It need not surprise us that Prior gives us (II, 154-155) an entirely different account of the events of this same evening, quoted from J. C. Curwen's *Observations on the State of Ireland* (London, 1818), II, 93-94.

" 'The most powerful feelings,' says Mr. Curwen, 'were manifested on the adjournment of the House. Whilst I was waiting for my carriage Mr. Burke came up to me and requested, as the night was wet, I would set him down —I could not refuse—though I confess I felt a reluctance in complying. As soon as the carriage door was shut, he complimented me on my being no friend to the revolutionary doctrines of the French, on which he spoke with great warmth for a few minutes, when he paused to afford me an opportunity of approving the view he had taken of those measures in the House. Former experience had taught me the consequences of differing from his opinions, yet at the moment I could not help feeling disinclined to disguise my sentiments. Mr. Burke, catching hold of the check-string, furiously exclaimed, "You are one of those people! set me down!" With some difficulty I restrained him;—we had then reached Charing Cross—a silence ensued, which was preserved till we reached his house in Gerrard Street, when he hurried out of the carriage without speaking, and thus our intercourse ended.' "

Either Mr. Curwen or Mr. Therry must have misdated his reminiscences. It is not unlikely that Burke was as excited by the debate of May 11—also on the Quebec Act—as he was by the debate of May 6; either of the reminiscents might have made so minor a slip as five days; hence both stories may be substantially accurate though one mistaken as to date.

79. Magnus, p. 220.

be. Actually, he had no need of the hint. He had already made up his own mind to the fact that he would be happier outside of the House; if it had depended upon his wishes, rather than on the duration of the Hastings Impeachment—to which he had committed himself—there can be little doubt that he would have retired at once. As it was, he behaved very much as if he had accepted retirement. In the whole year following the break with Fox he scarcely rose in debate more than half a dozen times, and never for more than a few minutes. This was not because he had turned his thoughts away from politics. Quite the contrary. Outside the House he was more active and more influential in this period than at any other time in his career. His pamphlets and letters on the French Revolution were reaching an audience in England and in Europe such as Burke had never previously reached. He had only concluded that his activities in Parliament had lost most of their value, and he was not eager to appear in that arena. In the three years before his ultimate retirement he scarcely made a major speech which was not required of him by the course of the Hastings Impeachment; when in the spring of 1794 the Impeachment finally came to its close, he immediately applied for the Chiltern Hundreds and retired from Parliament.

The moment of his retirement, in spite of some uncomfortable circumstances, might have been one of the happier moments of Burke's life. He was throwing off a fearful load of labor and responsibility which had increased steadily upon him through three decades of public service. The Impeachment, which had occupied him in one form or another for fourteen years, was finally concluded. His party was temporarily prosperous. By a coalition arrangement the Duke of Portland, Earl Fitzwilliam, Windham, and other of his friends were coming into government. This was the long-delayed moment at which they were able to reward Burke. He was to have his pension, and also a peerage; he had already chosen the name of Lord Beaconsfield. More important, at least to Burke's happiness, a political opening had been found at last for his beloved Richard. By Earl Fitzwilliam's generosity Richard was to have the closed borough which his father had held till his retirement; he was also promised a post of responsibility as chief secretary to Fitzwilliam when he became

Lord Lieutenant of Ireland. It would be hard to think of a conjunction of circumstance better able to rouse Burke's hopes again.

It proved to be the last of the terrible disappointments of his career. In the midsummer of 1794, within ten days of his election to Parliament, Richard died suddenly of a tubercular complaint. He was at that time in his thirty-seventh year.

The effect of the event on Burke was appalling. He abandoned himself utterly to grief and despair. For many days after he heard the news he had scarcely enough control of his feelings to eat or sleep; for months afterward he could be reduced to uncontrollable weeping when anything reminded him of his loss. He felt, and many of his friends felt too, that he himself might not survive the blow; indeed he scarcely seemed to want to revive his interest in life.

A great deal of his unhappiness was caused by a feeling that he himself had not been perfectly just to his son. Richard had been deeply devoted to his family, and had sacrificed himself to the all but hopeless task of straightening out their tangled affairs; Burke saw, too late, that he himself had neglected a duty. "When I consider," he said,

. . . that his natural gay season of enjoyment was clouded with cares and solicitudes which more fitly belonged to me, and were caused by my faults, and chained down by unworthy occupations, I cannot help impressing it on all parents, who are but too apt to think more of what their children owe to them than of what they owe to their children, to consider with more than usual seriousness, everything which, by self-indulgence, dissipates and distracts their affairs. . . . Parents, in the order of Providence, are made for their children, and not their children for them.[80]

Richard had never married, and his efforts to make a name for himself in politics and in the practice of law had been only partly successful. That the embarrassment of the family affairs was a great cause of his want of success Burke had long believed:

. . . on the first favorable turn of fortune I was unalterably resolved to make some amends to him by a "bona fide" retreat; to put myself into his hands, and to substitute him in everything, public or private, for myself. A poor retribution! but one which my offenses toward God and toward him, have not suffered me to make. It was indeed too much for me. I looked to it, in prospect, as the crowning felicity of my life.[81]

When Burke's pension was finally granted him he wrote his friend Walker King: "Oh my dear friend, how many pangs attend this satisfaction! That he, for whom I lived, did not live to see this, and to dispose of money so justly his. Oh, pray for my pardon!" [82]

The period between his son's death and his own, three years later, is the last of the shadowy periods of Burke's existence. He consciously avoided society, as if his frayed nerves could no longer bear the rays of light from an outside world. For months he would not look at a newspaper or inform himself of public affairs. He lived wholly at Beaconsfield. When it was first necessary for him to undertake an errand to London, he protested that he could not bear to "show to the world the face of a man marked by the hand of God." [83] Later he made such trips as were necessary—to London, or to Bath for his health—but seldom without expressing reluctance at the thought of facing numbers of people. When he returned home he would take back roads to avoid passing through the town of Beaconsfield, where he would have had to greet his neighbors. He and Mrs. Burke did not dine out of their own house for two years after Richard's death.

Such a retirement by a man of Burke's prominence could not escape comment. In one period when he had not been seen in London for an unusually long time rumors began to spread that he was actually mad, and *obliged* to stay in the country. One of his old friends heard that he was wandering about the fields of his estate kissing the cows and horses. When the friend investigated, it turned out that the story had a basis in an actual incident. Burke had been walking in his fields as he loved to do, when a horse that had been a favorite of Richard's came close to him and, for some

81. *Ibid.*, p. 269.
82. *Ibid.*, p. 268.
83. John Campbell, *Lives of the Chancellors* (2d American from 3d London ed. Philadelphia, 1851), VI, 214.

odd reason, pressed its head against his bosom as if offering him sympathy. It was too much for Burke's self-control. All his woes rushed over him again, and he threw his arms around the horse's neck and wept and sobbed convulsively.[84]

VI

"What I most envy Burke for," said Dr. Johnson in 1773, "is his being constantly the same." [85]

Johnson and Boswell on this occasion were discussing Burke chiefly in his social and conversational capacities: "never unwilling to begin to talk, nor in haste to leave off." Johnson would have been ready, however, to make nearly the same observation upon Burke's temperament in general—at least if we can judge by a later conversation Boswell recorded in 1777: "The hypochondriack disorder being mentioned, Dr. Johnson did not think it so common as I supposed. 'Dr. Taylor (said he) is the same one day as another. Burke and Reynolds are the same. . . . I am not so myself; but this I do not mention commonly.'" [86] Boswell had a rather similar opinion concerning Burke's fortunate temperament. Discussing the miseries of hypochondria in a letter to his friend Temple in 1775, he moralized nobly: "But, it is absurd to hope for continual happiness in this life. Few men, if any, enjoy it. I have a kind of belief that Edmund Burke does. He has so much knowledge, so much animation, and the consciousness of so much fame." [87]

It is interesting that two such keen observers as Johnson and Boswell should have made what was really so external a judgment of Burke. In the very same period of his career when he appeared to be continually happy and "constantly the same," we have the evidence of Burke's private correspondence to tell us what his inward feelings really were. He was writing to the Marquis of Rockingham in the latter part of 1774:

84. John Timbs, *Anecdote Biography* (London, 1860), p. 348.
85. Boswell's "Journal of a Tour to the Hebrides" (Aug. 15, 1773) in *Life of Johnson*, V, 32–33.
86. *Life of Johnson*, III, 192.
87. Boswell, *Letters*, I, 238.

. . . sometimes when I am alone, in spite of all my efforts, I fall into a melancholy which is inexpressible, and to which, if I gave way, I should not continue long under it, but must totally sink; yet I do assure you that partly, and indeed principally, by the force of natural good spirits, and partly by a strong sense of what I ought to do, I bear up so well, that no one who did not know them, could easily discover the state of my mind or my circumstances.[88]

The truth is that Burke, though it would probably be wrong to classify him as a hypochondriac, was subject to his periods of despair, like all the rest of us, and indeed had years of his life when he wrestled continually with drooping spirits. What was remarkable in his make-up was far less an untroubled equability than an extraordinary power of concealing his periods of inner distress. This power did not serve him equally well in every period of his career; toward the end of his parliamentary ordeal it even seemed to desert him entirely, leaving him more painfully exposed than public men usually are. But that was exceptional; during the greater part of his career Burke's powers of concealment served him astonishingly well. Probably most of his friends at any time up to the very last years would have agreed with Johnson and Boswell in thinking him a fortunate, contented spirit. The sentiment with which he concluded the passage just quoted from the letter to Rockingham would have startled many of those who thought they knew him well: "Whether I ought not to abandon this public station, for which I am so unfit, and have of course been so unfortunate, I know not."

Such an expression if it stood by itself might be dismissed as rather unimportant—perhaps as the result of a momentary fit of low spirits. One can duplicate its thought, however, in almost every period of Burke's career, sometimes asserted in ways which are far from sounding ill considered or accidental. Five years after the letter to Rockingham Burke was writing to Shackleton:

I should not hesitate a moment to retire from public business, if I were not in some doubt of the right a man has, that goes a certain length in those things; and if it were not from an observation, that

88. Burke, *Correspondence*, I, 480–481.

there are often obscure vexations and contests in the most private life, which may as effectually destroy a man's peace, as any thing which may happen in public contentions.[89]

In the following year, when his constituents in Bristol failed to renominate him, Burke was not only ready but eager to make good a retreat from politics; his friends overbore his own judgment in urging him to go on.[90] He went on, but not without sinking spells. Readers of Boswell will remember a conversation Johnson had in 1783 with a gentleman whom Boswell did not name:

A gentleman talked of retiring. "Never think of that," said Johnson. The gentleman urged, "I should then do no ill." JOHNSON. "Nor no good either. Sir, it would be civil suicide." [91]

There is scarcely any doubt from the context that the gentleman was Burke, who in 1783 had been in British politics for nearly twenty years.

There has been a great deal of discussion of the question whether Burke should have been offered a cabinet post at the two times very close to this when his party came into power. When the possibility of it was mentioned in the House just before the first Ministry was to be agreed on, Burke himself made an emphatic statement on the subject:

God knew, Mr. Burke said, he had no such views, nor had he a right to have any such. The thing was not within probability. . . . He was neither a man who had pretensions to it from rank in the country, or from fortune, nor who aspired to it from ambition. He was not a man so foolishly vain, or so blindly ignorant of his own state and condition, as to indulge for a moment the idea of his becoming a minister . . .[92]

This statement was made before the death of Rockingham—indeed before one could say that the full extent of Burke's parliamentary weakness had been exposed to the House. There is no reason to doubt that it was sincerely meant. Burke had, and surely

89. *Ibid.*, II, 278.
90. *Parliamentary History*, XXI, 1151.
91. *Life of Johnson*, IV, 223.
92. *Parliamentary History*, XXII, 1228.

knew that he had, at that time both political intelligence and parliamentary experience superior to those of any single individual likely to be placed in that ministry. He was merely wise enough to see that intelligence and experience alone are not enough for success in politics. While outsiders who were not very conscious of his weaknesses might be thinking seriously of his rising to cabinet rank, he himself was thinking seriously of total retirement.

Under the increasingly unfriendly treatment which he received after the death of Rockingham, both his discomfort and his sense of inadequacy inevitably grew. A kind of frantic anxiety began to creep into his speeches on public affairs, and he was aware that he was making himself ineffective often by his very intensity. There is a rather pathetic passage in a letter he wrote to William Windham in 1789, in which he explained why he had absented himself from the House for a while and retired to Beaconsfield: "I began to find that I was grown rather too anxious; and had begun to discover to myself and to others a solicitude relative to the present state of affairs, which, though their strange condition might well warrant it in others, is certainly less suitable to my time of life, in which all emotions are less allowed . . . I sincerely wish to withdraw myself from this scene for good and all . . ." [93]

It was ever harder for Burke to do what he had once found easy: conceal the strains of his career, and appear "constantly the same" while suffering the shocks of defeat and disappointment. When Fanny Burney, who had met and infinitely admired him in the early 1780's, met him again in the 1790's, she recorded in a letter to some of her friends the impression he made upon her: "How I wish my dear Susanna and Fredy could meet this wonderful man when he is easy, happy, and with people he cordially likes! But politics, even on his own side, must always be excluded; his irritability is so terrible on that theme that it gives immediately to his face the expression of a man who is going to defend himself from murderers." [94] Things had advanced to rather a painful point when Edmund Burke could not endure the strain of any kind of discussion of politics!

93. Burke, *Correspondence*, III, 89.
94. *Diary and Letters of Madame d'Arblay*, V, 92.

The question has been raised in all seriousness whether Burke in the last years of his career did not succumb to the mounting strains of his life and become actually irrational.[95] It is not a question that can be airily dismissed. There were several occasions, especially when the French Revolution was involved, when Burke's utterances could easily be taken as evidence of a state of mental unbalance. When a man says "I fear I am the only person in France or England, who is aware of the extent of the danger, with which we are threatened," [96] he is at least talking the *language* of paranoia. Burke made a good many such remarks in the 1790's. "I cannot persuade myself," he would say of the war with France,

. . . that this war bears any the least resemblance (other than that it is a war) to any that has ever existed in the world. I cannot persuade myself that any examples or any reasonings drawn from other wars and other politics are at all applicable to it; and I truly and sincerely think, that all other wars and all other politics have been the games of children, in comparison to it. [97]

It is only a step from that to saying (as he also did), "The world seems to me to reel and stagger," [98] or "The abyss of Hell itself seems to yawn before me." [99]

It would be a mistake to ignore the significance of expressions of this kind. They may not be quite enough to convince us that

95. It is argued at some length by Henry Thomas Buckle (*History of Civilization in England* [Am. ed. from 2d London ed. New York, 1858], II, 334 f.). Buckle hardly treats the matter as still a question. His passage reads in part: ". . . at this distance of time, when his nearest relations are no more, it would be affectation to deny that Burke, during the last few years of his life, fell into a state of complete hallucination. When the French Revolution broke out, his mind, already fainting under the weight of incessant labour, could not support the contemplation of an event so unprecedented, so appalling, and threatening results of such frightful magnitude. And, when the crimes of that great revolution, instead of diminishing, continued to increase, then it was that the feelings of Burke finally mastered his reason; the balance tottered; the proportions of that gigantic intellect were disturbed."

96. Charles Butler, *Reminiscences* (4th ed. London, 1824), I, 171.

97. Burke, *Correspondence*, IV, 219.

98. *Correspondence of Edmund Burke and William Windham*, ed. J. P. Gilson (London, 1910), p. 157.

99. Letter to Earl Fitzwilliam, Nov. 29, 1793, cited by Magnus (p. 249) from MSS at Wentworth Woodhouse.

Burke was, in any ordinary sense, irrational when he uttered them, but they put it beyond all doubt that his mind was under fearful strain, and that we are justified in guessing that its balance was threatened repeatedly. It is not a disparagement of Burke to say this. What he saw outside him and in his own life would have driven almost any man to something approaching frenzy. Any statesman who sensed the oncoming dangers of the French Revolution, and of the twenty years of international chaos to which it was a prelude, might be expected to use strong language to express his horror. Any private person who had undergone the crescendo of social, economic, professional, and psychological strains which had fallen upon Burke might be excused for speaking at times in the language of paranoia.

In his later years, too, Burke seems to have had a kind of positive belief in the value of giving vent to his feelings. He did not struggle to avoid violent, extravagant utterance; sometimes he rather appeared to seek it. Private sorrows which in an earlier period we can be almost sure he would have concealed he now proclaimed with shameless abandon; letters and even works carefully prepared for the press were filled with bitter laments over the death of his son or over his own forlorn and broken condition. But if this was true in private matters, it was even more true when he spoke of public affairs; he now habitually used the unmeasured language of an Old Testament prophet. And why should he not? Was it to preserve his own reputation that he was to avoid extravagance? He cared nothing for such reputation. "Indeed, my lord, I greatly deceive myself, if in this hard season I would give a peck of refuse wheat for all that is called fame and honor in the world." But would his cause, perhaps, be injured by his unrestraint? There too Burke saw no danger. His cause was the anti-Jacobin cause, and it demanded vehemence. The real danger, he thought, was that he might not rouse himself or his contemporaries to feel its importance half strongly enough:

Indeed, it is when a great nation is in great difficulties that minds must exalt themselves to the occasion, or all is lost. Strong passion under the direction of a feeble reason feeds a low fever, which serves only to destroy the body that entertains it. But vehement passion does not always indicate an infirm judgment. It often accompanies, and actuates, and is even auxiliary to a powerful understanding; and when they both conspire and act harmoniously, their force is great to destroy disorder within and to repel injury from abroad. If ever there was a time that calls on us for no vulgar conception of things, and for exertions in no vulgar strain, it is the awful hour that Providence has now appointed to this nation.[100]

It is well to remember that Burke's sober judgment did not wholly disapprove of the bursts of passion which we very frequently find in the *Reflections on the Revolution in France*, in the *Letter to a Noble Lord*, and in the *Letters on a Regicide Peace*.

Those who find it hard to believe that Burke's passion was not inevitably destructive of the strength of his solid argument should subject themselves anew to the full impact of the four *Letters on a Regicide Peace* which Burke wrote in the last year of his life. They will discover, perhaps to their surprise, that the peculiar quality of those letters is the cogency of their reasoning. They are, certainly, full of passion and of emphatic language, but at bottom they are as grounded and rational as any political tracts in the language. Burke himself spoke of them as his political testament; they have the seriousness of a dying man's words. At the same time they have an intellectual range that could belong only to a first-rate mind in the fullest vigor of its powers. Strangely, they have even a kind of exuberance and vivacity that many of Burke's earlier writings lack.

But Burke is perpetually puzzling. When one has entirely re-gained one's faith in the sovereign strength of his reason, one can be shaken all over again by a new fact. There is a curious but well-authenticated report about Burke's burial. His bones are not now under the slab which marks them in Beaconsfield church. They are not even in the same coffin in which they were originally buried. By his own direction they were first put in a wooden coffin but later transferred to a leaden one placed in a different spot. Burke did not wish it to be known exactly where he was buried. He feared that the French revolutionaries, if they tri-umphed in England, might dig up and dishonor his corpse.[101]

100. Burke, *Works*, V, 407.
101. See an article entitled "The Grave of Edmund Burke," *Notes and Queries*,

CXLIX, 80. The writer of this article says: "It may not be known that Edmund Burke is not buried in Beaconsfield Church at the spot indicated by the inscribed slab. An old resident informs me that when the church was restored many years ago, he saw the coffins of Edmund Burke, his son and his brother under one of the arches separating the nave from the aisle, and that Edmund Burke wished the place of his interment to be kept secret for fear of desecration by French revolutionaries." See also some unpublished papers of L. J. Mitford in the British Museum (Add. Mss. 32566). Mitford says: "Burke buried in a wooden coffin. Afraid the French should find his body; his bones moved from that coffin to a leaden one later."

III

A CAREER IN JOURNALISM

HORACE WALPOLE remarked, of course, upon Burke's impressive début in the House of Commons. Walpole usually succeeded in sizing up New Men at the moment they emerged into prominence. Commenting on the debate of January 27, 1766, in the House of Commons, he said:

> There appeared in this debate a new speaker, whose fame for eloquence soon rose high above the ordinary pitch. His name was Edmund Burke . . . an Irishman, of a Roman Catholic family, and actually married to one of that persuasion. He had been known to the public for a few years by his "Essay on The Sublime and Beautiful," and other ingenious works; but the narrowness of his fortune had kept him down, and his best revenue had arisen from writing for booksellers.[1]

With an infallible eye, Walpole had managed to discern the four weakest spots in this new man's social armor. Burke was an Irishman; he was related to Roman Catholics; he was poor; he was rumored to be "writing for booksellers."

To posterity three of these social weaknesses are obvious enough, but the fourth might not appear to be a weakness at all. Burke's productions for the booksellers, insofar as they are known to us, might seem among the most creditable achievements of his early life. One of them in particular could be warmly praised. While a young man not yet out of his twenties Burke had agreed to edit a "magazine" which should appear annually, and review the "History, Politics, and Literature" of the day. He had planned its form, in conjunction with Robert Dodsley the publisher, and then singlehanded he had managed the writing and compiling of it. It had been an immensely successful venture. Issues for the early

1. Horace Walpole, *Memoirs of the Reign of King George the III*, II, 273. Burke's first speech in the House was at least ten days earlier than Walpole thought. See Dixon Wecter's article "David Garrick and the Burkes," *Philological Quarterly*, XVIII, 369–370.

years sometimes ran to as many as eight or nine editions, which can pretty certainly be taken as a sign of the magazine's success. The principal annual feature, a Historical Article which reviewed British and European events of the previous year, won high commendations from contemporaries, and indeed is still, in the twentieth century, regarded as a leading authority on events of its day. One might think that "Edmund Burke . . . an Irishman" should have been highly applauded for his achievements connected with the *Annual Register*.

Unfortunately the eighteenth century had a rather strong prejudice against journalists as a group. They were under a general suspicion of being venal libelers, or at least hard-driven hacks who were not likely to be socially acceptable. From what we know of the press of the time it is probable enough that they were usually one or the other. Whether or not they really were, however, we know that their trade bore that stigma. It was usually practiced anonymously, even in its upper reaches; and many of the most gifted writers for the reviews would have been deeply humiliated to have had it known that they were "writing for booksellers."

This partly explains a fact which would otherwise strike us as peculiar, namely, that Burke, so far as we know, never admitted publicly that he was the editor of the *Annual Register*.[2] Some of his contemporaries seem to have heard rumors that he was.[3] His biographers are nearly unanimous in believing that he was, and that his relations with the magazine continued for over thirty

2. The nearest approach to an acknowledgment by Burke of authorship of any part of the magazine is perhaps recorded in the *Annual Register* itself in its notice of Burke's death (1797, p. 41), which thus describes his work upon the historical department of the magazine: "In 1757 he engaged with Dodsley to compile the History of Europe in the Annual Register. This work he did not always acknowledge; but Dr. Leland [doubtless Thomas Leland of Trinity College, Dublin, one of Burke's earliest and closest friends], accidentally or by design, by criticizing the off-spring, discovered the genuine fondness of the parent."

3. Burke's enemy Major John Scott, in an open letter to James Dodsley (printed in the *St. James Chronicle*, Jan. 18–20, 1791), said of the *Register's* Historical Article: "Mr. Burke has been for some time generally deemed the writer of that part of your *Register*." Samuel Denne the antiquary, in a letter of Sept. 12, 1795 (printed in Nichols' *Literary History of the Eighteenth Century*, VI, 649), said of the *Register*: "For many years it was surmised that Mr. Burke took the lead in that miscellaneous work . . ."

years. But there has till recently been scarcely a proved fact to support the rumors and beliefs.[4]

I

James Prior, Burke's first thorough biographer, described and proved Burke's association with the *Register* thus, writing in 1824:

This work also he never thought proper to claim. The fact of his participation in it has been always matter of doubt, though, from an attentive examination of circumstances minute in themselves, added to the modesty with which he speaks of himself at all times, and even the suppression of his name on important occasions, when some extraordinary compliments were paid him, both in and out of the House of Commons, the present writer was satisfied of the affirmative, even before he received more positive information. The sum allowed for it by Dodsley was only £100; several of the receipts for the copy-money, in his own handwriting, are still extant; the two following, for the year 1761, as being at hand, are given for the satisfaction of the reader:

"Received from Mr. Dodsley the sum of £50 on account of the Annual Register of 1761, this 28th March, 1761.

"Edm. Burke."

"Received from Messrs. R. and T. Dodsley, the sum of £50 sterl. being in full for the Annual Register of 1761, this 30th day of March, 1762.

"Edm. Burke." [5]

4. I believe that the first careful study of Burke's relations with the *Register* was made in my own Ph. D. dissertation, submitted at Yale in 1933. This study was later digested into two articles which appeared in *P.M.L.A.* (LIV [March, 1939], 223–245, and LVII [June, 1942], 446–468). Sir Philip Magnus included a brief treatment of the *Annual Register* in his biography of Burke in 1939 (pp. 333–335). Donald C. Bryant had a somewhat fuller treatment in his *Edmund Burke and His Literary Friends* (1939), pp. 289–297. Both of these scholars were generous in acknowledging their indebtedness to my studies.

The present essay covers nearly the same ground as the first of my articles in *P.M.L.A.*: "Burke and Dodsley's *Annual Register*." A few facts have been added, and I have altered both the form and the emphasis to suit the purpose of the present work.

5. Prior (1st ed.), p. 61. The "R. and T. Dodsley" in the second receipt is a mistake: it should be "R. and J. Dodsley."

Prior had a cut made of these two autograph receipts, and included it as an illustration in his *Life of Burke*. This is the only evidence presented by any of Burke's biographers in considerably over a century to prove that he was ever editor of the *Register*.

And obviously the receipts tell very little about the terms or the duration of Burke's editorship. Prior believed, as have most of Burke's other biographers, that after launching the magazine singlehanded in 1758, Burke conducted it by himself for a time and then, as he grew busier in other affairs, delegated either a part or the whole of the task of management to one or more other workers, but continued to make some contributions to the magazine himself during a period of about thirty years. Apparently Prior was not in a position to prove even that indefinite account of things, and still more apparently he was not sure of what is after all the important fact: the time of Burke's resignation as editor. In the list of Burke's writings which he included in his biography he named the "Annual Register—at first the whole Work, afterwards only the Historical Article," [6] without committing himself as to the time at which Burke ceased to write the whole work. In his *Life of Goldsmith* Prior did indeed make the statement that the *Annual Register* was "commenced and conducted by Burke for the first seven years," [7] but there the statement was made quite incidentally and by its context need not be taken at all as proving that Burke conducted it for no more than seven years; and of course it may also be significant that Prior never repeated the statement in the *Life of Burke*, which was extensively revised after the *Life of Goldsmith* had appeared.

There was actually a little more evidence scattered about than Prior ever realized, and admitting that the sum of it does not give us any adequate account of Burke's connection with the magazine, still it gives us a kind of skeletal outline of such an account.

Burke's agreement with Robert Dodsley and his brother, by which the magazine was inaugurated, was discovered among Robert Dodsley's papers. It is in Burke's handwriting, and describes as follows the plan of the *Register:*

6. *Ibid.*, p. xx.
7. James Prior, *Life of Oliver Goldsmith* (London, 1837), I, 309.

MEMORANDUM it is agreed this twenty fourth day of April 1758 between Edmund Burke Gent on one part & Robert & James Dodsley Booksellers on the other part, as follows viz The said Edmund Burke doth agree to write collect & compile from such materials as may arise a work entitled the Annual register or Retrospections on men & things for the year 1758 to be printed in octavo in the manner of Millers Kalender 800. & to make not less than thirty sheets nor more than thirty four, according to a plan agreed upon. The first Volume to commence from New Years day 1758 & to conclude with the End of the said Year, & to be finished so as that [sic] it may be corrected from the press & published by the Lady day following. And the sd. Edmund Burke doth agree that in case he should find reason to discontinue his writing the said work to give the said Robert & James Dodsley three months Notice of such his design and the said Robert & James Dodsley so reciprocally agree in Case they should chuse to discontinue the said work, or to employ any other person in the execution thereof to give the like Notice of three months to the said Edmund Burke. & the said Robert & James Dodsley in consideration of the said Edmund Burkes performing the said Work according to the above Articles do agree to pay the said Edmund Burke the sum of one hundred pounds for the first Volume of the said Work, one moiety of the said payment to be made on or before Michaelmas day next ensuing, and the other on the publication of the said Volume, and to find him all books & Pamphlets necessary for his carrying on the said Work. In witness whereof we have hereunto set our hands the day & year above written.

EDMUND BURKE
RDODSLEY
J DODSLEY.[8]

This is as full an account as one could hope for of the original plan of the magazine and of the original intention as to Burke's duties as editor. He was to take the responsibility for writing and compiling it alone. It was to be prepared for the press in time to be published on Lady Day each year. He was to be paid in two installments of £50 each, one to be received at the time of publication, the other on the following Michaelmas. It is natural to

8. Ralph Straus, *Robert Dodsley* (London, 1910), pp. 257 f.

assume that for the first few years Burke worked under this original agreement. It will be noted that Prior's receipts are for £50 each, and dated in the neighborhood of Lady Day. There are two other receipts of the same kind for the *Annual Registers* of 1762 and 1763.[9] A letter Burke wrote Dodsley from Dublin, February 9, 1764, may be evidence that the agreement was unaltered as late as that year. It reads:

Dear Sir,

I suppose, that by this, our Work is in the press, & advances prosperously. The part immediately in my hands is in considerable forwardness, so that next week, please God I propose to send over a good part of it, executed rather more to my satisfaction than I could have flattered myself was practicable, considering what we had to go upon. I have occasion to pay some money in London pretty speedily. I beg therefore you will pay Dr. Nugent fifty pounds on my receipt, wch. you will have along with this. Be so good to remember me affectionately to yr Brother, & believe me

Dr Sr

Y.r most obed.ᵗ serv.ᵗ & friend
E. Burke [10]

This sounds as if Burke were still doing the writing himself; the salary payment mentioned is again £50; and the transaction is in the neighborhood of Lady Day (a little early, possibly indicating that Burke was in need of money and forced to touch Dodsley in advance).

It is not likely that Burke would have attempted to carry the burdens of the magazine single-handed for very long after 1764. When he became secretary to the Marquis of Rockingham in

9. That for 1762 is now in the Morgan Library, New York, and reads as follows: "Received from Messrs. Dodsley the sum of fifty pounds ster in part of the annual Register for 1762 this 4th June 1762. (Signed) Edm. Burke." The receipt for 1763 is mentioned but not quoted in an article of James Crossley the antiquary in *Notes and Queries*, 1st ser., III, 441, treated more fully below.

10. British Museum, Add. Mss. 22130, f. 10. This letter does not specifically mention the *Annual Register*, but again from its date and the sum £50, for which a receipt is given, I think it is probably evidence that the first agreement was still being carried out. We know of no other work of Burke being published by Dodsley at this time.

1765, and certainly when he entered Parliament in 1766, other calls upon his time became very much more pressing. We have evidence that another worker was employed on the *Register* at nearly this time. James Crossley, the antiquary, in an article in *Notes and Queries* in 1851, described and proved as follows the activities of this man:

. . . for the *Annual Registers* beginning with 1767, and terminating in 1791, I have the receipts of Thomas English, who appears to have received from Dodsley, first £140, and subsequently £150 annually, for writing and compiling the historical portion of the work. Burke's connexion with the publication must therefore have lasted a much shorter period than Mr. Prior appears to have supposed, and apparently was not continued beyond seven or eight years, from 1758 to 1766, after which year, English seems to have taken his place.[11]

Crossley did not, incidentally, disagree with Prior as much as he believed he did, for his guess of seven years as the period of Burke's editorship happens to agree with that mysterious remark in Prior's *Life of Goldsmith* about the *Register* being "commenced and conducted by Burke for the first seven years."

Crossley's inference, however, that Burke's connection with the publication must have ceased when English's began, is only an

11. *Notes and Queries*, 1st ser., III, 441. Two autograph receipts of English now in the Morgan Library, New York, supplement those which Crossley described. The first of these reads: "Rec'd Nov. 6, 1767, of Mr. Dodsley One Hundred and Forty pounds in full for writing & compiling the Annual Register for the Year 1766 Thos. English." The second reads: "Rec'd Jan. 30, 1793, of Mr. Dodsley One Hundred and Fifty Guineas in full for Writing and compiling the History of Europe as contained in eight chapters in the Annual Register for the year 1790. Thos. English."

If one can place any reliance on wording, these receipts show that English's responsibilities on the *Register* lessened with the passage of time: he began by writing and compiling the whole magazine, and ended with only the Historical Article. Perhaps his period of responsibility for the whole magazine didn't last beyond 1766, the first year of his employment. A passage in Prior's *Life of Goldsmith*, II, 347–348, quotes an Irishman named O'Donnell as saying that English "had been, if I mistake not, a college friend of Edmund Burke; at any rate he was patronised by him, and upon the accession of the latter to parliament, English conducted the Annual Register under his direction, or at least those parts which merely required compilation." *The Diary of William Windham* (ed. Mrs. Henry Baring [London, 1866], p. 234) refers to "Mr. English, an Irishman, who writes the historical part of the 'Annual Register.'" The extent of Burke's intimacy with English is proved by many passages in his letters.

inference, however plausible. It contradicts the assumption of nearly all of Burke's biographers that he maintained some connection with the *Annual Register* for a period of thirty years; and there happens to be some evidence to substantiate the assumption of the biographers. It is printed in the *Register* itself for the year after Burke's death, in a review of Charles M'Cormick's *Memoirs of Edmund Burke*. The reviewer, whom one would judge by his language to be well informed as to the past and future of the magazine, says:

Having already in our Chronicle [another part of the magazine] given the prominent features of the character and fortunes of Mr. Burke, we shall content ourselves now with giving a few extracts from Mr. M'Cormick's book; reserving for a future volume, when we shall be furnished with ampler documents, a fuller account of this illustrious man, who claims particular regard from us as having been, during the space of one-and-thirty years, the principal conductor of the present undertaking; of which circumstance Mr. M'-Cormick takes notice in the following words:—

and the reviewer quotes the highly laudatory account M'Cormick gives of the magazine's immediate success on Burke's first launching of it. M'Cormick's quotation concludes:

The beams of public favour did not relax but invigorate the writer's efforts; and for more than thirty years the increase of merit and the increase of reputation were kept up by the continual display of new and extraordinary powers. In the year 1789, Mr. Burke declined this task, and transferred it to other hands.[12]

This evidence is not inconsistent with Crossley's receipts. The receipts prove that Thomas English worked on the *Register* for about twenty-five years; M'Cormick and the *Register's* reviewer assert that Burke was conducting the magazine for most of that period. Obviously Burke could have remained the responsible editor—"principal conductor"—and have had English working under him; and there is nothing to prevent the assumption that such was the case.

Nor are we bound to conclude what it is natural to suspect: that

12. *Annual Register*, 1797, p. 456.

after the engagement of English and perhaps other assistants Burke's own duties became nominal and the assistants really managed the editorial work. There seems to be evidence in the preface to the *Register* for 1774 that the "principal conductor" was at that time still necessary to the running of the magazine, and that the principal conductor was still Burke. The preface apologizes, as it usually did, for the late appearance of the magazine, but explains:

The time of publication we are sensible is a point which it is our duty and interest to attend to; and it is never without extreme regret that we have found the publication delayed beyond the beginning of the summer. But for the lateness of the present publication we have only one excuse to make—a very severe illness which for several weeks confined the gentleman principally concerned in the work to his bed. This created an unavoidable delay; but the first efforts of his returning health were employed in endeavours that the diligence and attention in the execution might in some measure compensate for the lateness of the publication.

We know that Burke suffered quite a serious illness at almost exactly this time. He wrote in a letter to Lord Rockingham, August 4, 1775: "I have been very far from well for some weeks past; but I am, thank God, perfectly recovered." [13] The *Annual Register* for the year 1774 was published at the end of August, 1775. [14]

But if Burke did continue to manage the magazine, in fact as well as in name, it certainly is a question why he was willing to do so when his political duties were so pressing and so much more important. The *Annual Register* was a successful and an influential periodical, but it was only a periodical. The work it offered Burke even as chief editor was only a rather exalted form of hack work, mostly compilation. The greater part of the magazine was made up of extracts from other books and magazines, and even those portions which the editor could write himself were always anonymous.

13. Burke, *Correspondence*, II, 39.
14. *London Chronicle*, Aug. 29–31, 1775.

One feature and only one in the *Annual Register* seems significant enough to have continued to attract Burke strongly after he had become involved in politics. The famous Historical Article might still have appealed to him as a creative outlet, and he might well have felt reluctant to resign it entirely. Though he could not have helped feeling that it was a long and exhausting annual task—the article normally ran from 50 to 100 and later to 200 and 250 pages of closely set double-column type—yet he may well have felt, even after his entry into Parliament, that it was a kind of work capable of stimulating and using his best abilities. And it was certainly a kind of work that was valuable to him, more than ever when he was launched in active politics. Burke was at all times laborious in his preparation for his parliamentary duties, and was celebrated for his immense range of information on current affairs, and for his readiness on all points in debate. M'Cormick and Prior both suggest that his work on the historical portion of the *Annual Register* may have been one of the chief reasons for that readiness, and that he made the work on the *Register* a regular part of his preparation for Parliament.[15] If so he had an excellent reason for being willing to continue his connection with the magazine even during his busiest years.

It was probably the most important reason, but it may not have been the only one. The state of Burke's finances made even a small salary, if it was certain, of some importance to him. He did not, of course, remain at exactly his original £100 a year; we are told (in a roundabout way) that Dodsley considerably increased the figure. A contributor to *Notes and Queries* in 1855 quoted the following information about one of Burke's successors as editor of the *Register*, a certain Dr. William Thomson:

Towards the latter end of his life, the Doctor was chiefly employed in bringing up the long arrear of Dodsley's *Annual Register*. Of this employment he was not a little proud, as he now considered himself the legitimate successor of Edmund Burke. We understand that he compiled the historical part from 1790 to 1800, inclusive; and if paid as liberally as the Right Honourable gentleman just alluded to,

15. M'Cormick (1st ed.), pp. 36–37; Prior (1st ed.) p. 62.

his remuneration would have exactly amounted to £3000 for ten
volumes . . .[16]
Burke was at no time in a position to scorn £300 a year.

II

Thomas English was not Burke's only collaborator in the task
of bringing out the *Register*. From various sources we learn of
several other gentlemen who also gave their assistance. There is to
be sure very little agreement as to who the gentlemen were or as
to the nature of their contributions to the magazine; but there are
enough miscellaneous references to their existence to give us some
curiosity about them. M'Cormick, in the passage we have already
quoted concerning Burke's editorship, says: "In the year 1789,
Mr. Burke declined this task, and transferred it to other hands.
Dr. Laurence, the reverend Dr. King, Mr. Inglish, and two or
three subordinate writers, have since compiled the Annual Register." [17] Robert Bisset, the second biographer, says, indefinitely:
". . . the work was carried on for several years, either by Burke,
or under his immediate inspection. Afterwards, when he was
immersed in active politics, it was conducted under his general
superintendence, with only occasional exertions of his own genius." [18] Prior makes a similarly vague remark about "many of the
sketches of contemporary history, written from his immediate
dictation for about 30 years," which remark he explains further
in the early editions of his *Life of Burke* by saying: "Latterly a
Mr. Ireland wrote much of it under Mr. Burke's immediate direction . . ." But in his revised fifth edition he changes this last
remark to: "Latterly a Mr. English and Dr. Walker (afterwards
Bishop) King, the Editor of his works, wrote much of it under
Burke's immediate direction." [19] Prior also has a long footnote in
his second edition—excluded, perhaps as irrelevant, in his fifth—
in which he quotes a lengthy newspaper obituary of Burke's
friend Dr. French Laurence, who was his literary executor along
with Dr. Walker King. The obituary says, in part:

16. *Notes and Queries*, 1st ser., XII, 62.
17. M'Cormick (1st ed.), pp. 30–31.
18. Bisset (1st ed.), p. 50.
19. Prior (1st ed.), pp. 60–61; (2d ed.), I, 85; (5th ed.), p. 55.

As one of the executors of the late Edmund Burke, it became the province of Dr. Laurence, in discharge of the trust so reposed in him, to superintend the posthumous publications, together with the other literary property, of his illustrious friend. Amongst these works, the conducting of the original Annual Register, in the composition of which Dr. Laurence had long assisted, came, on the death of Mr. Burke, entirely under his direction.[20]

Perhaps it was an oversight that Prior did not incorporate in his text any direct reference to Dr. French Laurence as either a collaborator or a successor of Burke as editor. Robert Murray also failed to mention him when treating the *Register*. Murray's passage on Burke's connection with the magazine reads:

He never acknowledged his editorial labours on behalf of the *Annual Register*, yet it is a valuable source of information on the growth of his thought from 1758 to 1791, and a source hitherto but little tapped. In the latter years he ceased to write for it, though even after 1791 he continued his guidance of it. He so directed Mr. English and Dr. Walker King.[21]

Murray also in another place makes a passing reference to William Markham as having assisted Burke on the *Register*.[22] Finally, the *Encyclopaedia Britannica* in its article on the *Annual Register* says that Burke ". . . is thought to have continued in charge till about 1788, and to have inspired his successors (Dr. Walker King, afterwards bishop of Rochester, and Dr. Richard Laurence, afterwards archbishop of Cashel) till his death." This Richard Laurence is not to be confused with the French Laurence mentioned above, who was his elder brother.

Richard Laurence's name completes the list of those we are told were contributors to the magazine. Besides the "two or three subordinate writers" to whom M'Cormick refers, there are six names in all: Dr. Richard Laurence, Dr. French Laurence, William Markham, Dr. Walker King, Thomas English (or Inglish), and "Mr. Ireland." If we could discover the nature of the contributions of these six, the periods during which each was at work, and the

20. Prior, II, 450 n.
21. Murray, p. 83.
22. Murray, p. 86.

relationship of each to Burke, we should have nearly the whole story of the *Register* in Burke's day. Of course most of this information we do not have. What scattered hints we can rake together from obituary records and similar sources must constitute for the present our sketchy account of the subject.

Of the names suggested, probably two can be discounted at once as of little importance. William Markham,[23] mentioned by Murray, may have given Burke some aid in the inception of the magazine, and perhaps a little paternal counsel for a time thereafter, but there is no clear evidence that he was ever regularly engaged in the work of writing and compiling it. He was ten years Burke's senior, and already well established in the world as an active churchman and headmaster of Westminster School at the time Burke first launched the magazine. He probably talked over many details with Burke, encouraged him, discussed matters of policy with him, but never wrote for the magazine or assumed any part of the responsibility. What slight importance he may have had would probably be only in the earliest years of the *Register*.

The "Mr. Ireland" mentioned in Prior's early editions is probably also unimportant, if not nonexistent. He might be one of the "two or three subordinate writers" referred to by M'Cormick, but from the fact that Prior cut his name out of the revised fifth edition, after including it in his earlier editions, it is not unlikely that "Mr. Ireland" was a mistake of Prior's, which he later discovered and corrected. We shall perhaps be wiser if we disregard him, too, and concentrate our attention on the four definite names of Thomas English, the two Laurences, and Dr. Walker King.

Of these four, Thomas English is the least obscure to us, chiefly because Crossley's receipts, referred to above, give us definite dates for his connection with the *Register*. We do not know much

---

23. Who later became Archbishop of York. See Clements Markham, *Memoir of Archbishop Markham* (Oxford, 1906), where among other details of the intimacy of the churchman with Burke, it is said (p. 12): "he also assisted and advised Burke in his work connected with the *Annual Register*." This probably refers to the early years of the magazine, for it immediately follows the statement that Markham corrected the *Sublime and Beautiful*—published in 1757—and precedes another statement that in 1758 Markham stood godfather to Burke's son.

about English independently; and from what we do know he would not seem to have been a very conspicuous person. His obituary in the *Gentleman's Magazine* describes him vaguely and hints still more vaguely at the nature of his literary employments, which were concealed perhaps from some of the same social considerations as caused Burke to conceal his editorship. The obituary is dated May 21, 1798, and begins:

At his lodgings, No. 9. Orange-street, Leicester-square, aged 73 (and not long after some of his last labours were prepared for the press), Thomas English, esq. a gentleman deservedly regretted by the circle of his friends and acquaintance. Mr. E. was a man of very considerable literary talents. His name, it is believed, has not been annexed to any of his writings; but some productions of his pen have been highly esteemed by the publick. He appears, however, not only to have been perfectly pure from the vanity of an author, but nearly to have wanted that degree of allowable ambition, which serves as the usual spur to pursuits in this line. His manners were plain and direct; his temper warm, perhaps hasty . . .

and the article continues with an account of his character, too general to be very interesting. It refers later, however, to his devotion to Burke:

In the circle of his friends, Mr. Burke was known to be the particular object of his admiration and attachment. He considered him as the greatest man, of which all his extensive knowledge of life or of books afforded him an example. We have to add, that he possessed, very eminently, undiminished and uninterrupted, for a long series of years, the reciprocal esteem and friendship of Mr. Burke—a more eloquent monument (as will be allowed by men of genius and men of honour) than the most laboured panegyric could erect to his memory.[24]

This suggests at least the main outlines of Thomas English's literary character and of his relations to Burke and the *Register*. The receipts tell us a little more, and perhaps from the wording of Crossley's description of his receipts we can infer still a little more. Crossley says, as we have seen, that Thomas English "appears to have received from Dodsley, first £140, and subsequently

24. *Gentleman's Magazine*, 1798, I, 448 f.

£150, annually, for writing and compiling the historical portion of the work." We may be justified in inferring from the size of this salary—considerably more than Burke himself had received for the complete composition of the magazine in its early years— that English was expected from the start to do a fairly large share of the work. We might go farther and infer from the salary's having risen so little in twenty-five years, that English's share in the work of the *Register* never increased much. From Crossley's reference to "writing and compiling the historical portion of the work" we may undoubtedly infer that English had some part in the important Historical Article. There are, to be sure, other parts of the *Register* that could be called "historical portions"— notably the Chronicle, a rather mechanical calendar of events in their chronological order. But all of the hack work which might be involved in preparing these other possible "historical portions" would hardly seem to deserve English's salary. It is the more probable hypothesis that he was working on the main article, no doubt in addition to those others; that he was preparing materials for it (which would be rather a mechanical task), and doubtless also writing some of it, though Burke made himself responsible for its final form.

We have already suggested that the date of English's engage-ment—probably 1766, according to the evidence we have—may be of significance. It is the first moment at which we know of any worker besides Burke being engaged upon the *Register*. It occurs at just the time when Burke, if he had been carrying the magazine singlehanded, must surely have been forced to recognize that he could not do so any longer. It coincides almost perfectly with the period of a severe breakdown, caused by overwork, which Burke experienced at about this time. We have already cited, in the pre-vious essay, the passage in which Burke speaks of this break-down:

The first session I sat in Parliament, I found it necessary to analyze the whole commercial, financial, constitutional, and foreign interests of Great Britain and its empire. A great deal was then done; and more, far more, would have been done, if more had been permitted by events. Then, in the vigor of my manhood, my constitution sank under my labor. Had I then died, (and I seemed to myself very near death,) I had then earned for those who belonged to me more than the Duke of Bedford's ideas of service are of power to estimate.

Was this breakdown the immediate occasion for English's engagement?

III

Between English's appointment and Burke's resignation more than twenty years later we can be reasonably certain of at least two figures in the picture of the *Annual Register*. Burke during those years was always acting as "principal conductor," guiding mind in chief command (whoever else may have been employed upon it); and English, Burke's friend, admirer, and contemporary, remained a regular worker in some subordinate capacity.

It is much harder to make out what parts were played, and at what times, by the three other collaborators we have named: that is, the two Laurences and Walker King. We know as much of their biographies as we do of English's; for they were all rather prominent men in their day, and obituaries can be found for them. We also know much more of their relations with Burke, which were intimate. Walker King and French Laurence were perhaps his closest associates in his latter years, and became his literary executors.

As there are no receipts, we have no dates to tell us at what period each began or ended his labors on the *Register*. The most we can discover is that all three of them did work upon it during Burke's lifetime (not necessarily during his editorship); that Walker King was the first to be engaged; that French Laurence succeeded him; and that Richard Laurence followed his brother. This we have on the authority of Henry Cotton, author of the well-known reference work *Fasti Ecclesiae Hibernicae* and usually a reliable authority. Cotton should have known what he was talking about, for he had been a domestic chaplain to Richard Laurence, as well as his son-in-law, and had edited the poetical works of French Laurence and Richard Laurence, including a brief memoir of each author in his edition. Cotton wrote to *Notes and Queries* in 1855 in reply to a query about the authorship of the *Annual Register:*

I know that the historical portion of two or three years, perhaps more, was written by Dr. Richard Laurence, then vicar of Coleshill, Berks, afterwards Archbishop of Cashel; brother of Dr. French Laurence, the eminent civilian and intimate friend of Burke. Dr. French Laurence had engaged to carry on the work, when Mr. King gave it up; but the unceasing pressure of his professional business soon compelled him to desist from the task, which was then undertaken by his brother. I think that Dr. Richard Laurence wrote for the years 1791, 1792, and 1793; but, at all events, it was between 1790 and the death of Edmund Burke in 1797.

Perhaps I ought to have inserted these papers (with some others) in the list of the Archbishop's writings given in my *Fasti Ecclesiae Hibernicae;* but the truth is, that I did not know then, nor do I now, know exactly the amount of his contributions to the *Annual Register*, and other periodical publications.[25]

We know, of course, that both Dr. Walker King and Dr. French Laurence were ultimately so intimately associated with Burke that it was in the natural order of things that they should take a part in any literary works which he had in hand. We know that in the 'nineties they were working together among his papers, to which they had free access. Indeed, they began at that time to bring out their edition of his *Works*, of which the first three volumes appeared in 1792. The question in relation to the *Annual Register* is therefore only, *how early* do we judge that each became so close to Burke and so continually associated with his literary endeavors that he could have been asked to lend a hand in Burke's annual task of bringing it out?

Walker King[26] would hardly have had that honor before 1771, when he received his A.B. (at the age of 17) from Corpus Christi College, Oxford; but within a short time of that it would seem

---

25. *Notes and Queries*, 1st ser., XII, 171.
26. He later became Bishop of Rochester. The fullest biographical account of him is the obituary in the *Gentleman's Magazine*, 1827, I, 269 f. There is some further information in Foster's *Alumni Oxonienses*, 1715–1886 (London, 1887–88), II, 796; in Foster's *Register of Admissions to Gray's Inn* (London, 1889), p. 501; and in Burke's *Landed Gentry* (16th ed. London, 1939), p. 1294.

to have been easily possible for him to be involved. He and two of his brothers were "intimate friends of the Burkes" as early as 1773.[27] One of the brothers was chosen as tutor and companion for young Richard Burke when he went to France in January of that year. Walker himself through Burke's influence got a post as tutor to the young Duke of Richmond in 1774.[28] Except for his holding that post for a year, and getting an M.A. from Oxford some time in 1775, we know very little of his career until he became private secretary to the Marquis of Rockingham (the position Burke had once held) in 1782. Burke was the chief worker and guiding mind of the "Rockingham Whigs"; as soon as King became an active member of that party he would have been working with and under Burke constantly,[29] and could with the greatest ease have fallen into a share of Burke's yearly task of preparing the *Register* for the press.

Since for the exact date of King's engagement there is so little proof, 1775 is offered merely as a probable guess.[30] King is mentioned by Cotton as having worked on the "historical portion" of the Register, and if this means the Historical Article, as no doubt it does, then it may be significant that this article had a very sudden increase in length in the *Register* for 1775. Originally, and for the first ten years of the *Register* the article had averaged about 60 pages a year, and perhaps this represents the idea of its character which Burke had formed for himself when he started the *Register* alone. In 1768, however, it had suddenly swollen to 84 pages—which may well represent the additional energy (or diffuseness) supplied by English; and from 1768 to 1774 it had continued to average around 90 pages, only once rising as high as 108. But in

27. Burke, *Correspondence*, I, 405 and note.
28. Unpublished letters relating to this arrangement are in the Morgan Library in New York.
29. We find him, for example, writing personal letters for Burke in 1782, with the explanation that Burke was so busy that he was obliged to correspond through King as a substitute. Burke, *Correspondence*, II, 476–477.
30. We pointed out that English's first engagement fell very close to the time of a severe breakdown of Burke's health, which might have convinced him that he could not get on without assistance; it may be permissible here to refer again to his other severe illness in 1775, which has already been mentioned as having delayed the publication of the *Annual Register* that year. Was this perhaps also the occasion of Burke's being forced to admit that he would have to have more help?

1775 it suddenly jumped again to 158, and the next year to 188, and from then on for the next ten years it averaged 200 pages or over.[31] Are we justified in guessing that this represents the additional energy supplied by King? There is also a remark in the *Register's* Preface for 1776 which may be taken as referring to the engagement of new editorial assistance at about this time. It reads:

Our publisher has liberally seconded our views in affording the expense consequent of so great an extension of the Historical Article. He thinks he cannot do too much to testify his gratitude to the Public, and desires we would observe, that from the abundance of matter which is now necessarily discussed, it trebles in extent the amount of the History in any year of the late war.

The "late war" refers to the Seven Years' War, in progress during the period of Burke's first—probably singlehanded—work upon the article in the first seven years of the magazine.

If we could trust these hints and guesses, we might be justified in believing that Walker King came to the assistance of Burke and English on the *Register* at about 1775, not long after completing his work at Oxford, but before his deepest involvement in the affairs of the Whig party in the early 'eighties. It is rather probable, as we have seen, that as he became closer and closer to Burke's concerns, and worked more and more with him, he would have taken a hand in this affair. There must have been a period during which he and English and Burke were all at work on the *Register*.

How long this period lasted is again a subject for guessing, because we are uncertain of when King's collaborations ended. As Cotton's account tells us that "Dr. French Laurence had engaged

31. The variations in length of the Historical Article of the *Annual Register* are as follows in the period of Burke's editorship:

Year	Pages	Year	Pages	Year	Pages	Year	Pages
1758	77	1766	48	1774	78	1782	244
1759	56	1767	45	1775	158	1783	180
1760	64	1768	84	1776	192	1784–85	192
1761	58	1769	73	1777	188	1786	177
1762	64	1770	95	1778	236	1787	232
1763	49	1771	94	1779	214		
1764	44	1772	105	1780	234		
1765	56	1773	108	1781	202		

to carry on the work when Mr. King gave it up," we know at least that our guesses must depend upon two preliminary questions. First, at what period in King's career would he be most likely to have resigned his task?

We know that Walker King was turning his attention to a career in the Church, and during the late 'eighties must have been giving an ever larger percentage of his time to his ecclesiastical duties. In 1786 he became Preacher of Gray's Inn, and in 1788 took his degrees of Bachelor and Doctor of Divinity at Corpus Christi College, Oxford. He was already well started on his way to a bishopric.

Second, at what period in French Laurence's career did he in turn become intimate enough with Burke to have been associated with him in his personal and even secret work of preparing the *Register?* What evidence there is points also to the late 'eighties. Laurence's obituary in the *Gentleman's Magazine* shows that he must have been known to Burke by that time. It says:

He first became known to the Publick by the active part which he took in the contest for Westminster, in the year 1784, in writing for Mr. Fox, particularly in the Opposition News-papers of that period; and he was author of most of the popular ballads which appeared during the course of that memorable election. By his superior talents Dr. L. was introduced to the notice and friendship of Mr. Burke; and in consequence of that gentleman's influence, was appointed one of the Lawyers retained by the Managers on the trial of Warren Hastings; during the whole of which prosecution he was indefatigable in exploring and arranging the documents necessary in so arduous and complicated a transaction; and the advantage derived from his exertions was ever acknowledged by his friend and associate as of the utmost importance.[32]

And this is confirmed by the most dependable biographical account of French Laurence, written by his brother Richard, which says: "The intimate friendship between Mr. Burke and Dr.

---

32. *Gentleman's Magazine*, 1809, I, 281. This gives a reasonably full account of French Laurence; the article in the *Annual Register*, 1809, pp. 605 f. gives much the same account; the article in the *Dictionary of National Biography* is fuller than either; the Preface of his brother's edition of his correspondence with Burke, referred to below, gives the fullest account of him we have.

Laurence commenced with the trial of Mr. Hastings. When that friendship was duly cemented, the former took no literary or political step without consulting the latter, who entered into all his views, and assisted in all his undertakings, with warmth and sincerity." [33] Laurence was taking a very active part in the Hastings Impeachment as early as 1786, when perhaps their close intimacy can be assumed.[34]

Richard Laurence's account, incidentally, also confirms Cotton's remark about French Laurence, that "the unceasing pressure of his professional duties soon compelled him to desist from the task." Richard Laurence's account reads:

In consequence of the credit he obtained by the trust, which the House of Commons reposed in him during this memorable impeachment, his professional employment at the civil law bar so rapidly increased, as to leave him very little time for literary pursuits. His intervals of leisure were usually spent at Beaconsfield; where he experienced, from every part of the Burke family, an attention and attachment, which, had he been united to them by the ties of blood, as well as of friendship, could scarcely have been exceeded.[35]

It might be natural here to suspect Richard Laurence of wishing to exaggerate the intimacy of his brother with Burke. Yet other accounts show that he hardly did so. French Laurence was probably Burke's most intimate associate and co-worker from the time of the Hastings trial until Burke's death. The extent of their correspondence from 1788 on gives some measure of this, as does the fact of Burke's having procured Laurence a seat in Parliament by his own influence with Lord Fitzwilliam. The latter event is commented upon as follows in the *Gentleman's Magazine* obituary on Laurence:

Through Mr. Burke's interest with Earl Fitzwilliam he obtained a seat in Parliament; from which time he considered himself rather

33. *Epistolary Correspondence of Edmund Burke and French Laurence* (London, 1827), p. iv.

34. In a letter to a relation, Laurence boasted of being sole author of one of the charges against Warren Hastings which Burke had presented to the House of Commons, and which had been printed in 1786. See *Correspondence of Burke and Laurence*, pp. xxii–xxiii.

35. *Correspondence of Burke and Laurence*, p. xxiii.

as the adherent of that great man than an implicit follower of the Party with which he had hitherto acted; and when the French Revolution induced Mr. Burke to withdraw himself from Mr. Fox and his friends, Dr. L. traced the steps of his Patron, and remained invariably attached to his principles, till the Country was deprived of one of its greatest ornaments.[36]

Indeed, Laurence's devotion to Burke's principles continued even after Burke's death, according to the *Dictionary of National Biography's* account of Laurence. That account says:

His speeches in parliament were marked by learning and weight rather than brilliance and force, and except on questions of international law, in which he was a recognized authority, evinced a mind so dominated by the influence of Burke as almost entirely to have parted with its independence. In opposing the union with Ireland he insisted that Burke, had he lived, would have done so likewise.

So complete a submergence in another man's mind must have come about only gradually, and this quotation refers to a period at least ten years later than that time in the late 'eighties when we are inclined to believe that Laurence took King's place on the *Register*. Nonetheless, the relationship which it suggests between Laurence and Burke has an important bearing on our account. For it shows that Laurence became to Burke just such an *alter ego*—such a cross between an intimate friend and an all-useful private secretary—as could be entrusted to undertake such a confidential task as the yearly preparation of the *Register*.

It will be noticed that there is a remarkable similarity between the early careers of Laurence and King, particularly as to their relationships with Burke and the *Register*. Indeed, the similarity amounts to a pronounced parallel, if we may add our guesses thus far to the biographical facts we know. King took his B.A. at Oxford in 1771 and his M.A. in 1775. Shortly afterward he became intimate with Burke and deep in the affairs of the Whig party, where he must have been working under Burke. For a while he worked on the *Annual Register* along with Burke and English, but ultimately his own career absorbed his energies; in 1788 he

36. *Gentleman's Magazine*, 1809, I, 282.

took his degree of Doctor of Divinity, and he must have given up his work on the *Register* about that time or not long after. We may follow Laurence through that same career, almost point by point. He took his B.A. at Oxford, from the same college as King, Corpus Christi, in 1777, and his M.A. in 1781. Shortly afterward he became associated with the Whig party, came to know Burke intimately, and worked under him in party affairs. For a while he worked on the *Annual Register* along with Burke and English, but he took his degree of Doctor of Civil Law at Oxford in 1787, and as his professional career developed he was forced to recruit the services of his younger brother to carry on the *Register*.

It is even interesting—though less important in relation to Burke, since Richard Laurence's services on the *Register* do not fall within the period of Burke's editorship—that Richard Laurence too had a very similar career. At least, he took his B.A. and M.A. at Corpus Christi College, Oxford, he too contributed to the *Annual Register* during the period when he was getting started in his profession, he too gave it up as his career developed, and like King he too ultimately became a dignitary of the Church.

IV

It is the place occupied by the *Annual Register* in the parallel careers of King and the two Laurences that has the greatest significance for this study. To all three of the men the time they spent on the magazine was an intermediate period between college and professional life. None of them went into journalism as a life work; perhaps they were all from a social class which regarded that as impossible. Yet one can easily believe that the few years spent in editorial tasks, and especially the task of reviewing British and European affairs for the Historical Article, would have proved of the utmost value to "young men on the make" who had not yet fully committed themselves to any full-time professional work.

But the character of the young men and of their attitude toward the *Register* has still another bearing on our account, for it does a great deal to explain what at first seemed rather difficult to understand: the question of how Burke found it possible to keep the editorship and the ultimate control of the magazine in his own hands almost to the end of his career, during years when he obviously could give it very little of his time. If his subordinates were young men very close to him, often in his house and at his table, looking to him as a party leader from whom they might expect advancement, and bound to him as disciples to their master, from whom they were to absorb experience and political wisdom —it is not hard to see that Burke could continue to hold the nominal and the real headship of their joint enterprise with hardly more exertion on his own part than it would take to give friendly advice to his attentive juniors. We have already seen that English— though he could not be classed as one of the young men, being nearly Burke's contemporary—was a man easily to be dominated: admiring Burke nearly to the point of adulation; and "perfectly pure from the vanity of an author" which might urge him to assert his independence. With English still at work on the *Register* and familiar with it by twenty years of experience, Burke could surely have trusted himself to dominate these younger men and to control the magazine even when he was no longer able to do any work on it himself.

And probably the magazine was already running on those terms well before 1789 when Burke resigned the nominal editorship. That date, though it is given us as the time when Burke ceased to be "principal conductor," can hardly mark any very sudden break in Burke's labors on the magazine, which must have been tapering off long before. Neither does it mark the end of his influence over the *Register*, which, being carried on by such avowed disciples as English and French Laurence, was sure to reflect Burke's ideas and policies till the time of his death and even beyond it. The likeliest guess is that either 1789 is the date at which Burke ceased to draw a salary from Dodsley, or it is the period when some specific change in the nominal headship was made—perhaps the likeliest of such changes being the succession of French Laurence to the editorship in Burke's place.

We have already suggested that changes in the editorial arrangements of the *Register* may reflect changes in Burke's own political career. The engagement of English was close to the time of Burke's entry into Parliament, and perhaps of a severe breakdown from overwork that he suffered shortly after that. We suspected that the engagement of King was at a time close to 1775, which was the date of another breakdown in Burke's health, doubtless also caused by overwork. This last change, in 1789, was at a time when Burke was sinking under the greatest pressure that he had ever borne—that in connection with the Hastings impeachment. Burke taxed all of his powers, and overworked himself and his subordinates then as he had never done before.

It is also interesting that these same periods of pressure, and particularly the last, will be found to be reflected in another way in the history of the *Register*. The magazine almost from the beginning of its history had been guilty of tardiness in making its annual appearance. It had literally never come out by Lady Day of the year following its date, as was the original intention; and apologies for lateness began early to appear in the yearly prefaces. What is curious to watch is the way in which those apologies became a sort of barometer of the intermittent but ever-increasing pressure of Burke's political life. The first of them appeared in the issue for 1761, when the magazine was only four years old. The second was in '65, just when Burke was entering Parliament, and probably just before English was engaged. There were two more in '69 and '70. In '74 there was one to which we have already referred, at the time of a serious illness of Burke's and perhaps close to the time of King's being engaged. After '74 there was none till '77, but beginning in '79 there were four in a row. In '83 apologies were omitted, but not for lack of cause, since this was the first issue of the magazine to be dated a full year late (that is, it came out in 1785 instead of some time late in 1784). By the issue for '84 the editors seem to have become resigned to disaster, for they never did get that issue out: an issue dated 1784-85 and intended to cover two years in one finally appeared in 1787 with even fuller apologies than usual. The editors explained in its preface that they had hoped to catch up to their schedule by this maneuver. But they had not succeeded in making the magazine less than a year late, and the issues for '86, '87, and '88 were each that far behind. The issue for '89 finally went even beyond that, for it did not appear till October, 1792, so that it was well over two years late. The *Annual Register* began to be something of a joke. There is an amusing advertisement in the *London*

Chronicle for January 18, 1792, which shows that other rival magazines were making fun of its chronic lateness. The advertisement begins as if it were the usual announcement of the appearance of the *Register*, but has a surprise ending. It reads:

The ANNUAL REGISTER; or, a View of the History, Politics and Literature, for the years 1789, 1790, and 1791, that has given such infinite satisfaction to the inquisitive mind, on the public events and literature of Europe, is best continued by the EUROPEAN MAGAZINE.

The arrears were never made up in Burke's lifetime. When he died in July, 1797, the *Register's* issue for '92 had not yet appeared.[37]

37. By combining what we learn from two sources—Ralph Straus's *Robert Dodsley*, and the yearly publishers' advertisements in the *London Chronicle*—we can establish nearly to the day the time of each *Register's* appearance during Burke's lifetime. The dates tell their own story.

Date of *Register*	Published	Date of *Register*	Published
1758	May 15, 1759	1775	Aug. 6, 1776
1759	May 21, 1760	1776	Sept. 25, 1777
1760	Apr. 25, 1761	1777	Nov. 5, 1778
1761	May 17, 1762	1778	Dec. 30, 1779
1762	May 5, 1763	1779	Jan. 13, 1781
1763	May 17, 1764	1780	Jan. 31, 1782
1764	May 18, 1765	1781	May 1, 1783
1765	May 28, 1766	1782	Nov. 23, 1784
1766	May 26, 1767	1783	Dec. 17, 1785
1767	May 19, 1768	1784–5	July 30, 1787
1768	June 22, 1769	1786	Aug. 30, 1788
1769	July 21, 1770	1787	Oct. 13, 1789
1770	July 20, 1771	1788	Dec. (30), 1790
1771	July 14, 1772	1789	Oct. 6, 1792
1772	July 22, 1773	1790	[Jan. 2, 1794]
1773	Aug. 4, 1774	1791	[July 9], 1795
1774	Aug. 31, 1775		

IV

A BODY OF ANONYMOUS WRITING

THE BODY of Burke's writing which is to be found in the *Annual Register* must amount, even at a low estimate, to thousands of pages; and of this great mass the part which we can be surest was Burke's falls into that period of his career which most needs to be illuminated. If we knew with any certainty what Burke wrote in the *Register*, we should be able to trace the lines of his mental development in his formative years as no one up to now has ever dared to trace them.

Unfortunately we have attained no such certainty. We know that the great mass of writing is there, but we cannot say of any single sentence or paragraph, this is undoubtedly Burke's. There is a high probability that any part of the magazine written before 1766 was written by Burke; we know of no other worker in that early period. But even this is speculative; there might have been such a worker, whose name did not happen to come down to us. After 1766 there was always at least one other worker, so that no single sentence or paragraph can be securely assigned to Burke. But (again we must remember) even after 1766 many scores, perhaps many hundreds, of pages in the magazine were assuredly his.

Naturally, conscientious scholars and biographers have been uncomfortable in this dilemma. Should they use the contents of the magazine when attempting to establish Burke's opinions, contacts, interests, and the like? Or should they shy away from its uncertainties? Some have risked it one way, some the other. Robert Murray quoted freely from any part of the magazine between 1758 and 1791 with apparent conviction that he was quoting Edmund Burke. Philip Magnus in his entire biography never once quoted the *Register* directly.

There is no solution for a problem which involves anonymous writing until the happy day when a signed confession by the author fixes his authorship forever. That day has not yet dawned for the *Annual Register*. Hence there is no alternative at present to the dusty task of assembling "evidence" that the dubious material was what we think it was. As to parts of the *Annual Register*, this means arguing that they were probably Burke's because they were before 1766; or because they follow the lines of Burke's interests; or because they correspond with his known opinions; or because they seem to be written in his style . . . It is a discouraging sort of work, the assembling of evidence.

There is, however, one part of the *Annual Register* which is at least as encouraging as anonymous writing usually is to this kind of investigation. This is the department of book reviews: a small but reasonably important section of the magazine. The *Register* did not attempt to review many books—not more than four or five in an average year—and its announced policy was to review only those which it was disposed to praise.[1] But this very fact made the department more nearly a reflection of the special interests of its author than otherwise it could have been. If we find that the books reviewed were in a considerable number of cases books which were in Burke's hands, or about which we can gain his opinions from other sources, or whose authors he knew, or whose lines of interest paralleled his, we are at least better placed than usual to set up a claim that the anonymous material must have been his. If we can establish such probability for a number of individual cases, the broader probability rises that this whole section of the magazine can be defended as his. It is hoped that there is enough evidence at hand to bring a cautious reader to grant that the whole section was his in the period before 1766, and that from 1766 at least through the issue for 1773 there are enough individual reviews which are probably his to establish the fact that he was maintaining his interest in this department of the magazine even if he did not write every line it contained.[2]

1. In the Preface to the first issue of the magazine, the editor says of the books reviewed: "We have observed upon none that we could not praise; not that we pretend to have observed upon all that are praise-worthy. Those that do not deserve to be well spoken of, do not deserve to be spoken of at all." The editor at this stage was *certainly* Burke.

2. Most of the material in this essay, though in a slightly different form, was presented in my article "Edmund Burke and the Book Reviews in Dodsley's *Annual Register*." *P.M.L.A.*, LVII, 446–468.

There is not a very large body of reviews altogether. From 1758 through 1765 the *Register* reviewed in all only forty-one books—never more than seven in one year. In the period from 1766 through 1773 only twenty-seven books were considered, and never more than five in one year. There was a steady decrease in the yearly number of reviews the *Register* chose to publish— which in itself might be an argument for assuming that an increasingly busy man, like Burke, was conducting this department of the magazine.[3]

I

One naturally considers first the rather small number of instances in which we know that Burke was acquainted with the specific books which the *Register* reviewed. Some of these, though they don't of course clear up the whole secret, give us more or less convincing glimpses of Burke's activities as a journalist and reviewer:

(a) When Adam Smith's *Theory of Moral Sentiments* was published in 1759, David Hume as a friend of Smith did what he could to get it a favorable reception among the London critics. He wrote to Smith on April 12 of that year describing his activities. "Wedderburn and I made presents of our copies to such of our acquaintance as we thought good judges and proper to spread the reputation of the book. I sent one to the Duke of Argyle, to Lord Lyttelton, Horace Walpole, Soame Jenyns, and Burke, an Irish gentleman who wrote lately a very pretty treatise on the Sublime." [4] And again on July 28 of the same year: "I am very well acquainted with Bourke, who was much taken with your Book. He got your Direction from me with a View of writing to you, & thanking you for your Present: For I made it pass in your Name. I wonder he has not done it: He is now in Ire-

3. The exact numbers of the reviews in each volume of the *Register* between 1758 and 1773 are:

1758	6	1762	4	1766	5	1770	3
1759	7	1763	5	1767	4	1771	3
1760	6	1764	4	1768	3	1772	3
1761	5	1765	4	1769	3	1773	3

4. *Letters of David Hume*, ed. J. Y. T. Greig (Oxford, 1932), I, 303.

land." [5] The review of the *Theory of Moral Sentiments* duly appeared in the *Annual Register* for 1759, published in the spring of the following year.

(b) When Burke's friend and frequent hostess Mrs. Elizabeth Montagu brought out her *Essay on Shakespear* in 1769 its author was supposed to be completely unknown. But apparently Burke was in on the secret—perhaps as the result of some good professional contacts. Mrs. Montagu wrote to her husband in September of that year:

Mr. Burke called on me this morning; he seems in health and good spirits. He tells me my book is very successful. Reynolds the famous Painter laid 5 guineas it was written by Mr. Warton who wrote the Essay on the Genius and writings of Pope, but said at the same time the essay on Shakespear was written with more imagination and fire. Reynolds has paid him his five guineas, so dangerous it is to guess at Authors when they dont put their names to their works. [6]

The book was very favorably noticed in the *Annual Register* for the year.

(c) James Beattie describes in his diary how he was introduced to Burke in 1773, and how flattering were Burke's remarks upon his recently published *Essay on Truth:*

Mr. Burke gave me as kind a reception as I ever received from anybody, and paid me many complimts, in the genteelest manner. Says that my postscript [an answer to his critics which Beattie appended to the second edition of the *Essay*] is one of the most manly & most masterly pieces of eloquence he has ever seen . . . says the publick will be very critical in regard to any future publications of mine, as I have taught them so well to distinguish what is good . . . spoke of the style of the Essay on Truth in the highest terms of approbation, and gave it such preference in point of variety harmony force and ease, as must have flattered the most exorbitant vanity. [7]

5. *Idem*, p. 312. For other evidence that Burke took an interest in the book, see James Prior, *Life of Edmund Malone* (London, 1860), pp. 368–369.

6. *Mrs. Montagu, Her Letters and Friendships*, ed. Reginald Blunt (London, 1923), I, 224.

7. *James Beattie's London Diary, 1773*, ed. Ralph S. Walker (Aberdeen, 1946), pp. 33, 54.

The *Annual Register* for 1771, which had appeared in the middle of 1772, had expressed similar admiration of the *Essay*, even to the point of singling out its postscript as "one of the finest pieces of writing we remember to have seen." On his visit to France in the early part of 1773 Burke had defended Beattie in the salons against the sneers of the freethinkers.[8]

(d) We get an incidental picture of Burke in the role of critic and literary promoter in a letter of his old Irish friend Thomas Leland in 1770. Leland was at that time planning to bring out a *History of Ireland;* and Burke had both encouraged him to undertake it and later supplied him with some important manuscript material. Leland wrote Burke from Dublin, urging him to assist still further the progress of the work:

I must tell you my scheme, for you may do me a little service. I wish to publish two volumes next winter, containing the history of Irish affairs from the first invasion to the final settlement of the kingdom in the reign of James I.; and if these should take, to publish a continuation in two vols. more. I should be much obliged to you, if, in some hour of leisure, you would mention this matter to your bookseller, and open a treaty for the two vols. (each of which will be larger than one of Robertson's Life of Charles, if printed in the same manner,) but without taking notice of my intention for a continuation. My reasons for desiring this are, that I have conceived some little dissatisfaction at Johnston, my old printer; and you are a person of great figure and consequence, and these fellows will think highly of any thing that Mr. Burke seems to interest himself in. Do, for Heaven's sake, puff me, as Charlemont and Flood and Michael Kearney do.[9]

It is obvious from such a letter that its author thought that Burke was willing, and able, to take a protective interest in a book of his friend's.

(e) There are a number of less explicit references to Burke's being engaged in such critical activities as advising authors or encouraging books. When Dodsley was preparing to print his

8. Chauncey B. Tinker, *The Salon and English Letters* (New York, 1915), p. 68.

9. Burke, *Correspondence*, I, 223–224. See also *ibid.*, I, 337–338; III, 441–442.

collection of *Fables,* we hear of Burke giving him advice as to typography.[10] Burke was one of the original subscribers to his friend James Stuart's *Antiquities of Athens* and his friend Joseph Priestley's *History of Discoveries Relating to Vision, Light and Colors.* He sent the new edition of Swift's posthumous work to Henry Flood in Ireland.[11] All of these books were reviewed in the *Annual Register.*

(f) There are one or two instances of books in which Burke's interest can easily be proved, though we do not find him carrying on any of the particular activities of a critic or reviewer. In his speeches and writings, for example, he makes several comments upon Dr. John Brown's *Estimate of the Manners of the Times,*[12] which was the first book reviewed in the first issue of the *Register;* apparently it had impressed its youthful reviewer. Later on Burke took a particular interest in Blackstone's *Commentaries on the Laws of England,* and went out of his way in writings and speeches to give it praise.[13] The *Register* noticed the *Commentaries* in two separate issues.

(g) There is perhaps one other legitimate means of inferring Burke's acquaintance with the books which the *Register* reviewed. There exists a catalogue of Burke's library, compiled when the library was sold after his death.[14] It lists a number of the books the *Register* reviewed in exactly the edition reviewed, as well as two or three which have Burke's name on their lists of subscribers.[15]

10. See a letter of Shenstone in *Works of William Shenstone* (3d ed. London, 1773), III, 323, discussing Dodsley's projected book: ". . . Spence, Burke, Lowth, and Melmoth, advise him to discard *Italicks.*"

11. Burke, *Correspondence,* I, 80.

12. See Burke, *Works,* I, 457 n.; V, 239; also Cavendish's *Debates of the House of Commons* (London, 1841), II, 106.

13. Burke, *Works,* II, 125; III, 272; XI, 38, 62 n., 88.

14. There are copies of this catalogue in the British Museum and the New York Public Library.

15. The following items in the catalogue have some significance for the present study. Except 383 and 561 these are the exact editions which would have been in the *Register's* reviewer's hands. The exceptions illustrate a connection of Burke with the author or book:

31 Baretti's Travels in Italy, 1769.

33 Brown's Estimate of the Principles of the Times, 1757.

171 Anderson's History of Commerce, 2 vol. 1764.

312 Marshall's Travels in Holland, &c. 3 vol. 1772.

335 Hume's History of England, 6 vol. 1762.

II

In a small number of the *Register's* reviews we might guess from the language used that the reviewer had some particular, perhaps personal, reason for being partial to the interests of his author. In these cases it is of interest if we know that Edmund Burke was well acquainted with the authors concerned.

(a) *Samuel Johnson.* The most interesting examples of this kind are the reviews of Johnson's *Rasselas* and of his edition of Shakespeare's plays. Both of these show that they were written by a reviewer who deeply admired his author, and indeed who wished to use the *Register's* pages to fight the author's personal battles. The review of *Rasselas* in 1759, almost certainly by Burke since it is only in the second year of the magazine, drops the following pregnant hint on the subject of Johnson's pension:

Though the author has not put his name to this work, there is no doubt that he is the same who has before done so much for the improvement of our taste and our morals, and employed a great part of his life in an astonishing work for the fixing the language of this nation; whilst this nation, which admires his works, and profits by them, has done nothing for the author.

And in the review of Johnson's much-criticized edition of Shakespeare in 1765 there is even stronger evidence of a wish to give aid to an old friend. After setting forth at considerable length the difficulties confronting an editor of Shakespeare, the *Register's* reviewer says:

---

355 Leland's History of Ireland, 1773.
383 Orme's Military Transactions of the British in Hindostan, *some passages marked by Mr. Burke,* 1775.
384 Ossian's Fingal, by Macpherson, 1762.
469 Rousseau, Emile, 2 vol. 1762. Rousseau's Emilius, by Nugent, 2 vol. 1763.
476 Shakespeare's Plays, with Notes by Johnson, 8 vol. 1765.
522 Webb on Painting, 1761. Webb on Poetry and Music, 1769.
547 Priestley on Vision, Light and Colors, 1772.
554 Swift's Works, with His Life and Notes by Hawkesworth, 6 vol. *plates,* 1755.
561 Sullivan's Lectures on the English Laws, *With a MS Inscription to Burke,* 1776.
617 Stuart's Antiquities of Athens, vol. 1, *Mr. Burke's Subscription Copy, with the list of Subscribers and the errata, uncut, plates,* 1762.

. . . we are still of the opinion, that notwithstanding the long delay of the work, and his not complying altogether with the expectation of the public, the public will be found considerably indebted to him; at least, till it can be proved, that the delay and deficiency have been owing to any wilful negligence on his part; a charge which it may not be so easy to prove, considering those vicissitudes to which, with regard to study, though not discernible, the mind of man is even more subject than his body is, with regard to labour; and from which the minds of the greatest geniuses are often less exempt than those of the meanest. The most, we think, that can be said of Mr. Johnson on this occasion, that he was rather rash in promising than backward in performing. It is, however, happy for the republic of letters that he promised as he did; since, otherwise, we should, probably, never have received Shakespeare through his hands.

(b) *Thomas Leland*. We have already mentioned Burke's Irish friend Dr. Thomas Leland, in whose *History of Ireland* Burke had a part. Both the review of that history and the review of Leland's *Life of Philip of Macedon*, published in the first issue of the *Register*, bear internal marks of the reviewer's partiality for his author: in frequent references to him in extremely complimentary terms, in allusions to the high reputation of his previous works, in mentions of the expectations naturally raised, and satisfied, in the scholarly world by the appearance of any book by Dr. Leland, and so forth.[16]

(c) Joseph Baretti. Another friend of Burke to whom we know he gave encouragement in his literary career was the Italian scholar Joseph Baretti. At the time Baretti was considering bringing out his *Manners and Customs of Italy* he wrote in a letter to his brother:

If Samuel Johnson, Edmund Burke, Dr. Goldsmith, and others among the leading men of letters and gentlemen of this nation do not deceive me, the work should win me an honorable position throughout England and make them all, ladies and gentlemen alike, eager to know an author who writes their language as I do.[17]

16. For evidence of Burke's acquaintance with Leland, see A. P. I. Samuels, *Early Life of Edmund Burke*, p. 94; Prior (5th ed.), p. 65; Burke, *Correspondence*, I, 109; *Correspondence of Edmund Burke & William Windham* (Cambridge, 1910), p. 3.

17. Lacy Collison-Morley, *Giuseppe Baretti* (London, 1909), p. 186.

In the review of *Manners and Customs of Italy* in 1768 full exposition is made of the book's and the writer's unusual merits—the reviewer's absorption in the latter topic extending to the point of his giving his readers a three-page account of a quarrel that had arisen between Baretti and another writer on Italy, all treated in a manner which highly favored Baretti. The reviewer also, like Burke, felt that Baretti's mastery of English should recommend him to English readers, and referred to it more than once. "There is perhaps a little," he admitted, "it is however but a very little, of the foreign accent, if I may use the word, in his writing: But on the whole, for correctness of language, and manliness of expression, his work would have done credit to the most approved English pen." Again, he speaks of the "wonderful perfection he has attained in our language."

And the later review of Baretti's *Journey from London to Genoa* in 1770 continues in the same vein. Its opening paragraphs begin:

The author of these volumes (whom we have formerly had occasion to make favourable mention of as a writer, from his account of the customs and manners of Italy, published in 1768) is a foreigner; nor will the attentive reader want any proofs of it. Indeed, from the *general* purity and propriety of the diction, we should almost suspect that these little trips in the language were not undesigned; but were left by the author as a sort of mark, to prove his title to the work.

We have mentioned the propriety of the diction: we must do him the honour of owning, that he has attained to that masterly command of the language, that would not discredit the very best of our own writers.

The review of the *Journey from London to Genoa*, like the review of the *Manners and Customs*, is given first place among the reviews for its year.

(d) *Elizabeth Montagu*. We have mentioned Burke's attention to the first launching of Mrs. Elizabeth Montagu's *Essay on Shakespear*. The opening paragraph of the *Register's* review of that book suggests a similar solicitude for the cause of its author. The lady having been a good deal criticized for her "defense" of Shakespeare against foreign critics (many English readers feeling that he needed no defense), the chivalrous reviewer came to the lady's own defense in a diplomatic and deprecatory passage; it is well worth examining as a possible instance of a reviewer's partiality. And if the hand of a friend should be found in it, perhaps a hint of the same hand might be granted in the earlier review of Lord Lyttelton's *Dialogues of the Dead* in 1760—to which collection Mrs. Montagu had contributed anonymously three dialogues. After admitting that some of the dialogues written by Lord Lyttelton himself were lacking in dramatic spirit, the reviewer says: "However, what little of that kind is wanting in these Dialogues, is abundantly made up in the three additional ones, which are by another hand. These are truly dramatic, and not inferior to the best dramatic dialogue." This certainly could be thought of as a bouquet to a charming and influential hostess who had "discovered" Edmund Burke in the late 'fifties.

(e) *Other writers.* These four writers, each treated in two reviews, and James Beattie, referred to above, are the best instances of our finding in the reviews themselves reasons to believe that Burke used the *Register* to puff personal acquaintances.[18] There are of course many other reviews of books written by friends of Burke. Lord Lyttelton as well as Mrs. Montagu was an intimate friend when the *Dialogues of the Dead* was reviewed in 1760, and still so when the *Register* reviewed with great fulness his *Life of Henry the Second* in 1767.[19] Burke knew Horace Walpole at the time the *Register* reviewed Walpole's edition of Vertue's *Anecdotes of Painting* in 1762 and his edition of the *Life of Herbert of Cherbury* in 1770; perhaps he knew him as early as 1758 when his *Catalogue of Royal and Noble Authors* was reviewed.[20] We have mentioned David Hume's friendship with

18. There is a slight hint of another such puff in the review of Benjamin Stillingfleet's *Miscellaneous Tracts* in 1759, where the reviewer says the merit of the work "will make everyone wish that learned author otherwise employed than in translation."

19. Their acquaintance began around 1757, and soon became intimate. See Robert Phillimore, *Memoirs of Lord Lyttelton* (London, 1845), II, 579; also Prior (5th ed.), p. 65.

20. A letter of Walpole to George Montagu in July, 1761 (*Letters*, ed. Mrs. Paget Toynbee, V, 86) says: "I dined with your secretary [this refers to William Gerard Hamilton] yesterday; there were Garrick and a young Mr. Burke, who wrote a book in the style of Lord Bolingbroke, that was much admired.

Burke as a means of introducing him to Adam Smith's *Theory of Moral Sentiments;* it might also be a reason for his interest in Hume's own *History of England.*[21] We have spoken of his giving advice to his friend Robert Dodsley on his collection of *Fables.* Dr. Charles Burney, whose *History of Music* was reviewed in 1773, was a fellow member of the Literary Club.

Inevitably, there are instances where we know that Burke was well acquainted with an author, but are not sure that the acquaintance dates from a period earlier than the *Register's* noticing of that author. He knew William Warburton at some time; [22] was it before the review of the *Doctrine of Grace* in 1762? He knew James Stuart well in 1764; did he know him when the *Antiquities of Athens* was reviewed in 1762? [23] When did he meet Adam Smith in the flesh? Was it as early as 1759? [24] Did he know Thomas Percy when the *Reliques* were noticed? [25]

We can perhaps ignore those other writers whom Burke "must have known." He must have known Benjamin Stillingfleet,[26]

He is a sensible man, but has not worn off his authorism yet—and thinks there is nothing so charming as writers, and to be one—he will know better one of these days."

21. Perhaps also for his interest in a book which attacked some of Hume's conclusions: William Tytler's *Enquiry into the Evidence against Mary Queen of Scots,* reviewed in 1760.

Mr. Robert A. Smith, now studying at Yale, called my attention to a copy of Burke's *Essay towards an Abridgment of the English History* (London, 1757) now in the Yale University Library. It bears a MS inscription: "This fragment given to me by Mr. Nicol the King's bookseller, was written by Edmund Burke and discontinued, on the publication of Hume's History."

22. See James Prior, *Life of Edmund Malone,* p. 370.

23. Burke's friend and protégé, the painter Barry, wrote from London to a friend in Ireland, either at the end of 1764 or early in 1765: "At present I am at a kind of journey work for Mr. Stewart, Hogarth's successor, where I am likely to have a great deal of satisfaction. This was brought about by your friend Mr. Burke . . ." *Works of James Barry* (London, 1809), I, 15. Barry also makes reference in another letter, after some mention of Burke, "to his friends, Athenian Stewart, to Sir Joshua, to myself, and others . . ." *ibid.,* II, 538. We have already referred above to the fact that the copy of Stuart's *Antiquities of Athens* in Burke's library was a subscription copy, which may be another reason for believing that Burke knew the author before the book appeared.

24. Bisset (2d ed.), II, 428 f. records the fact that Burke and Smith met and conversed, but he does not say when they first became acquainted.

25. He must have known him at least as early as 1768, when Percy became a member of the Literary Club.

26. Burke and Stillingfleet were both frequent attendants at Mrs. Elizabeth

Ferdinando Warner,[27] and Francis Sullivan.[28] We have no indubitable proof.

III

The evidence of authorship which is supplied by the quotation of parallel passages is almost always difficult to present convincingly. Therefore from a good deal of such material it will probably suffice to treat only three or four illustrative instances.

(a) *Opinion of lawyers and legal education.* At the time Burke began his labors on the *Register* he had very recently made up his mind to abandon the study of law. Apparently he had not given up the study without having formed a strong opinion of the narrowness and stupidity of the existing methods of legal education and a rather low estimate of lawyers as a group. Both opinions, or prejudices, he retained all his life; they appear repeatedly in his mature speeches and writings.[29] Part of the reason for his feeling is set forth in a passage of his *Essay towards an Abridgment of the English History,* an early and uncompleted work:

Thus the law has been confined and drawn up into a narrow and inglorious study, and that which should be the leading science in

Montagu's salons, and certainly had opportunities to meet. See, for example, a letter of Mrs. Montagu in 1764 referring to a dinner party to which both were invited, though Burke could not come. *Mrs. Montagu, Her Letters and Friendships,* I, 89. A remark of Burke to Boswell (*Boswell Papers,* XIV, 209) may also be evidence that he was acquainted with Stillingfleet.

27. In the composition of his *History of Ireland,* Dr. Warner made a trip to Dublin, where he applied to the Irish Parliament for permission to use state archives in the compilation of his work. Burke was at that period resident in Dublin where he had gone as Hamilton's secretary to act as a political manager of the Irish Parliament. If it is accepted as probable that Burke wrote the review of Ossian's *Fingal* in 1761, he very likely knew Dr. Warner as early as that, for the review quotes Warner's opinions on the authenticity of *Fingal* and also describes him "as an Englishman unbiassed to Ireland, and as an historian now compiling the history of that country."

28. As Burke through life maintained his acquaintance with several of the professors of Trinity College, Dublin, it is quite likely that he met Sullivan, who became Regius Professor of Law there in 1750. Burke certainly knew him by the year 1776: we have already referred to the copy of Sullivan's *Lectures on English Law* in Burke's library "*with a MS Inscription to Mr. Burke.*"

29. See Burke, *Works,* II, 37–38, Prior (5th ed.), p. 355; and for a more general prejudice against lawyers as a class, Burke, *Works,* II, 124 f., and III, 286.

every well-ordered commonwealth remained in all the barbarism of the rudest times, whilst every other advanced by rapid steps to the highest improvement both in solidity and elegance; insomuch that the study of our jurisprudence presented to liberal and well-educated minds, even in the best authors, hardly anything but barbarous terms, ill explained, a coarse, but not a plain expression, an indigested method, and a species of reasoning the very refuse of the schools, which deduced the spirit of the law, not from original justice and conformity, but from causes foreign to it and altogether whimsical. Young men are sent away with an incurable, and, if we regard the manner of handling rather than the substance, a very well-founded disgust.[30]

And Burke added to this a strong distrust of another illiberal practice of legal educators, namely, that of putting young men directly to work in attorneys' offices without having previously given them a broader background of education. Boswell's journal contains a record of Burke's opinion of this practice:

Burke said that it was a very bad plan to put a young gentleman who was to follow the law first to an Attorney; that considering the law solely as a *lucrative trade,* it might be well to do so, for thus he would form intimacies with Attornies and their clerks, and get sure business. But that it was very wrong to give narrow and contracted notions to men who might one day decide upon the lives and properties of the subjects of this Country, nay, arrive at the highest honours and have a great sway in the state.[31]

It is not hard to show that the *Register's* reviewer felt much as Burke did upon the subject. The choice itself of William Blackstone's *Discourse on the Study of Law* to review in 1758 shows the trend of his interest. The following passage introducing an extract from Blackstone will illustrate the reviewer's and the author's attitude toward the type of legal apprenticeship already mentioned. The reviewer writes:

The author has also the following most useful remarks on certain illiberal notions and practices with regard to legal education.

30. *Ibid.,* VII, 477.
31. *Boswell Papers,* XVII, 100.

"The evident want of some assistance in the rudiments of legal knowledge, has given birth to a practice, which, if ever it had grown to be general, must have proved of extremely pernicious consequence: I mean the custom, by some very warmly recommended, to drop all liberal education as of no use to lawyers; and to place them, in its stead, at the desk of some skillful attorney; in order to initiate them early in all the depths of practice, and render them more dextrous in the mechanical part of the business. A few instances of particular persons, (men of excellent learning and unblemished integrity) who, in spite of this method of education, have shone in the foremost ranks of the bar, have afforded some kind of sanction to this illiberal path to the profession, and biassed many short-sighted parents in its favour . . ."

The passage continues in the same strain for half a page. There is a similar passage, but in the reviewer's own words, in the review of Blackstone's *Commentaries* in 1767. It reads in part as follows:

In this situation of things, we must owe no trivial obligation to any gentleman of abilities equal to the task, who will take the pains to remove any part of the obscurity in which our system of laws is involved, and thereby contribute to render the whole more intelligible. It will increase this obligation, if we reflect, that the law has been long looked on as the most disagreeable of all studies; and of so dry, disgusting, heavy a nature, that students of vivacity and genius, were deterred from entering upon it; and those of a quite contrary cast, were looked upon as the fittest to encounter the great difficulties which attended a science, which, however excellent in its principles, lay in such a state of rudeness and disorder.

The review of Francis Sullivan's *Lectures on the Feudal and English Laws* in 1772 also begins in this vein:

Until our own times, the science of our common law lay a vast and confused heap, from whence, with infinite labour and difficulty, the practicioner at the bar only extracted a dry unpleasing knowledge, which, though it might enable him to raise his fortune, tended but little to enlarge his mind; few others attempted a study, which, separated from the interests of a profession, promised so little rational, and so little liberal enterment [*sic*].

Dr. Sullivan, though he has not the honour of being the first who has led his countrymen through a liberal and philosophical road to the study of the laws of his country, which undoubtedly is the palm of Judge Blackstone, has the no small merit of seconding that idea, and, as far as he has gone, of completing it.

(b) *Opinion as to the duties of a Member of Parliament.* One of Burke's best-known opinions after he entered politics was that a Member of Parliament when he had once been elected was not bound to obey precise instructions from his constituents; it was his duty to form his own judgments upon events. As Burke told the voters of Bristol in 1774:

To deliver an opinion is the right of all men; that of constituents is a weighty and respectable opinion, which a representative ought always to rejoice to hear, and which he ought always most seriously to consider. But *authoritative* instructions, *mandates* issued, which the member is bound blindly and implicitly to obey, to vote, and to argue for, though contrary to the clearest conviction of his judgment and conscience,—these are things utterly unknown to the laws of this land, and which arise from a fundamental mistake of the whole order and tenor of our Constitution.

Parliament is not a *congress* of ambassadors from different and hostile interests, which interests each must maintain, as an agent and advocate, against other agents and advocates; but Parliament is a *deliberative* assembly of *one* nation, with *one* interest, that of the whole—where not local purposes, not local prejudices, ought to guide, but the general good, resulting from the general reason of the whole. You choose a member, indeed; but when you have chosen him, he is not a member of Bristol, but he is a member of *Parliament*.[32]

It is interesting to note how closely this parallels the argument which is quoted from Bishop Ellys' *Spiritual and Temporal Liberty of Subjects in England* when the *Register* reviews that book in 1765:

32. Burke, *Works*, II, 96. See also a remark in his "Appeal from the New to the Old Whigs" (*Works*, IV, 95): "He was the first man who, on the hustings, at a popular election, rejected the authority of instructions from constituents,— or who, in any place, has argued so fully against it." See also *Works*, VII, 74, 99; *Cavendish Debates*, I, 287 f.

Monsieur Rapin de Thoyras looked upon it to be a considerable defect in our constitution, that the matters to be treated of in parliament are not expressed in the summons, as king John promised they should, and that members of our house of commons have not instructions about them, from the people whom they represent; or, if any such instructions be given them, that they are at liberty not to observe them. The matter of fact, indeed, is true; our members of parliament are not, by law, obliged either to consult those who have chosen them, nor to have any regard to their instructions, farther than they themselves judge them to be reasonable; for, though a man is chosen by a particular county or burgh, he is, by law, reputed to serve for the whole kingdom. But as these things could not be ordered otherwise, as the state of our nation is at present, so some persons are far from thinking, with Mr. Rapin, that these are circumstances of any disadvantage to our constitution.

and Ellys continues to argue against Rapin, at great length, in a strain entirely harmonious with Burke's later utterances.

(c) *Opinion of Lord Bolingbroke.* Like most of his contemporaries Burke was horrified by the irreligious tendencies of Lord Bolingbroke's posthumous works; and the *Vindication of Natural Society*, Burke's first book published in England, was, as is well known, an ironic attack on Bolingbroke's freethinking. Its preface states very clearly what was Burke's opinion of his opponent:

I cannot conceive how this sort of writers propose to compass the designs they pretend to have in view, by the instruments which they employ. Do they pretend to exalt the mind of man by proving him no better than a beast? Do they think to enforce the practice of virtue, by denying that vice and virtue are distinguished by good or evil fortune here, or happiness hereafter? Do they imagine they shall increase our piety, and our reliance on God, by exploding his providence, and insisting that he is neither just nor good?

Burke remained of this opinion till the end of his life. When he was writing on the subject of the French Revolution thirty years later, he showed an even stronger contempt and hatred for Bolingbroke, particularly exulting in the fact that by then his popularity had passed: "Who now reads Bolingbroke? Who ever

read him through? Ask the booksellers of London what is become of all these lights of the world." [33] And having, by some
chance, occasion to quote him, Burke took special precaution
against seeming to honor him by the reference: "I do not often
quote Bolingbroke, nor have his works in general left any permanent impression on my mind. He is a presumptuous and a super-
ficial writer." [34]

There are two reviews in the *Register* which will indicate how
closely the reviewer's opinions, and his manner of expressing them,
approximate Burke's. The first is the review of Swift's correspondence, published in 1765. The reviewer focuses attention on the
inconsistency of Lord Bolingbroke in writing Swift, September
12, 1724, a long letter, quoted in full, which condemns as subversive the work of freethinkers—a position regarded as hypo-
critical in view of Bolingbroke's strict injunction to Mallet to
publish his subversive *Philosophical Works*, after Bolingbroke's
death. The letter quoted (with other letters in point printed by
the reviewer from the originals) exposes Bolingbroke's lack of
consistency in permitting that publication. After seven full pages
of such quotation the reviewer comments:

The publication, however, of Lord Bolingbroke's works though it
leaves him without apology, as, whether his notions were erroneous
or true, he did what he professes he ought not to have done, has
eventually done rather good than harm; it has shown that the world
gave him credit for powers which he did not possess, and undeceived
those who imagined he had defended Deism, by a series of clear,
deep, and solid reasoning: his work is found to be lively, slight, and
unconclusive; its reputation has declined in proportion as it has been
known, and the great part of the impression, which was to enlighten
the world and enrich Mallet, is now rotting unsold in the warehouse.

The last sentence is strikingly reminiscent of Burke's contemptuous "Ask the booksellers of London what is become of all these
lights of the world."

The other review which treats Bolingbroke is that in 1770 of

33. Burke, *Works*, III, 349.
34. *ibid.*, III, 398.

Thomas Hunter's *Sketch of the Philosophical Character of the Late Lord Bolingbroke.* As that book is itself an attack on Bolingbroke, the reviewer expresses his own opinions by his hearty approval of Dr. Hunter's undertaking:

. . . there cannot be a greater service to men than that of exposing the futility and falseness of those bold and bad reasoners, who, like the serpent of old, pretending to raise and ennoble our nature, and to teach us wisdom, carry us away from that humble path of simplicity and obedience wherein it has pleased God to permit and direct that poor creature man to look for his salvation.

But the reviewer adds:

While we give every praise to the intention, and allow the merit of the execution of this work, we have still doubts whether these kind of writers, who dignify themselves by the style of freethinkers, are not, especially after a time, best answered with disdain: while the weakness of mankind, and their madness for novelty, give a kind of weight to these sorts of works, they seem to call for answers, lest a silence on the side of truth should give confidence to falsehood; but when the novelty is worn off, the less notice is taken of them, the less they are remembered.

This is surely reminiscent of Burke's protestation that he did not often quote Bolingbroke and had been very little influenced by him.

The reviewer also speaks scornfully of the style of Bolingbroke, which Burke had parodied: ". . . there is, however, a pompousness of phrase, a show and affectation of learning, and a sort of glair [*sic*] of elocution, that seems at least to excuse if not to justify the admiration his works once excited."

He also rebukes Dr. Hunter for being more tolerant of Bolingbroke's political than of his philosophical works: "Our author, with all his zeal against the philosophical or irreligious writings of Lord Bolingbroke, seems almost of an opinion with his Lordship in his political works, which, however, are fallen nearly into as much disrepute as his philosophical, and possibly not without reason . . ." Burke, according to John Morley, "trained his party to understand and resist" the political thought of Boling-broke.[35]

(d) *Opinion of Rousseau.* Burke's feelings about Jean Jacques Rousseau were in many respects like his feelings about Boling-broke; they were a mixture of apprehension and of dislike of the subversive elements in his philosophy. In the *Vindication*—though it cannot be proved that Burke had read Rousseau at the time it was written—we find him arguing Rousseau's own case for a "natural society," though of course arguing it ironically and with the definite purpose of demonstrating its fallacy. After exploring the possibilities and the dangers of these revolutionary ideas it is hardly thinkable that Burke should have ignored the rising popu-larity of Rousseau in England in the years around 1760.[36] The train of his interests, the fact of his being an editor and a book reviewer, the fact of his having been in France when Rousseau's popularity there was at its height—all make it almost impossible to imagine that he did not interest himself in Rousseau's books. We have already noted that two editions of *Emile* were in the list of books in his library.

Many years later, at the time he was attacking the French Revo-lution, Burke gave quite fully his opinions of Rousseau's writings. Those tendencies which he disliked and suspected in Rousseau, as well as the merits which he granted him, were very fully stated. It is not possible here to quote fully the several pages of that treat-ment, but the following passages are perhaps fair samples of its drift:

We certainly perceive, and to a degree we feel, in this writer, a style glowing, animated, enthusiastic, at the same time we find it lax, diffuse, and not in the best taste of composition,—all the members of the piece being pretty equally labored and expanded, without any due selection and subordination of parts. He is generally too much on the stretch, and his manner has little variety. We cannot rest upon any

35. John Morley, *Burke* (English Men of Letters series, London, 1892), p. 70.
36. Morley pointed out (*ibid.*, pp. 22–24) the nearness in time and also in subject of Burke's *Vindication* and Rousseau's *Second Discourse*. Mr. Richard Sewall has presented more fully the case for believing that Burke was familiar with Rousseau's work at the time the *Vindication* was written. *Philological Quarterly*, XVII, 97–114.

of his works, though they contain observations which occasionally discover a considerable insight into human nature. But his doctrines, on the whole, are so inapplicable to real life and manners, that we never dream of drawing from them any rule for laws or conduct, or for fortifying or illustrating anything by a reference to his opinions. They have with us the fate of older paradoxes:

> Cum ventum ad *verum* est, *sensus moresque* repugnant,
> Atque ipsa utilitas, justi prope mater et aequi . . .[37]

It is not that I consider this writer as wholly destitute of just notions. Among his irregularities, it must be reckoned that he is sometimes moral, and moral in a very sublime strain. But the *general spirit and tendency* of his works is mischievous,—and the more mischievous for this mixture: for perfect depravity of sentiment is not reconcilable with eloquence; and the mind (though corruptible not complexionally vicious) would reject and throw off with disgust a lesson of pure and unmixed evil. These writers make even virtue a pander to vice. . . .[38]

. . . they [the French who set up Rousseau as a model] infuse into their youth an unfashioned, indelicate, sour, gloomy, ferocious medley of pedantry and lewdness,—of metaphysical speculations blended with the coarsest sensuality.[39]

The *Annual Register's* reviews, though they do not manifest the violence of feeling which Burke showed after the French Revolution had begun, yet give nearly the same picture of Rousseau's merits and defects. In the review of Rousseau's *Letter to d'Alembert* in 1759 the reviewer says:

None of the present writers have a greater share of talents and learning than Rousseau; yet it has been his misfortune and that of the world, that those of his works which have made the greatest noise, and acquired to their author the highest reputation, have been of little real use or emolument to mankind. A tendency to paradox, which is always the bane of solid learning, and threatens now to

37. "Letter to a Member of the National Assembly," Burke, *Works*, IV, 32.
38. *Idem*, pp. 32–33.
39. *Idem*, p. 31. See also for other expressions of opinions of Rousseau, the "Reflections on the French Revolution," Burke, *Works*, III, 459. Mr. Reginald Buehler's Harvard dissertation entitled *Burke and Rousseau* should also be consulted.

destroy it, a splenetic disposition carried to misanthropy, and an austere virtue pursued to an unsociable fierceness, have prevented a great deal of the good effects which might be expected from such a genius. A satire upon civilized society, a satire upon learning, may make tolerable sport for an ingenious fancy; but if carried farther, it can do no more (and that in such a way is surely too much) than to unsettle our notions of right and wrong, and lead by degrees to universal scepticism.

The review of *Emile* in 1762 is in part more complimentary, though it refers to the defects and dangers of Rousseau's thinking. It begins:

To know what the received notions are upon any subject, is to know with certainty what those of Rousseau are not. In his treatise on the inequality amongst mankind, he has shown his man in the natural state; in his Emilius he undertakes to educate him. . . .

In this System of Education there are some very considerable parts that are impracticable, others that are chimerical; and not a few highly blameable, and dangerous both to piety and morals. It is easy to discern how it has happened that this book should be censured as well at Geneva as in Paris. However, with those faults in the design, with the whimsies into which his paradoxical genius continually hurries him, there are a thousand noble hints relative to the subject, grounded upon a profound knowledge of the human mind, and the order of its operations. There are many others, which, though they have little relation to the subject, are admirable on their own account; and even in his wildest sallies, we now and then discover strokes of the most solid sense, and instructions of the most useful nature. Indeed, he very seldom thinks himself bound to adhere to any settled order or design, but is borne away by every object started by his vivid imagination, and hurries continually from system to system, in the career of an animated, glowing, exuberant style, which points everything with great minuteness, yet with infinite spirit.

There is, it must be acknowledged, one considerable defect in his judgment, which infects both his matter and his style. He never knows where to stop. He seldom can discover that precise point in which excellence consists, where to exceed is almost as bad as to fall short, and which every stop you go beyond, you grow worse and worse. He is therefore frequently tiring and disgusting by pushing his notions to excess; and by repeating the same thing in a thousand different ways.

Allowing for the fact that thirty years separate the unacknowledged reviews from the acknowledged writings of Burke, it must be conceded that the parallels of thought are striking. And when the subject and intent of the *Vindication of Natural Society* are considered along with the parallels, perhaps the total argument for Burke's authorship of the reviews is strong enough to stand.[40]

IV

We pretty well expect that the main directions of interest reflected in the *Register's* reviews will parallel what we know to have been Burke's main directions of interest. Nonetheless this too is a kind of evidence, though it can hardly be more than corroborative.

(a) *Political interests.* For example, we suppose that if Burke were the reviewer, the *Register's* department of book reviews would give a special emphasis to books and discussions connected with politics. Actually this is far the strongest emphasis in the *Register's* reviews, and its relative importance mounts steadily during the period we are considering. Not only are political and constitutional history and law treated with great fullness, as might be explainable enough in a magazine like the *Register*, but very specific problems connected with the history of Parliament are given an amount of space that it is hard to imagine being granted them by any reviewer who was not himself a specialist.[41]

40. The *Register's* review of Adam Ferguson's *Essay on the History of Civil Society* in 1767 should be considered in connection with the question of Burke's attitude toward Rousseau. The reviewer's own words and a long passage which he quotes from Ferguson parallel strikingly Burke's opinions of the theory of Natural Society.

41. The following reviews give evidence of their author's rather special interest in politics, constitutional history, and law:

1759 Blackstone's *Discourse on the Study of Law.*
   Leland's *Life of Philip of Macedon* (containing a four-page extract on the Greek constitution).

(b) *Ireland*. The reviewer's interest in Ireland presents a rather similar case. We are not bound to assume that he was Burke just because he reviewed Irish authors and books upon Ireland.[42] But when his reviews contain notable parallels to Burke's highly specialized interest in Irish antiquarianism, there is much better reason for believing that the reviewer may have been Burke.[43]

Warner's *Memoirs of Thomas More* (containing an extract already cited on More's defiance of royal power in the name of the House of Commons).

1760 *Life of Edward, Earl of Clarendon.*
Robertson's *History of Scotland* (with a four-page extract on the Scotch feudal constitution).
Wallace's *Laws of Scotland.*

1761 Hume's *History of England* (extract on its constitutional bearings, and reviewer's comment on the extract).

1763 *Letters of Henry, Earl of Clarendon.*
Warner's *History of Ireland* (with remarks on the early Irish constitution).
Grey's *Debates of the House of Commons.*

1765 Ellys's *Liberty of Subjects in England.*

1767 Lyttleton's *Life of Henry the Second* (three extracts treating the constitutional aspects of feudalism).
Blackstone's *Commentaries.*
Ferguson's *Essay on Civil Society.*
Beccaria's *Essay on Crimes and Punishment.*

1768 Blackstone's *Commentaries.*

1771 Dalrymple's *Memoirs of Great Britain and Ireland* (with five pages of extracts describing constitutional crises in the reign of James II).

1773 Sullivan, *Lectures on the Feudal and English Laws.*

42. The following reviews may be noticed, however, as being either by Irishmen or about Ireland:

1758 Leland's *Philip of Macedon.*
1760 Webb's *Beauties of Painting.*
1762 Webb's *Beauties of Poetry.*
1763 *State Letters of Henry, Earl of Clarendon, Lord Lieutenant of Ireland* (with extracts of 1772 letters on the affairs of Ireland).
Warner's *History of Ireland.*

1764 Leland's *Christian Revelation.*
1765 Swift's *Works* (with a long extract relating to English treatment of Ireland).
1771 Dalrymple's *Memoirs of Great Britain and Ireland.*
1772 Sullivan's *Lectures on Feudal and English Laws.*
1773 Leland's *History of Ireland.*

43. Burke's lifelong interest in early Irish customs, laws, and language may easily be illustrated from Prior (5th ed.), p. 268, Bisset (2d ed.), II, 249 f., the *Letters of David Hume*, I, 400, the *Boswell Papers*, XVII, 51, 89–90, the *Works of James Barry*, I, 266, 445, or Burke's own *Works*, VI, 299. The reviewer shows various aspects of the same antiquarian interest in the following reviews:

1760 (Macpherson's) Ossian's *Fingal* (with a six-page discussion of the merits of the "Celtic Homer," comment on the question whether he was an

(c) *Aesthetics.* Burke's first thoroughly successful book had been his work on the *Sublime and Beautiful.* In the *Register's* department of book reviews similar lines of interest are not lacking, though reviews of books in the field of the fine arts are neither extremely numerous nor extremely enthusiastic. They are largely confined to the early years of the *Register.*[44]

(d) *Other directions of interest.* We may note the reviewer's interest in a rather technical work on commerce, at almost precisely the time when we know that Burke was plunging into that field of study; [45] the reviewer's interest in India is surely suggestive of Burke.[46] With these we may break off our recital of parallels of interest.

V

It may seem remarkable that we have not hitherto raised the question of literary style. It is not in this instance an unimportant question. On the contrary, it probably has been the determining

---

Irish or a Scotch bard, comment on the accuracy of his picture of ancient Irish customs).

1763 Warner's *History of Ireland* (a seven-page review dealing in detail with laws, customs, and manners of the earliest period of Irish historic and pre-historic times).

1766 Rowland's *Mona Antiqua Restaurata* (a seven-page review of this study of Celtic antiquities).

1773 Leland's *History of Ireland* (twelve-page review, entering into the details of the earliest period of reliable Irish history. Burke's own discovery of new manuscript material in this field is alluded to).

44. The following should be noted:

1760 Webb's *Beauties of Painting.*   1763 Stuart and Revett's *Antiquities of*
1762 Webb's *Beauties of Poetry.*   *Athens.*
        Walpole's *Anecdotes of Painting.*   1764 Algarotti's *Essay on Painting.*
                                                                          1773 Burney's *History of Music.*

45. The six-page review of Anderson's *History of Commerce* is given first place in the *Register's* reviews for 1764. We know that Burke was deeply absorbed in the study of commerce at this time. *Works,* II, 87.

46. Two reviews reflect this interest:

1764 Orme's *Military Transactions in Indostan.*
1766 Holwell's *Historical Events Relative to Bengal.*

Burke's interest in India was years in advance of that of most of his countrymen. (See Bisset [2d ed.] I, 63–64.) Burke later showed a thorough familiarity with Holwell (*Works,* IX, 396–493), quoting passages from the *Historic Events* three times in the course of the Hastings trial. *Idem,* 384–385, 389, 391. Orme's history was in Burke's library, "with some passages marked by his own hand."

reason that biographers such as Mr. Murray have felt justified in ascribing to Burke many parts of the *Annual Register*.[47] The book reviews in general "sound like" Burke, and perhaps that is the very strongest evidence we have that they are his.

Judgments of style, even when we can assume them to be highly accurate, depend upon incommunicable feeling. In the case of a writer like Burke, who has very few noticeable personal marks or mannerisms about his writing, explanations of how any given reader arrived at his feeling are almost sure to remain unconvincing. Yet two minor observations relating to style may be made. The first is that there is an unmistakable and steady improvement of the reviewer's style between the first issues of the magazine in the 'fifties and those of the late 'sixties and early 'seventies. The reviews not only increase in length and comprehensiveness with the years; they gain in originality and sureness of expression. Since we know with all but complete certainty that Burke was the writer of the first few years, it is natural to take the reviewer's steady progress toward maturity as evidence that the reviewer did not change his identity.

There is, however, one conspicuous interruption to the reviewer's steady improvement. One single review, that of Crantz's *History of Greenland* in 1766, is stylistically so different from all the other reviews of the early years of the magazine that it would seem to be almost certain that it was not written by the same hand. Its diffuseness (spending over eighteen pages on this comparatively insignificant book), its lack of organization, its mechanical differences from the other reviews (such as the practice, indulged in nowhere else, of embodying long quotations

47. In the course of this study I wrote to Mr. Murray to ask him whether he had any evidence besides the internal evidence of style for ascribing so many of the reviews to Burke. His reply read in part: "I am afraid I have no evidence to offer you that Burke wrote the reviews in the 'Annual Register,' though I am perfectly convinced that he did so. After all, what can be stronger than the internal evidence? Edmund Burke is written all over them." Other biographers and critics of Burke have presumably found themselves in Mr. Murray's dilemma; at least they have frequently enough made ascriptions of specific reviews to Burke without citing any external evidence. See Prior (5th ed.), p. 65; Macknight, *Life of Burke*, I, 33, 116, 235; also *Burke: Select Works*, ed. E. J. Payne (Oxford, 1877–78), I, 237, 243, 249, 277, 339, 377.

from the author in the review without any use of quotation marks)—all these, not to mention actual incorrectnesses of language, make it quite impossible to think it written by the previous reviewer, whether or not that was Edmund Burke.

The date of the Crantz review is of course significant. The *Register* for 1766 is the first on which we know that another worker besides Burke was employed. If the Crantz review is a fair sample of his competence, Thomas English had still a great deal to learn at the time he joined Burke on the *Register*!

VI

As has already been suggested, the case for Burke's authorship of the *Register's* reviews must be broken into two parts at the year 1766. Up to that year we have found no reason to doubt that Burke was writing the entire magazine singlehanded, so that taking the evidence we have been reciting as corroboration of what we already are disposed to believe, we should like to submit it as now very probable that Burke wrote all of the forty-one reviews which appeared up to that year. It is at least less probable that he wrote the twenty-seven which appeared in the issues from 1766 to 1773.

There are half a dozen of the reviews in the latter period however, in which Burke's authorship is supported by evidence full enough or striking enough to be almost completely convincing. These may be listed here, along with the types of evidence that connect them with Burke:

1766 *Letters of Swift.* Ed. John Hawkesworth. (Parallels to Burke's opinions of Bolingbroke; striking verbal parallel to Burke's acknowledged writing.)

1768 *Manners and Customs of Italy.* By Joseph Baretti. (Burke's acquaintance with Baretti; acquaintance with this book in manuscript; a copy in his library; indications in the review of a disposition to puff.)

1769 *Essay on Shakespear.* By Elizabeth Montagu. (Burke's acquaintance with Mrs. Montagu; with this book; copy in his library; indications in review of a disposition to puff.)

1770 *Journey from London to Genoa.* By Joseph Baretti. (Burke's acquaintance with Baretti; indications in the review of a disposition to puff.)

1771 *Essay on Truth.* By James Beattie. (Burke's acquaintance with Beattie; with this book; striking parallel between review and Burke's known opinion of the book.)

1772 *History of Ireland.* By Thomas Leland. (Burke's acquaintance with Leland; with this book; copy in his library; parallels to Burke's interest in Ireland and Irish antiquities; indications in review of a disposition to puff.)

These reviews might be ranked with those appearing in the first eight years of the *Register*, and called *very probable* instances of Burke's authorship. There are between 1766 and 1773 eight other reviews which though less striking cases may still be called *probable.* These are:

1766 *Historical Events of Bengal.* By J. Z. Holwell. (Parallels to Burke's interest in India; Burke's [later?] acquaintance with this book.)

1767 *Essay on Civil Society.* By Adam Ferguson. (Parallels to Burke's opinions on natural and civil society; copy in Burke's library.)

1767 *Life of Henry the Second.* By George, Lord Lyttelton. (Burke's acquaintance with Lyttelton; parallels to Burke's political opinions and interests.)

1767 *Commentaries on the Laws of England.* By William Blackstone. (Burke's acquaintance with Blackstone; with this book; parallels to Burke's opinions on law and lawyers; to his political opinions.)

1768 *Commentaries on Laws of England.* By William Blackstone. (Burke's acquaintance with Blackstone [?]; with this book; parallels to political opinions.)

1770 *Character of Lord Bolingbroke.* By Thomas Hunter. (Parallels to Burke's opinions of Bolingbroke.)

1771 *Memoirs of Great Britain and Ireland.* By John Dalrymple. (Parallels to Burke's political opinions; to his interest in Ireland.)

1772 *Feudal and English Laws.* By Francis Stoughton Sullivan. (Burke's acquaintance with Sullivan [?]; with this book [later?];

copy in his library [later?]; parallels to his opinions on law and lawyers; parallels to his political interests.)

It is scarcely wise to claim as probable any reviews with less evidence than these. The review of Rowland's *Mona Antiqua Restaurata* in 1766 may reflect Burke's interest in Irish antiquities; that of Walpole's *Life of Herbert of Cherbury* in 1770 may reflect an acquaintance with the author; that of Burney's *History of Music* in 1773 may reflect an acquaintance with the author or an interest in aesthetic subjects. But such hints are too slight for grounded argument.

V

BURKE, PAINE, AND JEFFERSON

A FOOTNOTE in Philip Foner's edition of the works of Tom Paine retails an account of a personal relationship between Paine and Burke well before the period of their historic controversy over the principles of the French Revolution:

In Croly's life of Edmund Burke there is the following interesting statement: "Among his (Paine's) earliest missives was a letter (from Paris) to Burke, whom he eagerly urged to introduce Revolution into England, by its established name of 'Reform!' Burke threw back the temptation, or the insult, at once. 'Do you *really* imagine, Mr. Paine,' was his reply, 'that the constitution of this kingdom requires such innovations, or *could exist with them*, or that any *reflecting man would seriously engage in them?* You are aware that I have, all my life, opposed such schemes of reform, because *I know them not to be Reform*.' Paine, however, continued his ill-received correspondence; and whether from the delight of molesting Burke, or the expectation of making him a convert to a side which had the grand charm for the conviction of his own profligate heart, plunder; he sent him narratives of the rapidly recurring triumphs of democracy. In one of these he stated that the Reformers had already determined on the total overthrow of the (French) monarchy, etc." According to Croly this letter was written by Paine "exactly three days before the storming of the Bastille." [1]

It is a story which Mr. Foner pretty obviously took whole from Conway's edition of Paine. [2] Conway got it directly from Croly's biography of Burke, [3] though why he chose to trust that inadequate and unscholarly source it is hard to see. He could have found the

1. *The Complete Writings of Thomas Paine*, ed. Philip S. Foner (New York, 1945), I, 244 n. This work will be cited in this essay as "Paine, *Writings*."
2. *Writings of Thomas Paine*, ed. Moncure Daniel Conway (New York, 1906), II, 269 n.
3. George Croly, *Life of Edmund Burke* (London, 1840), pp. 298–300.

same story in Prior.[4] If he had bothered to follow it back, he could have found the original version of the story, with a great many more details than Croly gave, in the second edition of Bisset's *Life of Burke*, published within three years of Burke's death:

Mr. Burke having long viewed with anxiety the new philosophy become fashionable in France, bestowed the most accurate attention on the designs of its votaries as they gradually unfolded themselves. In 1787 the noted Mr. Thomas Paine had been introduced to him by a letter from Mr. Henry Lawrence, and was treated by Burke with the hospitality which he thought due to an American stranger so recommended. He was frequently a visitor at Beaconsfield, and then informed his host that he had entirely given up politics, and was devoting his attention to mechanical enquiries. He had a model of an iron bridge, which he wished to be seen by eminent characters of Mr. Burke's acquaintance. Burke introduced him to Mr. Windham, Lord Fitzwilliam, the Duke of Bedford, and, during a summer's excursion to Yorkshire, he went with him to Rotheram's original manufactory at Sheffield. Not long after he spent a day with him at Lord Fitzwilliam's.

At this time Paine continued to abstain from political discussions. The following winter he went over to France, and became deeply connected with the anti-monarchical partisans at Paris. Returning in 1788 to England, his discourse took a new turn. Calling frequently on Burke, he endeavoured to impress on him the views which he himself had recently formed concerning French affairs. People in general, he asserted, did not know the change speedily about to take place in that country. The French, he averred, were determined to surpass every nation in liberty, and to establish a pure democracy. Mr. Burke saw that this was not an opinion resulting from Paine's penetration into principles and their probable effects, but from his knowledge of actually declared intentions. He was therefore the more certain that attempts would be made to carry these designs into effect. Paine prophesied that the same species of liberty would be extended to other countries; and, led away by his wishes, fancied all Europe would unite in overturning monarchy. Whether of himself, or from the suggestion of his French friends, Paine expressed his

4. (2d ed.), II, 122–125.

wishes that the British Opposition should coincide in the republican views, and *use parliamentary reform as the pretext.* Burke answered to him, "Do you mean to propose that I, who have all my life fought for the constitution, should devote the wretched remains of my days to conspire its destruction? Do not you know that I have always opposed the things called reform; to be sure, because I did not think them reform?" Paine, seeing Burke totally averse to his projects, forebore repetition. Burke, however, saw that Paine was well acquainted with the designs of the innovators; and from him learned many important facts, all tending to make a totally different impression on philosophic wisdom from that which they made on turbulent violence. The earliest particular information respecting the mischievous designs of the republican agitators communicated to Edmund Burke was by Thomas Paine.

Paine went to France early in 1789, and wrote several letters from Paris to Burke, explaining to him the schemes of the popular leaders. In one of these, dated July 11th, he copied a note received from a distinguished American gentleman, at whose house the republican chiefs held their most confidential meetings. "The leaders (said the note) of the assembly surpass in patriotism; they are resolved to set fire to the four corners of France, rather than not reduce their principles to practice, to the last iota. Do not fear the army, we have gained them." Here we see Mr. Burke learned from Paine, not only that they were determined to overthrow the existing orders, but that they had provided the most effectual means by debauching the army from their duty.[5]

The passage concludes somewhat repetitiously by pointing again to the irony of the situation, and to Paine's obvious error in giving Burke so clear an insight into French affairs.

It is the kind of passage which is certain to trouble any conscientious scholar. Its facts, if they could be trusted, have a real importance. The great controversy in which Burke and Paine were the principal antagonists was perhaps the most crucial ideological debate ever carried on in English. How each antagonist was prepared for the contest is an interesting matter in itself, but if either of them profited by a previous private friendship with the other,

5. Bisset (2d ed.), II, 283–287.

it is of special interest. The story also has implications for our judgment of the characters of both men. Bisset, who is clearly on Burke's side, nonetheless makes it appear that Burke was disingenuous in his treatment of Paine; Conway, Paine's principal biographer, goes so far as to speak of Burke's "treachery." [6] And perhaps we should ask too whether Paine confided his purposes too freely to a man he later thought his determined enemy. Finally, we wonder if the passage partly explains what has always been a great marvel: Burke's ability to prophesy the course of the French Revolution. Burke has been very highly praised for his acuteness in having seen the true character of the Revolution so far in advance of all his British contemporaries, but very little has ever been known about the sources of his information about French affairs. It would be most satisfactory if we could agree with Bisset that Paine was one of the most important sources.

Unfortunately Bisset's passage justifies a good deal of scholarly suspicion. Bisset's *parti pris* is evident; the whole story has the appearance of having been designed as an anecdote *against* Paine. (In the year 1800 in England Paine was rather widely confused with the Devil.) But besides the bias of the whole story, there are details which arouse suspicion. We are quite sure that Bisset could not have got at first hand the remark of Burke which he quotes. The "several letters" Paine is said to have written from Paris in the spring of 1789 have never come to light; indeed, there is no evidence at all that Paine was in Paris that spring. Paine's important friend whose note was transcribed for Burke is not identified, and though Bisset quotes whole sentences from the note, we are not told how he came to have a copy from which to quote.

Burke's later biographers have never quite known their duty in the matter. Prior, the most fact-minded and reliable of the nineteenth-century biographers, apparently was not worried by difficulties, for he embodied virtually all of Bisset's narrative in his own without either comment or acknowledgment. Murray and Magnus, the two leading twentieth-century biographers, took exactly the opposite course, apparently feeling that they had no right even to mention the acquaintance of Burke and Paine. It is not likely that this was pure oversight on their part. The ac-

6. Moncure Daniel Conway, *Life of Thomas Paine* (New York, 1892), I, 280.

quaintance has real interest and significance, which no biographer would entirely ignore. It is probable that both scholars knew the passage but were simply unwilling to trust it implicitly; a decision to reject it *in toto* rather than to enter into its critical difficulties is an understandable choice.

It is a question, nonetheless, whether the situation justifies this kind of rejection any more than it justifies Prior's entire trust. Admitting that Bisset's standards of accuracy might well scandalize twentieth-century scholars, there is an initial probability that some real facts are behind his account. It may at first seem a faint kind of corroboration but it is worth noticing Bisset's own solemn assurances that his narrative was authentic. At the end of the passage we have quoted from the second edition, he added: "These are facts which I did not know when I wrote the first edition. The evidence by which they are supported is such as to render their authenticity incontrovertible . . ." [7] Bisset did not present the evidence, probably because he had agreed not to name his informant. We know, however, that between his first and second editions he had obtained new biographical materials from James Mackintosh. In the last year of Burke's life Mackintosh had had a long talk with Burke on the subject of his antagonists in the revolutionary controversy, among whom Paine was by far the chief. [8]

We also have several scattered references in Paine's own writings to a time when he and Burke were friends. Paine was proud of the friendship while it lasted, and mentioned it often in his letters. After he had decided to attack Burke publicly, one might expect him to say less about their intimacy; he did, however, mention it occasionally, usually to establish some inconsistency between

---

7. Bisset (2d ed.), I, xi. It is quite certain that the reference is to Mackintosh, who perfectly fits Bisset's description of his informant—being young, a political theorist, and in at least an intellectual sense the "ablest of Mr. Burke's literary opponents" in the battle over the *Reflections*. Mackintosh met Burke for the first time about six months before Burke's death, which also matches Bisset's description. See *Memoirs of Sir James Mackintosh*, ed. R. J. Mackintosh (2d ed. London, 1836), I, 87–94.

8. The remark Mackintosh quotes from Burke about opponents who needed "no refutations but those of the common hangman" parallels a remark Burke had already made about Paine specifically. See "Appeal from the New to the Old Whigs," in Burke, *Works*, IV, 161.

Burke's public and private opinions or between his early and subsequent conduct.

One of the references, in the *Rights of Man*, might catch the eye as a minor corroboration of Bisset's idea that Paine taught Burke something about French affairs and thus indirectly contributed to the *Reflections*. It is in a passage about the Count de Broglie, one of the important actors in the early days of the Revolution. Paine says: "The character of this man as described to me in a letter which I communicated to Mr. Burke before he began to write his book, and from an authority which Mr. Burke well knows was good, was that of 'an high-flying aristocrat, cool, and capable of every mischief.'" [9] Paine does not name his good authority, but the phrase describing de Broglie is a rather striking one, and we pick it up at once in a letter from Paine's principal correspondent in France, the American Minister at Paris, Thomas Jefferson. In a letter to Paine with the significant date of July 11, 1789, Jefferson describes the machinations of the court party in France:

they had got the military command within the isle of France transferred to the Marshal de Broglio [*sic*], a high flying aristocrat, cool and capable of every mischief.

Jefferson then continues the letter with a sketch of the French situation as it appeared to him three days before Bastille day. [10] It is a sketch which is interesting in itself, but considerably more so in the light of the passage in Bisset which we have been considering:

. . . but it is now out that those troops shew strong symptoms of being entirely with the people, so that nothing is apprehended from them. The *National assembly* then (for that is the name they take)

9. Paine, *Writings*, I, 261.

10. A letter-press copy of this letter of Jefferson is in the Library of Congress in Washington. The letter has never been printed correctly; a truncated version of it, altered in detail, is printed in *The Writings of Thomas Jefferson*, ed. A. A. Lipscomb and A. E. Baugh (Washington, 1904), VII, 404–408. Jefferson's editors omit the phrase about de Broglie, "cool and capable of every mischief." When the phrase occurs later in a softened form, "cool and capable of everything," in a letter of Jefferson to John Jay, July 19, 1789 (VII, 412) and again in Jefferson's "Autobiography," written years later (I, 143), the editors do not omit it.

having shewn thro' every stage of these transactions a coolness, wisdom, and resolution to set fire to the four corners of the kingdom
and to perish with it themselves rather than to relinquish an iota from
their plan of a total change of government, are now in complete &
undisputed possession of the sovereignty. The executive & aristocracy
are at their feet: the mass of the nation, the mass of the clergy, and
the army are with them. They have prostrated the old government,
and are now beginning to build one from the foundation.

The phrases about setting fire to the "four corners of the kingdom," and not relinquishing "an iota from their plan," taken with
the date of July 11, make it certain that Bisset was quoting from
this letter. True, he was quoting inaccurately. It was misleading
too for him to say that "the republican leaders held their most
confidential meetings" at the house of Paine's correspondent,
implying that the American Minister habitually entertained and
abetted the revolutionary party. There was, however, one famous
occasion when by Lafayette's indiscretion rather than Jefferson's,
the leading "patriots" of the French Assembly did hold a confidential meeting in Jefferson's house at Chaillot.[11] Bisset's phrasing
merely distorted and magnified a genuine fact.

It is therefore time we gave up the supposition that Bisset's
narrative was a baseless fabrication which careful biographers
should try to ignore. It was rather a mixture of truth and distor-
tion, from which it is not too late to recover several facts about the
relationship of Burke and Paine.[12]

I

When Tom Paine set sail from America in the spring of 1787,
it was ostensibly on a business trip rather than a political mission.
Much as Paine loved politics, he had found it hard to live by it
after the close of the American war. He had therefore been forced
to interest himself in another field, which even in his rationalistic
century must have seemed remote from the political. He had

11. *Writings of Jefferson*, I, 155–156.
12. For the established facts of Paine's biography I follow Conway's *Life of
Paine*, still the most thorough and reliable biography.

become an inventor of mechanical contrivances. His inventions (most of which we know only by chance references in letters) sound sufficiently bizarre: a smokeless candle whose draught was *downward*, a "wheel of concentric rim," a motor which used gunpowder as its fuel, and various other novelties. There was, however, one far more promising invention: an iron bridge of Paine's own design. He had spent a great deal of time in perfecting this, and a good deal in trying to find a market for it in America. As it had not yet been built, he had difficulties in promoting it, the upshot of which was that he had decided to submit his designs, and a small wooden model of the bridge, to the inspection of the Academy of Science in France and the Royal Society in England. He hoped that the scientists of these academies would certify their approval of his plan, after which he could use the prestige of their names in the business of selling his product.

If Paine knew the tendencies of his own nature he may have suspected even in the spring of 1787 that he had other reasons for this trip which was to turn out so fatefully. Whatever his worldly interest might be, Paine was not a man who could find his whole mind absorbed by the promotion of a commercial project. His enthusiasms were peace, equality, reform, and the American political system; a very important reason for his mission to Europe was that Europe was by no means sufficiently awakened to those enthusiasms. In the midst of the American war Paine had had an eager desire to go to England in the character of a secret agitator: he wanted to travel incognito, mix with the English, and ultimately exert his influence by pacifistic and perhaps revolutionary pamphlets which would stir the minds of the common people. Was his mission now—in spite of the bridge—so utterly different? A careful observer might have seen significance in the fact that the bridge was to have "thirteen ribs, in commemoration of the thirteen United States." The invention of a motor to be run by gunpowder seems never to have been reduced to actuality. Perhaps the symbolic triumph of pacifism in the *idea* of such a motor was of more interest to Paine than any merely mechanical energy which might have been developed.

Paine decided to go to France before England, possibly because he had a more impressive set of introductions there. His friend

Franklin, only recently returned to America, had known most of the leading scientific and political figures in France. His friend Lafayette was well connected and had patronage to bestow. His friend Jefferson was American Minister, *au courant* with the political and intellectual worlds. Between the letters of introduction Paine carried, and the strong friends he had on the ground, he was ready to make his way pretty well in the influential circles of Paris.

He spent the three summer months of 1787 in and around Paris,[13] making useful contacts with scientific and political men. He met Condorcet and Achille Duchâtelet, who were later to be his associates in campaigning for a French republic. He is supposed to have met Danton. He became intimate enough with Loménie de Brienne, secretary to the reigning Minister, to get himself trusted with a kind of informal diplomatic mission to England. Paine and de Brienne conversed about pacifism and found that they were in agreement on the subject; to make the most of their generous sentiments, and perhaps also with a calculation that a correspondence might be of some future use to himself, Paine wrote de Brienne a long résumé of his own opinions, to which de Brienne wrote an approving letter in reply; it was understood between them that Paine was to carry this correspondence to England to show to any British statesman who seemed to manifest an interest in peace.

While he was in France Paine also composed a fair-sized political pamphlet, which he could take to the printer as soon as he arrived in England. Called *Prospects on the Rubicon*, it was chiefly a protest against a current supposition that France and England were about to go to war; it was very likely written at the suggestion of de Brienne and Paine's other French friends. It was, for Paine, a rather feeble composition, though it contained one or two striking passages about the awakening of a new spirit in France. Paine compared the French people, who he said were beginning to think for themselves, with the English, who he said in the same period were ceasing to think at all. As he usually did, Paine appealed to the Common Man to distrust those who gov-

13. Paine arrived in Paris at the end of May, 1787 (Paine, *Writings*, II, 1262); he left for London at the end of August (*idem*, p. 1266).

erned him; in this case the Common Man in England was to distrust the warmongering of the upper classes.

Paine's stay in England in the fall of 1787 was of about the same length as his stay in France in the summer had been. It was a good deal less of a social success. He managed the business of getting his designs and model into the hands of the Royal Society, and he paid a long visit to his native village of Thetford in Norfolk; otherwise he seems to have done little. He was in London only once or twice. He presented himself by letter to the Marquis of Lansdowne, some of whose friends he had met in France. Very likely he called upon Burke in person to present a letter of introduction he had brought from Henry Laurens in America.[14] Bisset's assertion that he was "frequently a visitor" at Beaconsfield is not at all corroborated by what we know of him this year. It is not unlikely, however, that if he met Burke in 1787, he would have acted the part of an inventor looking for patronage rather than a political missionary bringing new ideas from France.

Paine returned to Paris in December of 1787, and so far as we know he remained there until June of 1788.[15] It is plausible that, as Bisset asserts, it was in this second stay in Paris that his revolutionary ideas ripened. The fate of the bridge was now largely out of his hands, since the Royal Society had the designs but had not yet pronounced upon them; Paine was free to devote himself to the social and political interests which had always attracted him more. He continued to be well received. His friends —Lafayette, Condorcet, Jefferson, and the rest—could give him an entrée into the best intellectual society. His own fame was also

14. Bisset gives this name as "Henry Lawrence," but Prior is certainly right (5th ed. p. 323) in assuming that it is Henry Laurens, formerly President of the American Congress, whom Burke had befriended when he was imprisoned in England during the American war. Paine would not have been completely unknown to Burke. Discussing the currents of public opinion in America in his "Letter to the Sheriffs of Bristol" (*Works*, II, 211), Burke had spoken, somewhat critically, of "the author of the celebrated pamphlet which prepared the minds of the people for independence."

15. There is apparently some doubt about this, which I believe is resolved by a more careful examination of Paine's correspondence than has hitherto been made. See below, Appendix A. Certainly Paine arrived in Paris in December, 1787. Paine, *Writings*, II, 1266. The first clear evidence of his being back in London is in an unpublished letter in the Library of Congress, dated from London June 15, 1788.

considerable in a world very appreciative of writers. The fashionable topics of the day were reform and revolution, "first principles," and the role of Reason in political affairs; on all of these Paine felt that he had an unusual competence to speak. He had been through the much-admired American Revolution—had been perhaps its most articulate prophet. That revolution had proved how much can be changed, with very little bloodshed, when men go about their political tasks with common sense. Paine *was* Common Sense; he habitually signed his name with those two words. The French, though they may not have understood everything he had to say—he had no use of their language—were surprisingly ready to take him at the highest valuation. Perhaps they thought him a man like Franklin, whom they knew better; Franklin had proved himself a wise man, yet *he* might appropriately have called himself by the name of Common Sense . . .

When Paine crossed to England again in the summer of 1788 he was undoubtedly a vastly more confident man than he had been in the previous fall. Now we begin to hear of his being "taken up" in British circles, as he had been in French. Burke wrote to John Wilkes in mid-August: "I am just going to dine with the Duke of Portland, in company with the great American Paine, whom I take with me" [16] The "great American" was at the time on a week's visit to Beaconsfield; his introduction to the Duke of Portland led to a visit of several days at the Duke's country estate near by.[17]

Burke may at the start have introduced Paine to such men as the Duke of Portland, under the impression that the one thing needful was to find patronage for the bridge; at least we hear of a second introduction a couple of months after the visit to the Duke, which would suggest this kind of a motive. By October Paine's promotional activities had reached the stage of his having commissioned a firm in Yorkshire to manufacture an iron model of the bridge. While Paine was in Yorkshire superintending arrangements, Burke paid him a visit at the ironworks, in company with Earl Fitzwilliam, then Burke's own principal patron. Paine described the visit in a letter: "A few days after I got there, Lord

16. Prior, II, 123.
17. Paine, *Writings*, II, 1270.

Fitzwilliams [*sic*], heir to the Marquis of Rockingham, came with Mr. Burke, and the former gave the workmen five guineas, and invited me to Wentworth House, a few miles distant from the works, where I went, and stayed a few days." [18] Earl Fitzwilliam was one of the richest noblemen in England—an excellent contact for any needy inventor.

Paine was not likely, however, to overlook the fact that the Duke of Portland and Earl Fitzwilliam, besides being very rich men, were leading magnates in a political party. Portland was the nominal head of the "Rockingham Whigs" after Lord Rockingham's death; Fitzwilliam, being Rockingham's heir, was at the head of a large interest in the party. This was the leading party in opposition—hence the party with which a man of Paine's principles could have the most sympathy. He improved his acquaintance with them, and we soon hear of him on familiar terms with Charles James Fox, Sir George Staunton, and other important figures of the connection.[19]

On their side these gentlemen could have expected to find a political utility in Tom Paine. They had always been, and they still were, the party in England most sympathetic with America and most closely tied to the commercial interests which profited by American trade. The war had defeated their policies temporarily, but they had still an eager desire to bring America and England onto a friendly footing. Paine's writings during the war had exerted more influence on public opinion in America than those of any other individual, unless it were Jefferson. Why should not the great pamphleteer assist the process of re-cementing the friendship of a new independent America with its mother country?

Unfortunately there was one excellent reason he should not, in the fact that Paine had no desire to serve this purpose. Quite the contrary, indeed. Far from wanting to see America more closely tied to the old home, Paine had high hopes that the new republican principles of America would supersede and destroy the traditional

18. *Idem*, p. 1281.
19. I have found no corroboration for Bisset's statement that Burke introduced Paine to Windham and to the Duke of Bedford. The former is probable, from Burke's close familiarity with Windham in this period.

government of England. He had no desire by trade or otherwise to strengthen the status quo and make radical change more difficult. In one of his letters to Jefferson in France he commented on his relations with one of his English friends who seemed to have such hopes: "I believe I am not so much in the good graces of the Marquis of Lansdowne as I used to be. I do not answer his purpose. He was always talking of a sort of reconnection of England and America, and my coldness and reserve on this subject checked communication." [20]

Burke must have had some of the illusions with which the Marquis of Lansdowne started out, and perhaps a few more as well. There was very little, on the surface, to warn him that in important respects he was playing at cross-purposes with Paine. When they deviated from the subject of the bridge to the subject of politics, Burke must have believed that he was dealing with a man whom he could welcome freely as an ally. Burke had always been the single member of his party most wholeheartedly committed to friendship with America. He was also the one whose own situation would give him the greatest sympathy with Paine. In a sense he and Paine had played the same role in the American war. The speeches Burke made on Conciliation and on American Taxation reached a different public from that which read *Common Sense* or the *Crisis* pamphlets; they were different in their language, and in their method of argument; nonetheless, they had served the same cause. Burke and Paine had been the two great publicists on the American side of the war. Burke was not the man to overlook the foundation thus laid for a close political friendship. He welcomed Paine warmly, was soon discussing political questions with him, giving him information, admitting the limits of his own information—in a word, treating him as an ally. It is probable, though we have only Bisset's phrase as authority, that Paine was "frequently a visitor" at Burke's house during the latter part of 1788 and the early part of 1789.

Paine was as eager and sanguine as Burke about the development of a friendship between them. He enjoyed being "taken up" —as how many men do not?—and had a proper sense of the importance of connections with the socially prominent Whigs.

20. Paine, *Writings*, II, 1283.

". . . I am in pretty close intimacy," he wrote to one of his correspondents in America, "with the heads of the opposition—the Duke of Portland, Mr. Fox and Mr. Burke . . . I am in as elegant style of acquaintance here as any American that ever came over . . ."[21] He told the correspondent (female) that he had sent a letter of hers to Mrs. Edmund Burke "as a specimen of the accomplishments of the American ladies." Meantime he was cultivating Burke by more important attentions. He turned over to him the correspondence he had had with de Brienne on the subject of peace.[22]

Though it should not be unduly emphasized, there was probably a fair amount of worldly calculation in Paine's cultivation of Burke, which fitted in extraordinarily well with some other plans he was laying at the time. Paine had told his friends when he set out from America that he expected to return there within a few months, once the affair of the bridge was settled. For various reasons only partly connected with the bridge he had somewhat altered this resolution. He enjoyed the attention he was getting in France and England and began to look about for an excuse to remain abroad. As it happened there was a situation that offered him just the kind of excuse he wanted. America had been represented in England between 1785 and the spring of 1788 by John Adams. In February of 1788 Adams was called home, and at least temporarily America had no official ambassador in England. Though Paine for several reasons was not a man the new nation would normally have selected as its representative, he was on the ground, from the early summer of 1788, and had certain qualifications which made him useful. He was in correspondence with such leading Americans as Washington, Franklin, Madison, Jay, and Adams himself—the men who were leading the course of events at home. He had excellent contacts in France. He had an adequate if small income to live on, and there was no compelling reason for him to return to America at once. His bridge was an ostensible and partly a real reason for him to cultivate the acquaintance of influential people, and his connections when made for a private purpose could be useful in gaining him information of public value. His facility in writing, both as pamphleteer and correspondent, was a useful gift. Why should he not try his skill in the part of an amateur diplomat?

How soon Paine realized that he was offered this opportunity it is hard to know. Perhaps as early as his visit to Burke and the Duke of Portland in the summer of 1788 he had an idea that he was getting access to information by which his countrymen could profit. He wrote to Jefferson in Paris about that visit:

Some time ago I spent a week at Mr. Burke's and the Duke of Portland's in Buckinghamshire. You will recollect that the Duke was the Minister during the time of the coalition—he is now in the opposition, and I find the opposition as much warped in some respects as to Continental Politics as the Ministry. What the extent of the treaty with Russia is Mr. B[urke] says that he and all the opposition are totally unacquainted with; and they speak of it not as a very wise measure, but rather tending to involve England in unnecessary continental disputes. The preference of the opposition is to a connection with Prussia if it could have been obtained. Sir George Staunton tells me that the interference with respect to Holland last year met with considerable opposition from part of the Cabinet. Mr. Pitt was against it at first, but it was a favorite measure with the King, and that the opposition at that crisis contrived to have it known to him that they were disposed to support his measures. This together with the notification of the 16th of September gave Mr. Pitt cause and pretence for changing his ground.[23]

This was the kind of news and comment Paine might have expected a man in Jefferson's position to find useful. When there seemed a chance that Burke's party would come into power about three months later, Paine clearly anticipated getting even greater advantage from his contacts:

I am in some intimacy with Mr. Burke, and after the new Ministry are formed he has proposed to introduce me to them—The Duke of Portland, at whose seat in the Country I was for a few days last summer will be at the head of the Treasury—and Mr. Fox secretary for foreign Affairs." [24]

23. *Ibid.*, II, 1270.
24. Unpublished letter (Jan. 15, 1789) in the Library of Congress, Washington.

Though the party did not come in, Paine felt that his contacts with it gave him unusual sources of information. He urged Jefferson to discourage the American Congress from appointing any successor to Adams, since he, Paine, was on the ground:

. . . I do not think it worth while for Congress to appoint any minister to this Court.

The greater distance Congress observes on this point the better. It will be all money thrown away to go to any expense about it—at least during the present reign. I know the nation well, and the line of acquaintance I am in enables me to judge better than any other American can judge, especially at a distance. If Congress should have any business to state to the government here, it can be easily done through their Minister at Paris; but the seldomer the better. . . .

Should anything occur worth communicating while I am here and you in France, I will inform you of it. If nothing comes to you, you may conclude there is nothing . . .[25]

Jefferson seems to have agreed to the proposal that he so rely upon Paine. He forwarded this portion of Paine's letter to Washington in America. Meantime he and Paine put their correspondence on a more formal basis than it had hitherto been. Both wrote copious comments on the political situations, in France and England, in letters which were now interchanged frequently and more or less regularly, until Jefferson's recall to America in the latter part of 1789.

The establishment of this correspondence naturally had two results for Paine. In the first place it made it desirable for him to cultivate his English connections, as it was from them that he could obtain the confidential information he promised Jefferson. But in the second place the letters which he received gave him advantages from the other end: they too were confidential and from an exceptionally well-informed source; obviously they were useful to British politicians who wished to see behind the scenes in France.

It is against this background that we should set such knowledge as we have about the acquaintance of Burke and Paine at any time after the end of 1788. Paine was not, admittedly, in an offi-

25. Paine, *Writings*, II, 1283-1284.

cial position, but it is quite possible that both Burke and his party regarded him as a valuable channel of information as to what was going on in France, which gradually became one of their leading concerns.

II

It was all but universally agreed in the spring and summer of 1789 that the great movement for reform in France would succeed in its aims. It was led by as public-spirited and as rational a set of reformers as ever initiated a great political movement. Its plans were the ripe product of a century of intense intellectual activity in the most enlightened capital in Europe. It began well. The first events which followed the convocation of the Estates General vastly encouraged those who expected France to move peaceably toward its goal of a limited monarchy. A new spirit seemed to be at work in politics, capable of making France, and other nations too, follow in the train of advanced and idealistic leaders. "Bliss was it in that dawn to be alive," as Wordsworth later sang of the period. The critical spirit which usually watches and checks political changes seemed almost irrelevant in such a time of glorious hopes. Even when violence and bloodshed actually showed themselves in the events of July 14 intelligent observers preferred to ignore their warning. Charles James Fox's comment on Bastille day was: "How much the greatest event that ever happened in the world, and how much the best."

Edmund Burke was the one great statesman in France or England who had substantial doubts about the Revolution almost from the start. The earliest comment upon it which we have from him was made about three weeks after Bastille day; it is cool, not to say suspicious. Writing to his friend Lord Charlemont in Ireland, Burke said of the recent events:

As to us here, our thoughts of everything at home are suspended by our astonishment at the wonderful spectacle which is exhibited in a neighboring and rival country. What spectators and what actors! England gazing with astonishment at a French struggle for liberty, and not knowing whether to blame or to applaud! The thing indeed, though I thought I saw something like it in progress for several years, has still something in it paradoxical and mysterious. The spirit it is impossible not to admire, but the old Parisian ferocity has broken out in a startling manner. It is true that this may be no more than a sudden explosion. If so, no indication can be taken from it. But if it should be character rather than accident, then that people are not fit for liberty and must have a strong hand like that of their former masters, to coerce them. Men must have a certain fund of natural moderation to qualify them for freedom, else it becomes noxious to themselves and a perfect nuisance to everybody else. What will be the event, it is hard, I think, still to say. To form a solid constitution requires wisdom as well as spirit, and whether the French have wise heads among them, or, if they possess such, whether they have authority equal to their wisdom, is to be seen.[26]

Burke has been both praised and blamed for having been capable of such remarks at the time he made them. They show an astonishing political foresight, because only one outbreak of disorder had yet betrayed that *character* the French Revolution was to have. On the other hand, as John Morley complained, they show an almost inhuman detachment from the enthusiasms of the rest of mankind: Morley felt that Burke should, at least for a moment, have shared the generous delusions of his contemporaries.[27] It is hard to say, especially a century and a half after the event, whether Burke would have been more admirable in showing optimism than perspicacity; it does not seem a very important question to be settled now. What we would rather know if we could is how Burke was able to penetrate the French situation so much more successfully than other statesman. What in his temperament or background or information made him pay attention to those remote dangers he could so easily have overlooked?

The most obvious answer to the question would be to say that

26. Historical Manuscripts Commission, 13th Report, Appendix VIII (Charlemont Mss.), p. 106.
27. *Burke*, p. 211. After quoting Fox's comment on Bastille Day, Morley says: "Is it an infirmity to wish for an instant that some such phrase of generous hope had escaped from Burke; that he had for a day or an hour undergone that fine illusion which was lighted up in the spirits of men like Wordsworth and Coleridge?"

Burke had a special competence for predicting the outcome of a series of reforms, being himself a veteran reformer. Burke had been in politics for over thirty years at the time the Revolution began, and almost every major effort of his career had been reform in one shape or another. Against the bitter opposition of George III and the "King's friends" he had put through his Bill for Economical Reform in the early 1780's—probably the most important single act of reform achieved in England in the eighteenth century. Against an even more determined "Indian interest" he was struggling in the late 'eighties to reform the administration of British India. He had fought against the misgovernment of Ireland, against the African slave trade, against the oppression of Catholics and dissenters, against the imprisonment of debtors. There were very few causes of reform agitated in that day in which Burke had not taken a leading and effective part. Naturally he had not done all this without learning something of the trade of the reformer: the temptations and dangers which beset it, the mistakes reformers can make in their means, and the chance the best-intentioned always have of defeating their own most cherished ends. Undoubtedly all this bitter wisdom had a great deal to do with Burke's attitude toward the innovations in France. When he saw men as inexperienced, but withal as confident, as Lafayette, Condorcet, Bailly, Camille Desmoulins, André Chenier, setting about the stupendous task of recasting the whole Constitution of France, he wanted to know what sort of competence they had for the trade they were adopting. When he found that they were soldier adventurers, mathematicians, astronomers, youthful journalists, literary men, but none of them seasoned reformers, it was easy for him to guess that their way might very well lead them into disaster. They were hopelessly inexperienced amateurs in a field in which he himself had seen long and arduous service.

Though Burke knew a good deal about the situation of reformers in general he admitted, and his writings show clearly enough, that he had no unusual familiarity with the internal affairs of France. In his pamphlets on the Revolution there is nothing remotely comparable to the encyclopedic knowledge he had had of America when that was his major interest, or of India or Ireland when he was called on to speak of them. He had very few personal acquaintances in France; his use of the French language was halting; he lacked any well-developed sense of the political realities of the French situation. But on the other hand, if one examines his writings, one can be surprised at how early Burke had become aware of at least one important aspect of France in the eighteenth century, namely, its national inclination toward some kind of revolution. As early as 1769, at almost the beginning of his political career, Burke had seen a distinct possibility of a violent upheaval in France. In a comparison of the national finances of Britain and France, he gave it as his opinion that the latter were so dangerously strained ". . . that no man, I believe, who has considered their affairs with any degree of attention or information, but must hourly look for some extraordinary convulsion in that whole system: the effect of which on France, and even on all Europe, it is difficult to conjecture." [28] Having once convinced himself that such a major convulsion could occur, Burke watched with attention for signs of the form it might take and the influences, other than financial, which might help to bring it about. What he discovered increased both his alarm and his interest in the French situation. When he visited Paris—though for only a few weeks—in January and February, 1773, he was entertained in the leading salons and introduced to the *philosophes*.[29] The most important effect of their conversation upon him was to fill him with dismay at the reckless tone of their thinking. Within a month of his return to England he was warning the House of Commons with desperate seriousness against the dangers of too much freedom of thought in the field of religion:

The most horrible and cruel blow, that can be offered to civil society, is through atheism. Do not promote diversity; when you have it, bear it; have as many sorts of religion as you find in your country; there is a reasonable worship in them all. The others, the infidels, are outlaws of the constitution; not of this country, but of the human race. They are never, never to be supported, never to be tolerated.

28. "Observations on a Late Publication Intitled *The Present State of the Nation*," in Burke, *Works*, I, 331.
29. Burke was in France on at least three occasions besides this one: in his youth, at some time before August, 1757, (*Correspondence*, I, 32); in the summer of 1772 (Prior, I, 246); and in the summer of 1775 (*idem*, 307).

Under the systematic attacks of these people, I see some of the props of good government already beginning to fail; I see propagated principles, which will not leave to religion even a toleration.[30]

But it was not only in the fields of finance and of religion that Burke sensed revolutionary possibilities in France. He attended with particular care to the political doctrines which were being discussed there. He read Rousseau, and reviewed him for the British public in the *Annual Register*. He saw the dangers to the settled order of society inherent in the perpetual discussion of abstractions like Liberty and Equality. The whole bent of his mind was hostile to reasoning about politics in such terms:

Abstract liberty, like other mere abstractions, is not to be found. Liberty inheres in some sensible object. . . .[31] The *extreme* of liberty (which is its abstract perfection, but its real fault) obtains nowhere, nor ought to obtain anywhere; because extremes, as we all know, in every point which relates either to our duties or satisfactions in life, are destructive both to virtue and enjoyment. Liberty, too, must be limited in order to be possessed. . . .[32] The idea of forcing every thing to an artificial equality, has something at first view very captivating in it. It has all the appearance imaginable of justice and good order; and very many persons, without any sort of partial purposes, have been led to adopt such schemes, and pursue them with great earnestness and warmth. . . . You know that it is this very rage for equality which has blown up the flames of this present cursed war in America. I am, for one, entirely satisfied that the inequality which grows out of the nature of things by time, custom, succession, accumulation, permutation, and improvement of property, is much nearer that true equality, which is the foundation of equity and just policy, than anything that can be contrived by the tricks and devices of human skill.[33]

30. *Parliamentary History*, XVII, 779–780.
31. "Speech on Conciliation with America," in Burke, *Works*, II, 120.
32. "Letter to the Sheriffs of Bristol," in Burke, *Works*, II, 229.
33. Bisset (2d ed.), II, 147–148. Burke sometimes goes even further in his scorn of "that doctrine of the equality of all men, which has been preached by knavery, and so greedily adopted by malice, envy, and cunning . . ." *Correspondence*, II, 242.

Even when Burke was fighting passionately on the side of the Americans against the policies of George III, he took special care to deny that it was because the Americans had Natural Rights to things like Liberty and Equality. He had an aversion to all reasonings about Rights. "I do not enter into these metaphysical distinctions," he said; "I hate the very sound of them." [34] What to Paine and even Jefferson was the very heart of the American cause to Burke was an alien intrusion of "metaphysics."

Burke did not, of course—he hardly could, while he remained in active politics—try to separate himself from contact with either individuals or groups whose habits of reasoning he deplored. He cooperated with the Americans against George III, in spite of his opinion of their Rights. He pursued his reforms in company with a great many lovers of "metaphysics." Even the philosophical foes of religion he did not cast off. "I doubt that keeping company with David Hume," he told Boswell, "in a strict light, is hardly defensible. But in the present state of society I see all men. 'Tis making myself of too much consequence not to." [35] If on the religious level he could be so broadminded, he was willing to do as much in politics. "A Republick never can be in this country, so I live in charity with my friends who think of it." [36]

Naturally he did not always pretend agreement with those with whom he continued to associate. He argued vehemently for his own principles. Horace Walpole said that when Burke was in Paris in 1773 "it grew the fashion to be Christians. Saint Patrick himself did not make more converts." [37] When in 1785 Mirabeau visited England, Burke entertained him and, we are told, debated eagerly with him in broken French:

It was very singular to see Mirabeau and Burke in controversy. Mirabeau could speak little English, Burke French imperfectly. Yet these celebrated men argued with as much earnestness and continuation as if they had been speaking a language common to both. Mirabeau was astonished at the eloquence and force with which Burke ex-

34. "Speech on American Taxation," in Burke's *Works*, II, 73.
35. *Boswell Papers*, XI, 268.
36. *Idem*, 268.
37. Horace Walpole, *Letters*, ed. Mrs. Paget Toynbee, VIII, 252.

pressed his meaning though he could only do it by uniting words of different languages.[38]

We are not told what topics the two men discussed, but it would be rather surprising if a contact with Mirabeau in 1785 did not increase both Burke's awareness and his curiosity concerning revolutionary currents in France, whether in religious or political or other intellectual fields.

If we accept Bisset's dates, Tom Paine first introduced himself to Burke in 1787, but first began talking at any length to him about politics in the following year. Whatever curiosity about the French situation Burke had acquired by that time would have contributed greatly to his interest in what Paine had to say. Paine had been convinced by even his short stay in France in the summer of 1787 that a new revolutionary spirit was stirring there; his longer stay in the winter and spring of 1788 had much increased his acquaintance with both the new ideas and their most active proponents. Paine was a man, like Burke himself, who lived in political ideas; we can be quite sure that he did not spend a week with Burke in August, 1778, without discussing much of what he had learned in his exciting stay in Paris.

The two men may not have realized at once how far apart they were ultimately to be on the subject of the Revolution, but some differences they did recognize at the start. We have already quoted the remark of Paine to Jefferson in the letter which described his week's stay with Burke: ". . . I find the opposition as warped in some respects as to Continental Politics as the Ministry." [39] When Paine talked to Burke of Revolution, Burke was at first skeptical. He did not think the French were prepared for it, or had the spirit or fortitude to go through with it.[40] Burke must also, before he had known Paine long, have seen the decided limitations of his political prudence. When in the winter of 1788 George III became temporarily insane, Paine pressed Burke's party to propose a kind of British National Assembly to take up the constitutional issues of a Regency.[41] Since this was at the time when

38. *The Farington Diary*, I, 5.
39. Paine, *Writings*, II, 1270.
40. *Ibid.*, I, 249.
41. *Ibid.*, I, 453; see also II, 1279, 1282.

plans for convening the Estates General in France were attracting wide attention, a move of the kind could not have been made in England without a clear implication that England, like France, was contemplating radical constitutional reforms; Paine should have known that Burke's party would not even consider taking the lead in such a direction.

Paine was, however, by nature a missionary, not at all likely to be daunted in his efforts by encountering a little indifference or opposition. Bisset's statement that he "went to France early in 1789, and wrote several letters from Paris to Burke, explaining to him the schemes of the popular leaders," is certainly wrong in its chronology, for Paine did not go to Paris *early* in that year; yet it may not be wholly misleading. Paine was probably making every effort, while in England and later when he did go to France, to arouse Burke's interest in the revolutionary cause. According to his own testimony, he put in Burke's hands at least one letter of Jefferson—the letter of July 11—which he must have expected to have that effect. One would like to know whether he showed him other letters as well. It would cast a strong light on Burke's early suspicions of the Revolution if we knew certainly that he had seen such a passage as the following, in which Jefferson described to Paine some of the preparations for the elections to the Estates General in the spring of 1789:

The D. d'Orleans has given instructions to his proxies in the Baillages which would be deemed bold in England, and are reasonable beyond the reach of an Englishman, who slumbering under a kind of half reformation in politics & religion, is not excited by anything he sees or feels, to question the remains of prejudice. The writers of this country, now taking the field freely, & unrestrained or rather revolted by prejudice, will rouse us all from the errors in which we have been hitherto rocked.[42]

The passage made an especial appeal to Paine, we know,[43] but perhaps it would have been one of those, in Bisset's words, "tend-

---

42. A letter-press copy of this letter is in the Library of Congress. The letter is printed with some alterations in *Writings of Jefferson*, VII, 315–319.

43. Paine commented on the passage in his next letter to Jefferson. Paine, *Writings*, II, 1287.

ing to make a totally different impression on philosophic wisdom from that which they made on turbulent violence." If Burke saw it, it ought to have done a great deal to rouse him to an (alarmed) interest in what was going on in France.

The letter of July 11 itself contained more than the single passage we have quoted to disturb Burke's conservative nature. It contained a long and pretentious recital of principles which Lafayette with assistance from Jefferson had drawn up to guide the reforms of the Estates General. The first of the principles was:

1. Every government should have for it's only end, the preservation of the rights of man: whence it follows that to recall constantly the government to the end proposed, the constitution should begin by a Declaration of the natural and imprescriptable rights of man.

That too was a subject on which Burke's "philosophic wisdom" might have been a little irritable. There is some irony, considering Burke's subsequent opinions of Lafayette, in Jefferson's concluding complacently:

You see that these are the materials of a superb edifice, and the hands which have prepared them, are perfectly capable of putting them together, & of filling up the work of which these are only the outlines.

Paine very likely *did* see this, but it is not so likely that he found Burke agreeing with him. Much later in his career Burke said, concerning his own views on the Revolution, that "the Rights of Man had opened his eyes." [44] Burke may have been referring to the formal Declaration of Rights debated and approved by the Assembly in late August, 1789, but it is not at all impossible that he was referring to this letter of Jefferson of a month and a half earlier.

Paine took a short trip to France in the summer of 1789, returning to England in the fall; we do not know whether he discussed his observations with Burke after his return, though it is fairly probable that he would have. He went over to France again in the winter of 1789–90, and if Bisset's "several letters" were

44. John, 1st Baron Acton, *Lectures on the French Revolution*, ed. J. N. Figgis and R. U. Laurence (London, 1910), p. 126.

actually written, it was probably during this winter. *One* letter was certainly written, for Paine himself describes its contents in a passage of the *Rights of Man:*

As I used sometimes to correspond with Mr. Burke, believing him then to be a man of sounder principles than his book shows him to be, I wrote to him last winter from Paris, and gave him an account how prosperously matters were going on. Among other subjects in that letter, I referred to the happy situation the National Assembly were placed in; that they had taken a ground on which their moral duty and their political interest were united.

They have not to hold out a language which they do not themselves believe, for the fraudulent purpose of making others believe it. Their station requires no artifice to support it, and can only be maintained by enlightening mankind. It is not their interest to cherish ignorance but to dispel it. They are not in the case of a ministerial or an opposition party in England, who, though they are opposed, are still united to keep up the common mystery.[45]

Burke, too, later referred to correspondence between him and Paine in this period. He told an acquaintance in 1791 that

. . . he had been in correspondence with Mr. Payne who was then (in 1790) living at Paris, with the American Minister Jefferson, Fayette and the Jacobins, and that in one letter he stated how much good the propagation of the French opinions throughout Europe and England by --- or Burke would advance [*sic*] the cause of Freedom— On this idea Burke broke off all intercourse with Payne— [46]

This is no doubt the interchange which Bisset described ambiguously in a passage we have already noticed:

. . . Paine expressed his wishes that the British Opposition should coincide in the republican views, and *use parliamentary reform as the pretext.* Burke answered to him, "Do you mean to propose that I, who have all my life fought for the constitution, should devote the wretched remains of my days to conspire its destruction? Do not you

45. Paine, *Writings*, I, 297.
46. Mrs. Aubrey Le Blond, *Charlotte Sophie, Countess Bentinck* (London, 1912), I, 163.

know that I have always opposed the things called reform; to be sure, because I did not think them reform?"

Bisset did not make it clear whether this was a conversation or an exchange of letters; Burke's description makes clear that it was an exchange of letters in the early months of 1790.

Presumably Burke's statement that he "broke off all intercourse with Paine" at that time gives us the terminal date of the wholly *friendly* relations of the two men.

III

On February 9, that is, at almost exactly the time of his break with Paine, Burke made his first important public declaration of opposition to the French Revolution. In the annual debate in the House of Commons on the Army Estimates, Fox and others had taken occasion to refer to the recent changes in France in strong terms of approval. Fox had especially praised the new democratic principles of the French army, which he hoped would change the whole international military situation for the better.

Burke dissented, in the most emphatic terms. Like Fox he did not confine his remarks strictly to the military problem. He expressed his opinion of the whole tendency of the French reforms to that date. What he said of the formation of the National Assembly by the merging of the Nobility, Clergy, and Third Estate perhaps gives the key to most of Burke's criticisms of the early career of the Revolution:

Instead of redressing grievances, and improving the fabric of their state, to which they were called by their monarch and sent by their country, they were made to take a very different course. They first destroyed all the balances and counterpoises which serve to fix the state and to give it a steady direction, and which furnish sure correctives to any violent spirit which may prevail in any of the orders. These balances existed in their oldest constitution, and in the constitution of this country, and in the constitution of all the countries in Europe. These are rashly destroyed, and then they melted down the whole into one incongruous, ill-connected mass.[47]

47. "Speech on the Army Estimates," in Burke, *Works*, III, 221.

Reflections on the French Revolution.

Reproduced by courtesy of The Pierpont Morgan Library from a contemporary caricature. The two daggers clearly allude to Burke's famous "dagger speech" of December 28, 1792.

But this radical want of balance at the start had immediate results which Burke disapproved as strongly:

When they had done this, they instantly, and with the most atrocious perfidy and breach of all faith among men, laid the axe to the root of all property, and consequently of all national prosperity, by the principles they established and the example they set, in confiscating all the possessions of the Church. They made and recorded a sort of *institute* and *digest* of anarchy, called the Rights of Man, in such a pedantic abuse of elementary principles as would have disgraced boys at school: but this declaration of rights was worse than trifling and pedantic in them; as by their name and authority they systematically destroyed every hold of authority by opinion, religious or civil, on the minds of the people. By this mad declaration they subverted the state, and brought on such calamities as no country, without a long war, has ever been known to suffer, and which may in the end produce such a war, and perhaps many such.[48]

Burke would not admit that these were the necessary effects of a desirable revolt against tyranny:

With them the question was not between despotism and liberty. The sacrifice they made of the peace and power of their country was not made on the altar of freedom. Freedom, and a better security for freedom than they have taken, they might have had without any sacrifice at all. They brought themselves into all the calamities they suffer, not that through them they might obtain a British constitution; they plunged themselves headlong into those calamities to prevent themselves from settling into that constitution, or into anything resembling it.[49]

Significantly, Burke warned his audience that he would break with his closest friends and join with his bitterest enemies on issues which he felt were as serious as those of the French Revolution. And when his colleague Sheridan opposed him in a bitter speech in defense of French principles, Burke did break with him forthwith.

It was perfectly clear, of course, that Burke's speech in this

48. *Idem*, pp. 221–222.
49. *Idem*, p. 222.

debate was intended as a public challenge to a wide discussion of the Revolution. Burke had not only made up his mind that the French were behaving very foolishly in their own country, but he was convinced that British sympathy with them and admiration of their courses were bringing England itself into danger. If he was right, it was time that his countrymen were warned of their situation. Burke's speech itself was such a warning, and deeply impressed the House. But Burke was not content with a mere parliamentary debate. He printed the speech for public distribution, and within a week was also advertising a much more important "public letter" in which his ideas on the Revolution would be set forth. This letter—when it finally came forth—was the *Reflections on the Revolution in France*.

Paine tells us of his own first knowledge of Burke's speech and of the projected letter: "At the time Mr. Burke made his violent speech last winter in the English Parliament against the French Revolution and the National Assembly, I was in Paris, and had written to him but a short time before, to inform him how prosperously matters were going on. Soon after this, I saw his advertisement of the pamphlet he intended to publish." [50] Paine saw at once his own proper course. He assured his radical friends in France that he would answer Burke's letter when it appeared.[51] Believing that that could not be long, he returned to England to be on hand for its appearance.

The morning after my arrival I went first to Debrets, bookseller, Piccadilly; (he is the opposition bookseller). He informed me that Mr. Burke's pamphlet was in the press (he is not the publisher), that he believed Mr. Burke was much at a loss how to go on; that he had revised some of the sheets, six, seven, and one nine times! I then made an appointment with Lord Stanhope, and another with Mr. Fox. The former received me with saying "have I the pleasure of shaking hands with the author of *Common Sense?*" I told him of the condition of Mr. Burke's pamphlet, and that I had formed to myself the design of answering it, if it should come out at a time when I could devote myself to it. From Lord Stanhope I went to Mr. Fox . . . I

50. Paine, *Writings*, I, 244.
51. *Idem*, p. 245.

talked to him of Mr. Burke's pamphlet, and said that I believed I should reply to it. I afterwards saw Sir George Staunton, to whom I mentioned the same thing.[52]

Paine's evident enthusiasm for the fray was to be disappointed for a while. The pamphlet did not appear. Whether, as the printer thought, this proved Mr. Burke "at a loss how to go on," or whether Mr. Burke had decided that the time was not yet ripe for the controversy, or whether Mr. Burke was simply too much engaged by other activities—for whatever reason, the fact was that there was a long pause in which nothing happened. Fully a month after Paine had set out from France so flushed with hope, he was confessing in a letter to his friend Christie: ". . . I am now inclined to think that after all this vaporing of Mr. B., he will not publish his pamphlet. I called yesterday at Debrets, who told me that he has stopped the work. (I had not called on Mr. Burke, and shall not, until his pamphlet comes out, or he gives it up.)"[53]

In all, Paine had to endure a delay of eight months between his first resolution to write an answer to Burke and Burke's final decision to give him something to answer. For a person of Paine's restless temperament that must have been a very serious trial. Paine no longer made any pretense that he was not vividly interested in politics above everything else. He talked politics continuously with his British acquaintances. In spite of his resolution not to see Burke, he soon found he wanted to talk it with Burke too. In May an international incident which took place on the west coast of America threatened to involve Britain and Spain in a naval war. Paine immediately absorbed himself in the details of the affair and shuttled eagerly from one of his political friends to another. He had some information which he wanted to convey either to Burke personally, or to Burke's party. He asked Burke for an interview "upon the condition the French Revolution should not be a subject." Burke complied, and they had a talk,[54] which in turn gave Paine more information he wanted to convey

52. *Ibid.*, II, 1300–1301. Foner lists this letter as to an unidentified correspondent. It is clear from its contents (n.b. the last paragraph on p. 1301) that it was addressed to Thomas Christie, also a correspondent of Burke's.

53. *Idem*, p. 1301.

54. *Idem*, pp. 497–498.

to Gouverneur Morris, the new American Minister; [55] and so forth. One can't help suspecting that Paine's visits were sometimes a little of a nuisance to busy men. "Paine calls upon me," Morris noted in his diary, "and talks a great deal on subjects of little moment." [56]

By the summer Paine himself was aware that his continuous activity was attracting attention to him. In a letter of August 3 he lamented that the British newspapers were beginning to print paragraphs about him, "sufficiently pointing me out as a person whom it is proper to have an eye upon—and that my erecting a bridge is but a cover." [57] In the fall—perhaps to be out of the way—he paid a brief visit to Paris: at least his fifth visit since he had come from America in 1787.

Finally, in the latter part of October, Paine got the good news he was waiting for. Mr. Burke, after all his delays, was at last going to bring out his letter; it was advertised to appear on November 1. Paine returned to England at once. When the *Reflections* was published on the promised day, Paine was already settled in rooms at the Angel Inn in Islington, ready to begin work on his reply.

IV

It is one of the characteristics of a public controversy that it must reduce almost every human affair it touches to an extraordinary simplicity. Problems which any of the controversialists might privately admit to be complex and bewildering have to be presented as very elementary choices between Right and Wrong. Personal relationships which may be subtle, or at least may be believably complicated, must fall into strong outlines as enmities and friendships, depending on which side of the controversy any given individual may have taken. No doubt this is inevitable, and hence acceptable to those who usually take part in public controversies. The not-very-sensitive electorate which ultimately makes the decisions on all public issues must have some picture in its

55. Gouverneur Morris, *A Diary of the French Revolution*, ed. Beatrix Davenport (Cambridge, 1939), I, 531-532.
56. *Idem*, p. 516.
57. Cited in Frank Smith, *Thomas Paine, Liberator* (New York, 1938), p. 128.

mind when it exercises its choice. The most brilliant public men have never been able to make that picture a thing of subtle lights and shadows.

Some such reflection is bound to occur to us when we see Burke and Paine facing each other in public debate. For we suddenly discover that the two men—who after all had seen and heard a good deal of each other over a period of three years—are inveterate enemies, who have scarcely a belief in common and not the most ordinary degree of respect for each other's characters. This might surprise us, for even in 1790, when we know that some disagreements had come to the surface, there was little evidence of any violent change in their relationship. Burke did say that he "broke off all intercourse" with Paine in that year, but that might mean no more than that he ceased to correspond with him, or ceased to encourage his visits. Paine on his side talked of his resolution not to call upon Burke till his pamphlet had appeared. But he changed his mind and himself proposed to call. His subsequent account of their interview sounds as if both men had managed to talk amicably, and Burke even somewhat unguardedly.

Nonetheless, by the time the first part of the *Rights of Man* appeared in March, 1791, there was no one in Paine's universe more hostile to truth and virtue than a certain "Mr. Burke." He is the general villain of the tract. He is, to begin with, completely wrong in his basic ideas. But he is also stupid, and argues badly from his wrong assumptions. He talks "nonsense, for it deserves no better name." One cannot respect his intelligence. "Mr. Burke," says Paine with heavy irony, "does not call himself a madman, whatever others may do . . ." But neither can one approve of his moral character. He is deserting his former principles, and Paine thinks he sees a ready and discreditable explanation of why: "there is a certain transaction known in the City, which renders him suspected of being a pensioner in a fictitious name. This may account for some strange doctrines he advanced in his book . . ."

Whether Burke himself was shocked at being so handled by a man he had once befriended, we do not know. If he was, he at least never allowed himself to show it publicly. He had his own manner—the opposite of Paine's—of being insulting. In his *Ap-*

peal from the New to the Old Whigs, published early in August, 1791, he devoted about a dozen pages to rebutting the *Rights of Man,* but without once mentioning the author's name or the fact that he himself had ever been acquainted with him. Paine, for all his abuse, had insisted eagerly on his former intimacy with Burke, whom he admitted having once regarded as a worthy man. Burke indulged in no such reminiscences. He preferred the cut direct. His manner of answering Paine's tract was to quote a long series of its more reckless and objectionable passages with the dry comment: "I will not attempt in the smallest degree to refute them. This will probably be done (if such writings shall be thought to deserve any other than the refutation of criminal justice) by others . . ."[58]

Paine made his public rejoinder to this in the second part of the *Rights of Man,* published in February, 1792. By that time— seven months after the appearance of Burke's *Appeal*—a good many events had occurred to change the political scene and the terms of the altercation. Paine was, or fancied that he was, a very much greater man in the early part of 1792 than he had been in the early part of 1791. A revolution in England appeared to be a genuine possibility; if it had occurred, Paine might well have been its principal hero. He would certainly have been its mouthpiece; we are told by his most recent editor that close to a million and a half copies of the second part of the *Rights of Man* were published in his lifetime! From the dizzy eminence he thus occupied, or looked forward to occupying, he affected to regard Burke as no longer his equal. "I will now, by way of relaxation, turn a thought or two to Mr. Burke," he begins one passage; "I ask his pardon for neglecting him so long." His attention on this occasion extends to only a few jokes upon certain arguments Burke had offered—but then, says he, "If Mr. Burke's arguments have not weight enough to keep one serious, the fault is less mine than his; and as I am willing to make an apology to the reader for the liberty I have taken, I hope Mr. Burke will also make his for giving the cause. Having thus paid Mr. Burke the compliment of remembering him, I return to the subject."[59]

58. "An Appeal from the New to the Old Whigs," in Burke, *Works,* IV, 161.
59. Paine, *Writings,* I, 385.

Paine did not overlook Burke's fleer about "criminal justice." On the contrary, he welcomed it. By the spring of 1792 he was so confident of his popular position as rather to hope that the government would try to bring charges against him. It would dramatize the situation. He had therefore a use for Burke in the role of a vindictive persecutor; in spite of the dearth of objective evidence he asserted repeatedly in the spring and summer of that year that Burke was working behind the scenes to get him arrested and his works suppressed. Paine now also asserted—instead of hinting—that this tool of reaction was a secret pensioner.

It would be hard to guess whether Paine himself fully believed his various assertions. The state of excitement in which he was living in 1792 made veracity a rather trifling matter. The fact is that he—like Burke himself—was a man who could not fight seriously over political principles without eventually attacking personalities; it was a kind of measure of his sincerity about essential issues that he *had* to malign his former friend. Burke had dared to set himself against all the apocalyptic hopes of the French Revolution; it necessarily followed that he was a monster of inhumanity.

Of course Paine never saw the fulfillment of the hopes of 1792. Long before that year was over he had been hunted out of England by the government he thought would be overturned. He went to France to become a member of the National Assembly, but there too he found himself ineffective and soon in danger. He bravely spoke for mercy at the trial of Louis XVI, when it was too late to obtain it. He struggled to help his friends, mostly ill-fated Girondists. When the Terror came he only saved himself from death by a kind of temporary self-annihilation; he went into close retirement and—we are told—remained in a state of intoxication for a matter of weeks. When the period of greatest danger was over he had what was probably the good fortune of being arrested and kept in prison for all the latter part of the Revolution.

At the time he wrote his *Appeal* in 1791, Burke had not wanted to comment publicly upon Paine, but at various other times between 1791 and his death he allowed opinions of him to come out, in letters, conversations, and even speeches. Most of them are of no great interest, being brief and in the scornful tone in which virtually all British conservatives spoke of Paine in the 1790's. One, which gives Burke's estimate of Paine's powers as a writer, may gain interest from that fact. A young man named William Smith had written an answer to the first part of the *Rights of Man.* When it was published he sent a copy to Burke. Burke's letter of acknowledgment says in part:

You talk of *Paine* with more respect than he deserves. He is utterly incapable of comprehending his subject. He has not even a moderate portion of learning of any kind. He has learned the *instrumental* part of literature; a *style,* and a method of disposing of his ideas; without having ever made a previous preparation of study, or thinking, for the use of it. *Junius,* and other sharply-penned libels of our time, have furnished a stock to the adventurers in composition, which gives what they write an air, (and but an air,) of art and skill; but as to the rest, Paine possesses nothing more than what a man whose audacity makes him careless of logical consequences, and his total want of honor and morality makes indifferent as to political consequences, can very easily write.[60]

Such a passage does not make it quite clear whether Burke was really angry at Paine or merely contemptuous. One would like to be sure which it was. There is another passage, from a record of Burke's conversation in 1796, which might help to settle the question. Burke was talking with James Mackintosh, and though (perhaps by Mackintosh's discretion this time) Paine's name is not mentioned in the record, it is not too long an inference that he was the principal person under discussion.

Talking of the anti-moral paradoxes of certain philosophers of the new school, he (Burke) observed, with indignation, "They deserve no refutation but those of the common hangman, '*carnifice potius quam argumentis egent.*' Their arguments are, at best, miserable logomachies, base prostitutions of the gifts of reason and discourse, which God gave to man for the purpose of exalting, not brutalising, his species. The wretches have not the doubtful merit of sincerity;

60. Prior, II, 180–181.

for, if they really believed what they published, we should know how to work with them, by treating them as lunatics. No, sir, these opinions are put forth in the shape of books, for the sordid purpose of deriving a paltry gain from the natural fondness of mankind for pernicious novelties. As to the opinions themselves, they are those of pure defecated Atheism. Their object is to corrupt all that is good in man—to eradicate his immortal soul—to dethrone God from the universe. They are the brood of that putrid carcass, the mother of all evil, the French Revolution. I never think of that plague-spot in the history of mankind, without shuddering. It is an evil spirit that is always before me. There is not a mischief by which the moral world can be afflicted, that it has not let loose upon it. It reminds me of the accursed things that crawled in and out of the mouth of the vile hag in Spenser's Cave of Error." [61]

It does sound as if Burke had permitted himself to express *some* anger at his former friend.

61. Mackintosh, *Memoirs*, I, 93–94.

APPENDIX A

CORRESPONDENCE OF PAINE AND JEFFERSON, *1788–1789*

Our knowledge of Paine's activities and his whereabouts in the years 1788 and 1789 depends considerably on what we can learn from his principal correspondence in those years: that with Thomas Jefferson. This correspondence has been somewhat neglected by scholars. Mr. Philip Foner, whose *Complete Writings of Thomas Paine* professes to cover Paine's correspondence, has omitted several important and easily accessible letters to Jefferson; he has also mis-dated letters, represented them as written from wrong addresses, and cut or garbled passages. Jefferson scholars, if they have not been quite so culpable as Mr. Foner, have certainly not done full justice to Jefferson's side of the correspondence. The twenty-volume edition of Jefferson's writings brought out by the Jefferson Memorial Association in 1904 did not profess to be exhaustive; hence we are not surprised that it omitted several of the letters to Paine. It might be condemned, however, for having omitted important passages in letters which it did include.

We shall soon be able to remedy our ignorance of at least Jefferson's half of the correspondence. The magnificent new edition of his writings now being compiled by the Princeton University Press will bring the full resources of twentieth-century scholarship to bear upon the unsolved problems of his letters. It is to be hoped that the comparatively easy task of printing Paine's surviving letters will attract some other scholar who will repair the deficiencies of Mr. Foner's edition.

Meanwhile a study such as the above, which has to depend frequently upon this correspondence, is obliged to make corrections in the versions of the letters now in print, as well as make use of many letters still in manuscript. The following is a list of the Paine-Jefferson letters now preserved in the Library of Congress in Washington. The Paine letters there are the originals; the Jefferson, letter-press copies. Those I list as "Ms. letters" have not been printed to my knowledge.

I give my reasons for occasionally differing from Mr. Foner or the editors of the Jefferson Memorial Edition on such matters as dates and place names.

1788   P to J. Feb. 19 [Paris]. Mr. Foner prints this letter (*Complete Writings*, II, 1267) as from "London, England." The original in the Library of Congress bears no place name. Since Paine refers to an enclosure and tells Jefferson "you can return it to me tomorrow," he cannot have been in London when he wrote the letter.

P to J. May [Paris]. Mr. Foner prints this letter (II, 1029–1031) also as from "London, England," for which again there is no authority. The letter begins, "Your saying last evening . . ."

1788(?) P to J. [Paris]. This letter, which Mr. Foner prints (II, 1034–1035) as written from "Paris, France, Sept. 7, 1788," bears no place name or date. It may well have been written from Paris; Paine refers to an idea which had come to him on his "walk to Chaillot." The letter was probably *not* written in September of 1788; we have no evidence whatever that Paine was in France after May of that year. I should be inclined to guess that it was written at some time in the spring. If the evidence is of any value, I notice that it and the previous letter (definitely dated May, 1788) as well as the next two letters I shall cite are all on the same type of stationery: a pale-green, over-sized sheet which so far as I know Paine did not use elsewhere.

1788(?) P to J. [Paris]. Mr. Foner prints (II, 1289–1290) a fragment of a letter which he labels "London, May, 1789." The original bears no place name or date, though "1789" has been penciled upon it. The stationery is a reason for thinking that this too might have been written in the spring of 1788.

1788(?) P to J. [Paris]. Mr. Foner prints (II, 1298–1299) another fragment which he labels "[1789]." The original bears no date. Again the stationery argues for the spring of 1788.

1788   P to J. June 15, London, *Ms. letter.*

J to P. July 3, Paris. *Ms. letter.*

P to J. Aug. 18 [Beaconsfield?]. *Ms. letter.* From a letter of Burke to Wilkes cited in our text we know that Paine was visiting Burke at Beaconsfield at this time; the two of them set out that day to dine at the Duke of Portland's estate, which was close to Burke's.

P to J. Sept. 9–Sept. 15, London. Mr. Foner prints (II, 1268–1272, 1272) two extracts from this letter, one of which he dates Sept. 9, the other Sept. 15; the original is a single letter, begun Sept. 9, continued September 15. Mr. Foner justifies long omissions from the text by saying that passages are illegible. The original in the Library of Congress is perfectly legible throughout.

P to J. Dec. 16, London. Mr. Foner prints this letter correctly (II, 1273).

J to P. Dec. 23–Jan. 5–Jan. 11, Paris. The Jefferson Memorial Edition prints the early portion of this letter in two parts (VII, 241–244; 245–247); both parts it dates Dec. 23, 1788. The latter portions, which are continuations dated Jan. 5 and Jan. 11, it does not print.

1789   P to J. Jan. 15, London. *Ms. letter.*

P to J. Feb. 16–Feb. 26–Mar. 12–Apr. 10–Apr. 13, London. Mr. Foner prints this letter (II, 1035–1040; 1281–1284; 1286–1289), not, however, indicating that it was a single continued letter.

J to P. Mar. 17, Paris. The Jefferson Memorial Edition prints this letter correctly (VII, 315–319).

J to P. May 19–May 21, Paris. The Jefferson Memorial Edition prints this letter correctly (VII, 361–364).

P to J. June 17, London. Mr. Foner prints this letter correctly (II, 1291–1292).

P to J. June 18, London. Mr. Foner prints this letter correctly (II, 1292–1293), except for one quite legible phrase which he calls illegible.

J to P. July 11, Paris. The Jefferson Memorial Edition prints this letter incompletely (VII, 404–408). See Appendix B below for the full text.

J to P. July 13, Paris. *Ms. letter.*

P to J. July 13, Rotherham. Mr. Foner prints this letter (II, 1293–1294) with only very minor inaccuracies.

J to P. July 17, Paris. *Ms. letter.*

J to P. July 23, Paris. *Ms. letter.*

J to P. Sept. 13, Paris. *Ms. letter.*

P to J. Sept. 15, London. Mr. Foner prints this letter correctly (II, 1295–1296).

P to J. Sept. 18, London. Mr. Foner prints this letter correctly (II, 1296–1297).

J to P. Oct. 14, Cowes. *Ms. letter.*

APPENDIX B

JEFFERSON'S LETTER OF JULY 11, 1789

The letter from Jefferson which we know Paine quoted to Burke, and which may have had an important effect in arousing Burke's distrust of the Revolution, is not printed entire in the Jefferson Memorial Edition. The following is a complete text, from the copy in the Library of Congress. I have followed Jefferson's punctuation exactly except in one respect. He habitually begins his sentences without using a capital letter; as this seems to me needlessly confusing here, I have altered it.

Paris July 11, 1789.

Dear Sir

Since my last, which was of May the 19th, I have received yours of June the 17. & 18. I am struck with the idea of the geometrical wheelbarrow, and will beg of you a farther account if it can be obtained. I have no news yet of my congé.

Tho you have doubtless heard most of the proceedings of the States general since my last, I will take up the narration where that left it, that you may be able to separate the true from the false accounts you have heard. A good part of what was conjecture in that letter is now become true history. A conciliatory proposition from the king having been accepted by the Nobles with such modifications as amounted to a refusal, the Commons voted it to be a refusal, and proceeded to give a last invitation to the clergy & nobles to join them, and to examine the returns of elections. This done they declared themselves the National assembly, resolved that all the subsisting taxes were illegally imposed, but that they might continue to be paid to the end of their present session & no longer. A majority of the clergy determined to accept their invitation & came and joined them. The king, by the advice of Mr. Necker, determined to hold a seance royale, and to take upon himself to decide what should be done. That decision as proposed by Necker was favorable to the Commons. The Aristocratical party made a furious effort, prevailed on the king to change the decision totally in favor of the other orders, and at the seance royale he delivered it accordingly. The Common chamber (that is the Tiers & majority of the clergy who had joined them) bound themselves together by a solemn oath never to separate till they had accomplished the work for which they had met. Paris & Versailles were thrown into tumult & riot. The soldiers in & about them, including even the king's life guard, declared themselves openly for the Commons. The accounts from the soldiery in the provinces were not more favorable. 48. of the Nobles left their body & joined the common chamber. The mob attacked the Archbishop of Paris (a high aristocrat) under the Chateau of Versailles, a panick seized the inhabitants of the Chateau. The next day the king wrote a letter with his own hand to the Chamber of Nobles & minority of the Clergy, desiring them to join immediately the common chamber. They did so, and thus the victory of the Tiers became complete. Several days were then employed about examining returns & it was discovered at length that great bodies of troops and principally of the ancien corps, were approaching Paris from different quarters. They arrived in the number of 25, or 30,000 men. Great inquietudes took place, and two days ago the Assembly voted an address to the king for an explanation of this phaenomenon & removal of the troops. His answer has not been given formally, but he verbally authorised their president to declare that these troops had nothing in view but the quiet of the Capital; and that that being once established they should be removed. The fact is that the king never saw any thing else in this measure; but those who advised him to it assuredly meant by the presence of the troops to give him confidence and to take advantage of some favorable moment to surprise some act of authority from him. For this purpose they had got the military command within the isle of France transferred to the Marshall de Broglio, a high flying aristocrat, cool and capable of every mischief. But it is now out that these troops shew strong symptoms of being entirely with the people, so that nothing is apprehended from them. The *National assembly* then (for that is the name they take) having shewn thro' every stage of these transactions a coolness, wisdom, and resolution to set fire to the four corners of the kingdom and to perish with it themselves rather than to relinquish an iota from their plan of a total change of government, are now in complete & undisputed possession of the sovereignty. The executive & the aristocracy are at their feet: the mass of the nation, the mass of the clergy, and the army are with them; they have prostrated the old government, and are now beginning to build one from the foundation. A committee charged with the arrangement of their business, gave in, two days ago, the following order of proceedings.

1. Every government should have for it's [*sic*] only end the preservation of the rights of man: whence it follows that to recall constantly the government to the end proposed, the constitution should begin by a Declaration of the natural and imprescriptible rights of man.

2. Monarchical government being proper to maintain those rights, it has been chosen by the French nation. It suits especially a great society; it is necessary for the happiness of France. The Declaration of the principles of this government then should follow immediately the declaration of the rights of man.

3. It results from the principles of monarchy that the nation, to assure its own rights, has yielded particular rights to the monarch: the constitution then should declare in a precise manner the rights of both. It should begin by declaring the rights of the French nation, and then it should declare the rights of the king.

4. The rights of the King & nation not existing but for the happiness of the individuals who compose it, they lead to an examination of the rights of citizens.

5. The French nation not being capable of assembling individually to exercise all it's rights, it ought to be represented. It is necessary then to declare the form of it's representation & the rights of it's representatives.

6. From the union of the powers of the nation & king should result the enacting & execution of the laws; thus then it should first be determined how the laws shall be established, afterwards should be considered how they shall be executed.

7. Laws have for their object the general administration of the kingdom, the property and the actions of the citizens. The execution of the laws which concern the general administration requires provincial and municipal assemblies. It is necessary to examine therefore what should be the organization of the provincial assemblies, & what of the municipal.

8. The execution of the laws which concern the property and actions of the citizens call for a Judiciary power. It should be determined how that should be confided, and then it's duties & limits.

9. For the execution of the laws & the defence of the kingdom,

there exists a public force. It is necessary then to determine the principles which should direct it & how it should be employed.

RECAPITULATION

Declaration of the rights of man. Principles of the monarchy. Rights of the nation. Rights of the king. Rights of the citizens.

Organisation & [function?] rights of the national assembly. Forms necessary for the enaction of laws. Organization & functions of the provincial & municipal assemblies. Duties & limits of the judiciary power. Functions & duties of the military power.

You see that these are the materials of a superb edifice, and the hands which have prepared them, are perfectly capable of putting them together, & of filling up the work of which these are only the outlines. While there are some men among them of very superior abilities, the mass possess such a degree of good sense as enables them to decide well. I have always been afraid their numbers might lead to confusion. 1200 men in one room are too many. I have still that fear Another apprehension is that a majority cannot be induced to adopt the trial by jury; and I consider that as the only anchor, ever yet imagined by man, by which a government can be held to the principles of it's constitution. Mr. Paradise is the bearer of this letter. He can supply those details which it would be too lengthy to write—if my congé comes within a few days, I shall depart in the instant: if it does not I shall put off my voyage till the Equinox is over. I am, with great esteem Dear Sir

your friend & servant

Th Jefferson

VI

"MONSIEUR DUPONT"

I N THE fall of 1789 a young gentleman in Paris wrote a letter
to Burke. Considering the circumstances, it was rather a
bold letter.[1] The young gentleman knew Burke slightly,
having visited him while in England a year or so before; on the
other hand he was none too sure that Burke would remember him,
and took care to recall details of their former meeting. The Burke
family had entertained him on that occasion, both in London and
at Beaconsfield; Burke had talked to him about Liberty in a way
that aroused for the first time his passion for Liberty. The young
man now asked whether Burke would care to renew their acquaintance. There was hope that he might be in England again the
following spring; perhaps he would be able to revisit his friends
the Burkes. Meantime how would Edmund Burke—a man of
sixty and one of the hardest-worked statesmen alive—care to
open a correspondence with him? What were Edmund Burke's
opinions of recent political events in France? Did he approve of
the reforms being undertaken by the National Assembly? Or
would he not allow that the French deserved the blessings of
Liberty?

In one respect the writer of this letter was an extraordinarily
lucky young man. The correspondence which he proposed to
Burke turned out to be one of the most significant political cor-
respondences in history. To be sure it was somewhat one sided.
The young man himself had not much to do with it. The fact is
that his letter reached Burke at almost precisely the moment
when he was ready to set down his ideas on the first phase of the
French Revolution; he set them down in a long letter to this
young man. Presently he followed the long letter with another,
shorter one. A month or so later (having received in the meantime
a response from his correspondent), Burke began writing what

1. Though it has apparently not survived, much of its contents can be inferred
from Burke's reply. *Correspondence*, III, 102 ff.

is very likely the longest human composition ever put in the form of a letter—his *Reflections on the Revolution in France.* This too is ostensibly addressed to the young Frenchman, though it grew into a "public letter" of several hundred printed pages. Its publication, nearly a full year after Burke began writing it, was a major historical event. The British edition sold 12,000 copies the first month—then an unheard-of number; the French translation had an even greater success. In its effect on public opinion it was certainly Burke's greatest work; it is usually regarded too as the highest achievement of his literary powers.

The individual who provoked such an outburst—who gave Burke the cue, as it were, for his greatest single utterance—surely deserved to be remembered. It is unfortunate that Burke saw compelling reasons for concealing his identity. What a British statesman had to say in criticism of the French Revolution was not likely to please the rulers of France; and Burke also thought there was a good chance, in the excited state of Frenchmen's minds, that his own opinions might be imputed to his young correspondent. Full of this idea, and also fearing that the post might be violated, Burke delayed sending the first of his letters for several weeks. When later, in the preface to the *Reflections,* he described the correspondence out of which the book had grown, he ventured no more than a vague reference to "a very young gentleman at Paris." So far as we know, from the publication of the *Reflections* to his own death in 1797 Burke never disclosed his correspondent's identity.

This was the beginning but not the end of a mystery. The young man, perhaps agreeing with Burke about the danger, seems never to have confessed his own share in the correspondence. No one else was able to clear up the story. There were scattered rumors that the young man's name was Dupont; there were other rumors about his circumstances; as time passed, it became evident that the public was to hear nothing better than rumors about him. We can see in Burke's early biographers how doubtful his identity finally became. Charles M'Cormick and James Prior mentioned the name of Dupont, but as the translator of the *Reflections* rather than its recipient; Prior also listed the name among Burke's correspondents around the year 1789, but without connecting it with the *Reflections* or discussing whether this was or was not the Dupont who had made the translation. Both Bisset and Prior thought the correspondent addressed in the *Reflections* was the same as the one addressed in *A Letter to a Member of the National Assembly*, Burke's second tract on the Revolution. Bisset did not say that this correspondent was named Dupont; indeed Bisset never mentioned that name. Prior, who had given the name in two other connections, did not repeat it in this one.

All the biographers naturally attempted, somewhat unimpressively, to narrow their descriptions of the lost young man, since they could not agree on his name. He was "a man of talents and connections who had visited [Burke] at Beaconsfield a year or two before." He was "of the reasonable class of well-wishers to freedom" and not a firebrand like Tom Paine. He was a "young statesman" (plausibly enough if it could first be shown that he was a Member of the National Assembly). He was a "near relation and confidential friend of the Baron de Menou, who afterwards filled the president's chair in the French Assembly." If the correspondent was the same as the translator, he was "an advocate formerly in Paris." [2]

Since for a period of over fifty years there was no authority to trust in the matter it is not surprising that the biographers confused themselves and contradicted each other. It was not until 1844, with the publication of the authorized edition of Burke's correspondence, that any reliable facts were brought forward. The editors of the correspondence printed two letters of Burke written to "Monsieur Dupont": one of them is the long letter which Burke wrote in the fall of 1789 and for a few weeks hesitated to send; the other was written late in 1790, apparently within a week of the publication date of the *Reflections*, answering "Monsieur Dupont's" objection to one passage in that work. Not to leave anything in unnecessary doubt, the editors of the *Correspondence*

---

2. It would be a complicated and not a very useful task to arrange all the con-flicting statements and conjectures of the biographers in a chronological series. The following references will permit the interested reader to review for himself the various assertions and retractions of the first three biographers. M'Cormick (1st ed.), p. 339 n., (2d ed.), p. 339; Bisset (1st ed.), p. 522, (2d ed.), II, 354; Prior (1st ed.), pp. 347, 379–380, 568–574; (2d ed.), II, 43, 100–101, 128, 135; (5th ed.), pp. 296 and n. 310.

stated in a footnote that their two letters were to the same person, that this was the person also addressed in the *Reflections*, that his name was Dupont, and that he later translated the *Reflections* into French.[3]

This was a great improvement on the previous uncertainties, but if the editors thought that this footnote was to end all difficulties they were entirely mistaken. Actually, explicit as it sounded, the footnote failed to settle the most crucial question. Prior and Bisset—the two most reliable biographers—had asserted that the same person was addressed in the *Reflections* and in the *Letter to a Member of the National Assembly*. One would like to know whether the editors agreed to that! It would make an important difference if they did. A Monsieur Dupont who was also known to be a Member of the National Assembly might be possible to identify; a Monsieur Dupont who merely lived "at Paris" was as good as anonymous. The editors had given very little positive help toward an identification.

In commenting on the first of their two letters the editors also started a serious difficulty. The letter, which they dated October, 1789, was nineteen pages in length in the printed version, and one of the most important of all Burke's letters; its prophecies about the French Revolution, written so early in its course, are of the greatest interest. But the editors found that parts of this important document—of which they themselves must have held Burke's copy—were already in print, in Prior's biography of Burke. In the first, second, and third editions of his work Prior had quoted passages amounting in all to about three pages and nearly if not precisely matching the corresponding passages in the authorized nineteen-page version; only Prior had asserted that these passages came from a letter addressed to a person named Monsieur de Menonville.[4] The official editors corrected Prior. Their footnote says:

Prior, in his Life of Burke, gives part of this letter as addressed to M. Menonville, but it seems without doubt to be the letter alluded

3. Burke, *Correspondence*, III, 102 n.
4. (1st ed.), pp. 347–351; (2d ed.), II, 43–47; (3d ed.), pp. 323–325. The editors did not observe it, but the passages Prior quoted had been printed still earlier by M'Cormick (1st ed.), pp. 322–326. They will be discussed below.

to in the introduction to the "Reflections on the Revolution in France" published the next year. That work, written in the form of a letter, was addressed to the same person as this letter of October, 1789; and the person was M. Dupont . . .

This should have settled the matter, but it was the beginning of further uncertainty. For Prior would not yield the point. When he made a thorough revision of his biography ten years later, he took account of the attempt to correct him, but only to rebut it. Having again quoted his passages as coming from Monsieur de Menonville, he added a footnote of his own: "Some portion of this communication but with several variations, appears in a letter addressed to M. Dupont . . . but as it is longer and more elaborate, we may consider it an improved version of hints first thrown out here to another." [5]

It is improbable, to say the least, that this can be taken as a final explanation of the conflict of authority. Though a few differences do distinguish Prior's passages from those in the official version, they are far too minor to justify supposing two separate letters; we know no instance of Burke's transcribing for one correspondent whole paragraphs which he had written for another. It is far easier to suppose that one letter existed, which the editors thought was written to Monsieur Dupont and Prior thought was written to Monsieur de Menonville. The real question is why Prior felt sure enough of his own belief to resist the strong authority of the editors. He was by no means an irresponsible scholar, and we have seen that he had every reason to be modest about his knowledge of Monsieur Dupont. Why did he feel so certain of the name of Monsieur de Menonville?

Whatever the reason, his stubbornness added the final straw to this accumulation of uncertainties. The whole correspondence became a species of puzzle. Each one of its parts—the contested first letter, the letter of 1790, the *Reflections*, the *Letter to a Member of the National Assembly*—seemed to dovetail with one or more of the other parts; what appeared absolutely impossible was to get them all to dovetail at once. But there was still another difficulty which no one had happened to mention. Prior

5. (5th ed.), p. 296 n.

had assigned to Monsieur de Menonville the letter about which he was corrected, but he had also assigned to him a second letter—or fragment of a letter. Should this too be regarded as in question: perhaps written to Monsieur Dupont? It would seem so; Prior said it was to the "same correspondent." One must consider, then, five letters, to be sure of embracing all difficulties. One must also admit the possibility that the correspondent may have been not Monsieur Dupont but Monsieur de Menonville. As if it were not bewildering enough to have him simultaneously a statesman, an advocate, a translator, a Member (perhaps President) of the National Assembly, and a "very young gentleman," he must be allowed to hover between two very dissimilar names.

Two scholars in the twentieth century have tried to cope with the complications which the problem presents. The first, a German named Meusel, starting from what seemed the most useful clue, examined the lists of men elected to the National Assembly in 1789. He found four Duponts; by analysis of their qualifications he had no difficulty in eliminating three, and accordingly proposed the fourth as doubtless Burke's lost correspondent.[6] The second scholar, a Frenchman named Mantoux, was more thorough in investigation than the German, and succeeded in eliminating the fourth Dupont along with the other three.[7] But he analyzed the whole problem with more care than any previous writer, and incidentally made one very illuminating suggestion. Had not the assumption always been made far too easily that only *one* correspondent was to be sought? It would be possible, from the facts we have, to argue that two or even three separate individuals might be involved.

Monsieur Mantoux's essay, at least in one passage, uses the hypothesis that there were three persons with whom Burke dealt. These were: the original correspondent—Burke's "very young gentlemen"—to whom the *Reflections* were addressed; the trans-

6. Fritz Meusel, *Burke's Schriften gegen die französische Revolution* (1790–97) (Wittenberg, 1904). This is a doctoral dissertation presented at the University of Heidelberg in 1904.

7. Paul Mantoux, "A qui furent addressées les 'Réflexions sur la Révolution française' de Burke?," published in *La Révolution française*, LXXXV (1932), 5–15.

lator, who need not be the same as the original correspondent; and
the Member of the National Assembly, who need not be the same
as either. Monsieur Mantoux then looks for three separate individuals, but has a varying success in his three quests. He finds
an entirely convincing candidate, supported by external evidence,
for the role of translator; a quite satisfactory candidate, whom
however he only asserts to be "probable," for the Member of the
Assembly. The most crucial of the three, the "very young gentleman," is his defeat. Having exhausted all the evidence at hand, he
resigns this quest in despair. "Only one conclusion remains ad-
missible," he says: ". . . it is that the young man to whom Burke
addresses himself at the beginning and end of the book is purely
and simply a literary fiction. The literature of the eighteenth
century, especially that of the pamphlets and occasional writings,
abounds in imaginary correspondents. Burke employed a de-
vice . . ."

Before attempting to alter Monsieur Mantoux's conclusions in
several respects, I should like to say that in my own treatment of
this problem I have been very much assisted by his essay. The
hypothesis that three separate individuals are to be sought has
seemed to me useful, and I have adopted it experimentally. As to
Monsieur Mantoux's most important conclusion, that Burke's
original correspondent did not exist, I disagree with him. I think
I can offer a real young man who is more satisfactory than the
supposed *fiction littéraire*. I accept, however, Monsieur Mantoux's
candidates for the roles of translator and of Member of the Assembly, and shall only try to produce more evidence of Burke's
relations with them than he chose to offer.

I

If we start from Monsieur Mantoux's hypothesis, obviously the
story of "Monsieur Dupont" falls into three parts:

(1) There was Burke's correspondence with the "very young
gentleman." This began in the fall of 1789 and entered its final
stage when the *Reflections* was begun as a personal letter, probably before January 1, 1790.

(2) There was the activity of Burke's translator. This must

have begun some time in the middle months of 1790; it ended with the publication of the Paris edition of *Reflections* in November of that year.

(3) There was an interchange of letters between Burke and some Member of the National Assembly. This began after the *Reflections* had appeared. The Member's original letter to Burke bore the date November 17, 1790; Burke's reply, which is the pamphlet *A Letter to a Member of the National Assembly*, bore the date January 19, 1791.

Burke himself in the preface to the *Reflections* gives us an account of the first correspondence. This has already been partly treated but must now be looked at again. It gives us the chronology of the correspondence:

It may not be unnecessary to inform the reader that the following Reflections had their origin in a correspondence between the author and a very young gentleman at Paris, who did him the honor of desiring his opinion upon the important transactions which then, and ever since, have so much occupied the attention of all men. An answer was written some time in the month of October, 1789; but it was kept back upon prudential considerations. That letter is alluded to in the beginning of the following sheets. It has been since forwarded to the person to whom it was addressed. The reasons for the delay in sending it were assigned in a short letter to the same gentleman. This produced on his part a new and pressing application for the author's sentiments.

The author began a second and more full discussion on the subject. This he had some thoughts of publishing early in the last spring; but the matter gaining upon him, he found that what he had undertaken not only far exceeded the measure of a letter, but that its importance required rather a more detailed consideration than at that time he had any leisure to bestow upon it. However, having thrown down his first thoughts in the form of a letter, and, indeed, when he sat down to write, having intended it for a private letter, he found it difficult to change the form of address, when his sentiments had grown into a greater extent, and had received another direction . . .

As will be noted, Burke mentions five letters in all:

(1) The letter from Paris which opened the correspondence.

(2) Burke's reply to it, written some time in the month of October, 1789, but not immediately sent.

(3) Burke's "short letter" explaining the delay.

(4) The "new and pressing application" which the "short letter" produced.

(5) The *Reflections* itself.

Of these five the *Reflections* and the letter of October, 1789, survive entire; fragments of another letter of Burke which may well be the "short letter" are also printed in early biographies, though they have never been studied as part of this correspondence.

The opening passage of the letter of October, 1789, tells us almost everything we can learn on Burke's authority about the "very young gentleman." Though the style has the slightly formal kind of informality suitable to a statesman of sixty unbending to an ardent youth, we catch a glimpse of a genuine, if not intimate, relationship:

Dear Sir:

We are extremely happy in your giving us leave to promise ourselves a renewal of the pleasure we formerly had in your company at Beconsfield and in London. It was too lively to be speedily forgotten on our part; and we are highly flattered to find that you keep so exactly in your memory all the particulars of the few attentions which you were so good to accept from us during your stay in England. We indulge ourselves in the hope that you will be able to execute what you intend in our favor; and that we shall be more fortunate in the coming spring, than we were in the last.

You have reason to imagine that I have not been as early as I ought, in acquainting you with my thankful acceptance of the correspondence you have been pleased to offer. Do not think me insensible to the honor you have done me. I confess I did hesitate for a time, on a doubt, whether it would be prudent to yield to my earnest desire of such a correspondence.

Your frank and ingenuous manner of writing would be ill answered by a cold, dry, and guarded reserve on my part. It would, indeed, be adverse to my habits and my nature, to make use of that sort of caution in my intercourse with any friend. Besides, as you are pleased to think that your splendid flame of liberty was first lighted up at my faint and glimmering taper, I thought you had a right to call upon me for my undisguised sentiments on whatever related to that subject.[8]

It is worth noting that two or three of the details mentioned here are of a sort Burke would not be very likely to invent for a fictitious relationship; the young man's having been entertained not by Burke alone but by the Burke family; their having entertained him in London as well as at Beaconsfield; the young man's having made a plan, never executed, of visiting them the *previous* year . . . Such matters only blur the outlines of an imaginary picture, though they would be likely enough to be part of a real one.

There is also a sentence near the opening of the *Reflections* which preserves a remark the young man must have made in his "new and pressing application" for Burke's sentiments. Burke says: "You imagined, when you wrote last, that I might possibly be reckoned among the approvers of certain proceedings in France, from the solemn public seal of sanction they have received from two clubs of gentlemen in London, called the Constitutional Society, and the Revolution Society." It is evident that the young man, having heard Burke talk highly of Liberty on a former occasion, was assuming that he would be at least as sympathetic with the French reforms as would other liberal Englishmen.

This misjudgment rather increases the likelihood that the acquaintance of the two correspondents had never been more than a slight one. That is no great addition to our previous knowledge; the sentence is, however, our last evidence from Burke's own writings of either the young man's character or his relations with Burke.

We have already surveyed the dubious and contradictory rumors we can obtain from several other sources. Most of these are not worth prolonged attention, but there is one which may have received less attention than it deserves. M'Cormick, the earliest and usually the least reliable of Burke's biographers, anticipated Prior in printing passages from two letters which have

8. Burke, *Correspondence*, III, 102–103.

already been mentioned: those Prior said were written to Monsieur de Menonville. M'Cormick gave no name to the correspondent, but in introducing the first of the letters he did try to explain its origin:

A near relation and confidential friend of the Baron de Menou, who afterwards filled the president's chair in the French assembly, had lately opened a correspondence with Mr. Burke, whose opinions upon what was then doing at Paris were eagerly requested by the young statesman. Mr. Burke's answer, which was written in October 1789, and which he then intended to publish, is a masterpiece . . .[9]

One would like to ask a question about the simple meaning of this. Did M'Cormick intend to say that it was the Baron de Menou, or was it the Baron's near relation, "who afterwards filled the president's chair in the French Assembly"? The order of the sentence leaves us in doubt.

Other questions, however, are more important. Where did M'Cormick get the story he gives us, and where did he get copies of the two letters? In introducing his passages from the second of the letters, he describes it as ". . . addressed to the same correspondent, but intended, as well as the former, for the people of England. We shall soon be able to trace the cause of their not having been printed . . ."[10] No explanations ever followed. It is hard to believe that M'Cormick did not have some genuine basis for his assertions, but if he did he never made it known to the public.

What is more surprising is that Prior, who was normally so much more reliable a biographer than M'Cormick, did not improve on him in this matter. Indeed, he deepened the difficulties. He quoted the same passages M'Cormick had quoted, only taking the occasional liberty of clipping off a phrase or so. But he supplied the correspondent a name, he dated the first letter more precisely, and apparently he decided that the correspondent was only a Member, not a President, of the French Assembly. His introduction runs: "To another correspondent, M. de Menonville, a relation of the Baron de Menou and a member of the National Assembly,

9. M'Cormick (1st ed.), p. 322.
10. *Ibid.*, p. 326.

who requested his opinion of their affairs towards the end of September, 1789, he wrote early in the following month . . ." [11] As Prior most certainly got his quoted passages from M'Cormick, we are bound to ask where he got his other, new facts. In particular, where did he get the name of Monsieur de Menonville? We are never told where. It is merely the last and most tantalizing of the unanswered questions concerning the "very young gentleman."

The complications of the problem have at least one heartening aspect. They suggest that there must have been a real individual. Monsieur Mantoux's *fiction littéraire* would surely have been a simpler outline! But we must ask, can an individual be found who will match any reasonable share of our various fragments of identification?

In Dixon Wecter's study *Edmund Burke and His Kinsmen* there is an anecdote concerning two Frenchmen, father and son, by the name of Dupont. They were in London in November, 1785, and Burke wished to entertain them; as he was prevented by another engagement, he asked his brother Richard to take them to a large dinner at the Guildhall. Richard was much amused by the actions of the father, who at one point in the dinner was sure he had been robbed. A letter of Richard's describes the scene:

At last the father got something on his plate, and searching in his pocket (for a knife I suppose) he gave a great start, and exclaimed par dieu on m'a volé; quoi says the Son? On m'a piqué le pocket, replyd the father. O Sir, said I, ce n'est q'une mouchoir.—O Mon dieu Monsieur J'ai perdu ma portefeuille. That is pocket book. This drew the attention of the neighbors, who hastily enquired if there were any notes in it, and were answered that it was full. The explanation followd quick that they were not bank notes, but notes of all that he had seen, and all that he had to see, and all his remarks. Here I seriously pityd him. [12]

The father and son were quite probably Pierre-Samuel Du Pont, the economist, and his elder son Victor. Pierre-Samuel had been

11. Prior (1st ed.), pp. 347–348.
12. Wecter, *op. cit.*, p. 74.

appointed the French representative for the negotiation of a commercial treaty with England at the close of the American war. Negotiations for the treaty had been begun while Burke's party was in power as early as 1783, and though they dragged out for years, we know that the international situation had brought them to something of a crisis in November, 1785; it is fair to assume that Pierre-Samuel Du Pont would have been in London for negotiations at nearly that time.[13] If he was the father in question, it is probable that the son who accompanied him was his elder son, Victor, rather than his younger son, Eleuthère. At this time Pierre-Samuel was in charge of the French Department of Commerce, and Victor held a post in that department; we know that Victor's duties required him to travel frequently.[14]

A fact which might further attract our interest to this pair of Du Ponts is that their family had been living for centuries near a small French provincial town by the name of Mignonville. In one of their family letters Victor speaks of their being the "elder branch of the Du Ponts of Mignonville," and refers facetiously to his brother as "head of the large and illustrious family of Du Pont of Mignonville, Beaumoulin, Frôles, Les Celestes, &."[15] In his early political career, before the Revolution, Pierre-Samuel had not found it necessary to call himself by any longer name than Du Pont, and it was only later, when three other Duponts were elected to the National Assembly, that he distinguished himself by the name of Du Pont de Nemours.[16] But it is not at all improbable that before this latter decision was made a member of the family might have chosen to identify himself as "Monsieur Du Pont de Mignonville." Nor is it very improbable that if he did so an Englishman not quite sure of his name could render it "Monsieur Dupont de Menonville," or in a shortened form, "Monsieur de Menonville." If that happened, we could easily explain why Prior, perhaps trusting to some early notes, refused to withdraw before the authority of the editors of Burke's *Corre-*

13. See G. Schelle, *Du Pont de Nemours et l'Ecole Physiocratique* (Paris, 1888), pp. 237–238.

14. See article on Victor du Pont in the *Dictionary of American Biography*.

15. *Life of Eleuthère Irénée du Pont*, ed. B. G. du Pont (Newark, Delaware, 1923), I, 72–73.

16. *Idem*, p. 110.

spondence. Though Prior may not have known it, Monsieur Dupont and Monsieur de "Menonville" could be the same individual.

The possibility directs our attention toward Victor Du Pont as a candidate for the role of the "very young gentleman." In 1789 Victor was twenty-two years old—which might seem "very young" to a statesman in his sixties. If he was introduced to Burke in 1785, he was eighteen at that time. We know nothing of his having been entertained at Beaconsfield, though if Burke had any considerable dealings with Pierre-Samuel Du Pont, it is obvious that both the economist and his son might have visited the Burke estate. Their being taken to dinner in London by a member of the Burke family would of course fit the phrasing of Burke's letter of October, 1789, where it is recalled that the family had enjoyed the young gentleman's company in London.

The letters of the Du Pont family give us rather an attractive picture of Victor as a young man. He was striking in appearance; six feet three inches tall and unusually handsome. We are told that his manners were engaging and that he was generally liked. The letters do manage to suggest that he was spoiled and never inclined to much exertion; he was very slow in placing himself in any settled profession. But he dressed well, entertained himself freely, and exploited the social position which his father had won for the family.

His most useful accomplishment was his mastery of English. In acquiring this he seems to have overcome some of his natural indolence. In June of 1787 one of his letters home shows him asking eagerly for English books:

. . . a Grammar by Tiret (if it is not there send and buy it at once); one by Boyer; a Dictionary, and the first volume of Grandison. Besides these you will find in my room either in the portfolio marked "English", or somewhere else, several English writing books and bits of translating, please send them with the books.

I will tell you why I need all this. It is that I may learn English as quickly as possible, for it is probable that I may be made Secretary of the Embassy in America within two or three months.[17]

17. *Idem,* pp. 90–91.

His ambition was rewarded. He obtained both the post in America and an excellent command of English. According to his father's boast on a later occasion, he knew English "perfectly, and succeeded better than his chiefs in America." [18] When in the course of the Revolution the family found themselves almost without resources, Pierre-Samuel found comfort for them all in Victor's accomplishment: "If peace is established, as seems possible, he will earn money for us all with his English, and his wife too, and our whole little Republic will live very comfortably in the great one, by dint of hard work." [19]

At the time Victor went to America he had already lost interest in two careers offered him in France; that in his father's Department of Commerce, in which he had begun; and later one in the Department of Agriculture. He was not content with the career he found in America. By the fall of 1788 he was writing home in the hope that his father might be able to arrange to have him shifted to another post: "I hope that by spring Papa will still have sufficient influence to get me a place as vice-consul . . ." [20] We know of no change in his situation in the spring of 1789, but by fall he was back in Paris,[21] where again he was somewhat at a loss to find himself occupation. He became a volunteer aide to Lafayette in the newly organized National Guard, and occasionally had a part in quelling a riot or assisting at a parade, but his letters show no more settled occupation for a period of nearly two years. He described his own life humorously in a letter to his brother: "Do I not have to find places to dine, to court some girl I might like to marry, to dodge creditors, deceive husbands . . . ?—all these things leave a poor fellow but little time." [22]

It may have occurred to him while thus at leisure that it would be a pleasant gesture to renew acquaintance with Edmund Burke in England. Who could tell what a friendly letter might initiate?

18. *Ibid.*, II, 55.
19. *Idem*, p. 374.
20. *Ibid.*, I, 104.
21. Victor's superior in America was recalled to France in the fall of 1789 (*idem*, pp. 121-122). It is possible that Victor returned earlier than his chief. A letter of Sept. 16, 1789 (*idem*, p. 116) leaves it in doubt whether he was at that time in America or in France
22. *Idem*, p. 130.

At the least it could lead to a social visit; if one were luckier it might open up some useful employment for a young man whose principal asset was a proficiency in English.

II

If Victor Du Pont can be admitted as a plausible candidate for the role of Burke's "very young gentleman"—as perhaps he can, in the present absence of any other candidate—he might at first seem about equally likely to have been Burke's translator. He knew English; we have undertaken to show that he knew the Burke family; he was in a position to pay just such a visit to Beaconsfield in the spring of 1790 as Burke's young correspondent was proposing; such a visit could have led very easily to his being asked to undertake a translation.

The little one can infer from the single letter of Burke to his translator which is printed in *Correspondence* [23] might also encourage this idea. Burke writes as to a younger man; to a man, too, more in sympathy with French liberalism than Burke himself was; to a man who, as Burke happens to mention, had received his education in France. The occasion of the letter is that the translator had protested against what he thought an illiberal passage in the *Reflections;* Burke's tone in reasserting his position against an ardent but inexperienced young patriot is not unlike his tone in replying to the "very young gentleman."

It is fortunate that we are saved from this attractive line of inferences. Monsieur Mantoux, though he was willing to dismiss the first correspondent as *une fiction littéraire,* presents a solid and persuasive account of the translator, who is evidently not young Victor Du Pont. Monsieur Mantoux writes from better evidence than the usual inference or rumor:

M. d'Anglezan, in the preface of his translation of the *Reflections on the French Revolution* [Paris, 1912] tells us that the first translator, M. du Pont, was his great-great grandfather. Here are the details which, on my request, he was so obliging as to send me from his

23. III, 155–162.

family papers: Pierre-Gaëton du Pont, son of Laurent-Octave du Pont, Intendant of the Military School, and of Jeanne Caulet d'Hauteville, was born in Paris at the end of 1759, or the beginning of 1760. He entered the magistracy and was selected, being a Counsilor to the Parlement in 1788 or 1789, to go to England to study the institution of the jury. His activities brought him into relations with various political figures, magistrates, and lawyers; it is thus that he was led to make the acquaintance of Edmund Burke and of his son Philippe, with whom he linked himself speedily and very intimately. The first outbreak found him in England, where he remained, and it was there that his intimacy with the Burke family decided the author of the *Reflections* to ask him to translate his work. This translation was made extremely rapidly and under the eyes of Burke himself, which did not prevent it, however, from being rather inexact. As soon as the manuscript was finished, M. du Pont crossed the sea and came to Paris to have it printed. He did not stay in Paris, where he felt he was not safe; he lived for some time at Bordeaux; towards the beginning of 1794 he went to England on an American boat, and remained there this time more than three years. In 1814, Louis XVIII, to whom he was recommended by the duc d'Avaray, the duc de Rivière and M. d'Outremont, named him Naval Intendant at Toulon. He died on the 17th of April, 1817 . . .

One detail of this must be corrected. Burke's son, as we have seen, was named Richard, not Philippe. But he was practicing law in London in 1788, he was within a year or two of being the same age as Pierre-Gaëton du Pont, and incidentally he had a special interest in France and Frenchmen, having spent about two years of his early life in a small town near Paris, learning about the country and the language.

There is little reason to doubt the main facts of Monsieur Mantoux's account; indeed they will be found to harmonize with many facts and rumors which Monsieur Mantoux does not cite. Prior's reference to Burke's translator as "his friend M. Dupont, an advocate formerly in Paris" reinforces the story. A long footnote in M'Cormick's biography extends it somewhat. M'Cormick is describing the last-minute rush to get the *Reflections* to the press:

Mr. Burke's eagerness to have it published on the first of November is strongly marked in a letter written about a week before to a friend in town, who was to keep goading the printers to the utmost exertion and dispatch. "For God's sake," he says, "move heaven and earth to get it out at the exact day— Whether well, or ill—with convenience, or not— For otherwise, I may as well not print it at all. My reasons are solid." The new parliament was to meet on the 25th, and Mr. Burke hoped that his book would before that time make some impression. It appears from the same letter that he was no less urgent with Mr. Dupont, an emigrant, then at Lord Rivers's, who was engaged in a French translation of the work, for the purpose of its being circulated on the continent.[24]

The hasty and imperfect nature of the translation can be confirmed from two other sources. The Paris edition when it appeared contained an apology for the imperfection of its form:

There are few instances of such precipitation as has attended the publication of this translation. It was re-touched from the third London edition, which appeared on Tuesday the twentieth of this month. The author having made additions and transpositions, it was necessary to re-copy the manuscript, make the changes, and print the whole in eight days. This is little time to make it as correct as one would have wished it.[25]

The many errors caused comment. They were largely corrected in the third Paris edition, and a much longer apology given for their having occurred:

The first two editions of this book having been printed under fear of a piracy, there resulted an unfortunate precipitation which disappointed the anticipation of the public and the intention of the editor.

Except for the faults of printing and punctuation, which by an unlucky chance disfigured some of the most striking passages of the work, one could have guaranteed to the public the most essential merit of a translation: accuracy. The profound and sublime genius of the author, the fulness and eloquence of his style, and often the

24. M'Cormick (1st ed.), p. 339 n.
25. *Réflections sur la Révolution de France*, par Edmund Burke. Traduit de l'anglais sur la troisième édition (Paris, 1790). See "Avis au Lecteur," not on a numbered page.

finesse of his expressions, had rendered this task very difficult. An effort of zeal had completed it in a very short time, to the satisfaction of the author; and it is with distress that one realizes that he will have been able to peruse a printed version so little answering to the manuscript which he saw and which he had the indulgence to approve.

The circumstance of living in a foreign country and not having, to restore one's ear, any correctors not under the same disadvantage, made it needful to communicate this translation to a man of letters in France, and to submit it to a more elegant pen. If this project was not carried out, the public's impatience was the cause. Others were already working on translations which would not have been long in appearing. They were entrusted to many different hands and were being executed in haste, and perhaps the translators had to overcome, to discover the true sense of the original, the double difficulty of the language and of the difference of their own opinions; this might have been a true risk to the clarity of these opinions in themselves. Thus, out of regard for the author, it was better to give the public a translation a little less elegant, but one which he had approved on the score of its accuracy.[26]

These are strictly contemporary accounts; from the rapidity with which the French editions of *Reflections* poured from the press, they must have been written within a week or two of each other at some time around the first of December, 1790. An account with greater biographical interest appears in the preface to a later Paris edition. This is a more scholarly edition, brought out in 1819 when most of the heat of the Revolution should have passed. It tells nearly the same story as Monsieur Mantoux, adding colorful details:

The translation which we owe to M. Dupont, Naval Intendant at Toulon, a respectable magistrate too early lost to his country, his family and his numerous friends, was made under the eyes of Burke at the end of the year 1790. The English author himself corrected what seemed to him not sufficiently expressive, as we have proof in

26. *Réflexions sur la Révolution de France*, par Edmund Burke. Traduit de l'anglais sur la troisième édition; quatrième édition, revue, corrigée, et augmentée (Paris, 1790), pp. iv–v.

the manuscripts of the translator, left in the hands of his widow. M. Dupont often sacrificed his taste to the desires of his friend; and it is to this condescendence that one should attribute the turns of phrase more English than French, and sometimes scarcely intelligible, which are encountered in this translation.

M. Dupont, moved solely by the desire for public good which always animated him, had the courage to return to Paris, whence our first troubles had driven him, to have his work printed. Eighteen editions were published in a very short space of time and this prodigious success was the pleasing and the only recompense of his disinterested zeal; he had no other end than to spread abroad useful truths in the midst of a torrent of errors and a too general distraction. He was rewarded for his generous efforts by the esteem of honest men and by the hatred of the ill-intentioned; but the ill-intentioned were in the majority. Proscribed under the double stigma of member of Parlement and translator of Burke, he was obliged to flee, leaving to Mme. Dupont, his mother, all the materials he had brought back from a hospitable land, as well as the notes relative to his translation. But Mme. Dupont was herself arrested; and her faithful servants, fearing for the life of their worthy mistress, burned without pity all the papers of her son; in them there was some question of the *English*, of *England;* and at that time that was a crime of high treason.[27]

The inconsistencies of this account are obvious; papers which were burned while in the household of Monsieur Dupont's mother are cited as if still in existence in the hands of his widow; though they were completely destroyed, we can convince ourselves that Burke corrected them in his own hand; and so forth. Nevertheless, the number of details confirmed elsewhere is sufficient to forbid our discounting the story completely; intrinsically it is probable enough.

It ends the few scraps of knowledge about Burke's translator which we have found in external sources. There are a few references to "Du Pont" in Burke's private letters, which probably refer to the same person, and suggest that he was a close friend

27. *Réflexions sur la Révolution de France*, par Edmund Burke. Nouvelle edition avec des notes, par J. A. A[uvray] (Paris, 1819), pp. vi–vii.

of the Burkes. In a letter of January 27, 1792, in which Burke is urging a member of the French *noblesse* to answer an attack on his order, he also says: "I shall write to Du Pont, if he be still in England, to come to town, and to exert himself in the defense of his own corps." [28] In a letter undated but probably written in 1793 or 1794, "Du Pont" is mentioned as a visitor at Beaconsfield.[29] He was in contact with the Burkes at the time of Richard's death in August, 1794.[30]

What connection Burke kept with this "Du Pont" in the months immediately following the French publication of the *Reflections* it would be interesting to know. In two letters of Burke to his son Richard on August 16, 1791, there are mysterious references to a "Paris correspondent" who might well be he. Richard was on the continent at this time, visiting the temporary court of French émigrés at Coblenz; Burke in England was supplying him with information and advice likely to assist his mission. "I send you the letters which came hither, they will cost you something, but they may be necessary to you. I send you what I received from my Paris correspondent. I believe his fears are not without foundation." [31] Apparently the Paris correspondent was supplying Burke himself with advice. In another passage Burke tells Richard: "The enclosed letter, from our Paris correspondent, will show you where the danger lies." [32] In giving Richard news of the success of *An Appeal from the New to the Old Whigs*—published a couple of weeks before—Burke tells him: "A third edition is preparing. I don't know what to do about my Paris friend, who will wish to translate." [33] If Pierre-Gaëton du Pont was the "Paris friend" in question, Burke had some cause to think him a careless translator. Richard would of course have known the name, and it is not surprising that Burke should have refrained from using it; these letters were to follow Richard to the continent, and could very easily miscarry.

28. Burke, *Correspondence*, III, 382.
29. Now in the possession of Professor Frederick W. Hilles of Yale University.
30. See letter of French Laurence to Mrs. Haviland, Aug. 4, 1794, quoted in Prior, II, 273.
31. Burke, *Correspondence*, III, 253.
32. *Idem*, p. 275.
33. *Idem*, pp. 255–256.

III

The *Reflections* was duly published on November 1, 1790. On November 17 one of its French readers was addressing a long and serious letter to Burke. The letter has not survived, but Burke's reply to it, the *Letter to a Member of the National Assembly* makes several references to its contents; if we examine Burke's pamphlet carefully,[34] we can reconstruct a considerable part of what this correspondent said.

Burke begins:

Sir,—

I had the honor to receive your letter of the 17th of November last, in which, with some exceptions, you are pleased to consider favorably the letter I have written on the affairs of France. . . . Some of the errors you point out to me in my printed letter are really such. One only I find to be material. It is corrected in the edition which I take the liberty of sending to you.

The error to which Burke refers is itself not of great magnitude. The first edition had described in too exaggerated a manner the routing of all moderate elements in the Assembly:

There they sit, after a gang of assassins had driven away all the men of moderate minds and moderating authority among them, and left them as a sort of dregs and refuse, under the apparent lead of those in whom they do not so much as pretend to have any confidence.

The later, corrected edition softened the statement a little, especially omitting the word *all:*

There they sit, after a gang of assassins had driven away some hundreds of their members; whilst those who held the same moderate principles with more patience or better hope, continued every day exposed to outrageous insults and murderous threats.[35]

Apparently the French writer had been eager to see full justice done to the moderate members.

34. Burke, *Works*, IV, 3 ff.
35. E. J. Payne (*Selected Works*, II, 334–335) first pointed out this significant change between the first and subsequent editions of the *Reflections*.

He was also concerned for the safety of the King and Queen, and must have tried to restrain some of Burke's freedom in speaking of their vulnerable situation. Burke replies;

I am not apprehensive, that, in speaking freely on the subject of the king and queen of France, I shall accelerate (as you fear) the execution of traitorous designs against them. You are of opinion, Sir, that the usurpers may, and that they will, gladly lay hold of any pretext to throw off the very name of a king . . .

In later passages it is evident how far the Frenchman's alarms for the monarchy had gone. Burke says:

You ask me what I think of the conduct of General Monk.

And later:

I certainly agree with you, that in all probability we owe our whole constitution to the restoration of the English monarchy. The state of things from which Monk relieved England was, however, by no means, at that time, so deplorable, in any sense, as yours is now, and under the present sway is likely to continue.

Apparently the Frenchman was casting about for a solution to what he thought a desperate situation. Burke admits his inability to help him:

You gently reprehend me, because, in holding out the picture of your disastrous situation, I suggest no plan for a remedy. Alas! Sir, the proposition of plans, without an attention to circumstances, is the very cause of all your misfortunes . . .

After a passage on the futility of paper plans, Burke concludes:

. . . I have answered, I think, another of your questions,—Whether the British Constitution is adapted to your circumstances? When I praised the British Constitution, and wished it to be well studied, I did not mean that its exterior form and positive arrangement should become a model for you or for any people servilely to copy. I meant to recommend the *principles* from which it has grown . . .

But he is willing to enter into a comparison the Frenchman had suggested, of the English and the French constitutions:

You think, Sir, (and you might think rightly, upon the first view of the theory,) that to provide for the exigencies of an empire so situated and so related as that of France, its king ought to be invested with powers very much superior to those which the king of England possesses under the letter of our Constitution.

Burke is not unwilling to argue for the full adequacy of the power of the King of England, for however wide a scope of empire. Modern Frenchmen are not to look down upon any important part of the English Constitution:

You ask me, too, whether we have a Committee of Research. No, Sir,—God forbid! It is the necessary instrument of tyranny and usurpation; and therefore I do not wonder that it has had an early establishment under your present lords. We do not want it.

In this interchange there is material which can help us to form an estimate of the French correspondent. Indeed Burke in one passage gives us his own flattering opinion of him:

Your fundamental laws, as well as ours, suppose a monarchy. Your zeal, Sir, in standing so firmly for it as you have done, shows not only a sacred respect for your honor and fidelity, but a well-informed attachment to the real welfare and true liberties of your country. I have expressed myself ill, if I have given you cause to imagine that I prefer the conduct of those who have retired from this warfare to your behavior, who, with a courage and constancy almost super-natural, have struggled against tyranny, and kept the field to the last. . . . I assure you, Sir, that, when I consider your unconquerable fidelity to your sovereign and to your country,—the courage, forti-tude, magnanimity, and long-suffering of yourself, and the Abbé Maury, and of M. Cazalès, and of many worthy persons of all orders in your Assembly,—I forget, in the lustre of these great qualities, that on your side has been displayed an eloquence so rational, manly, and convincing, that no time or country, perhaps, has ever excelled.

It is quite possible that Burke had no knowledge of the corre-spondent other than that which he could collect from his letter. If so, it evidently left him in no doubt about the gentleman's con-servative zeal. The Abbé Maury and Monsieur Cazalès were at this time perhaps the best-known leaders on the Right of the Assembly.

Besides responding to his worthy sentiments, Burke must have tried to gauge his correspondent's political weight. One would like to know what opinion he formed. There are passages in letters to others in which Burke speaks most respectfully of him. In themselves these are not very informative. More enlightening is the fact that Burke left it entirely to the Frenchman's judgment whether the *Letter to a Member of the National Assembly* should be published in either France or England. Though the *Letter* itself contains no reference to this proposition—perhaps broached through an agent, or in a "covering letter" which has not survived —Burke described the arrangement to two of his other correspondents. In the early part of January, 1791, replying to a French lady who had written praising the *Reflections* he said:

I certainly never should have written one word more on the subject, convinced as I am of its utter inutility, if I had not been applied to by a gentleman at Paris, of rank and consideration, for an explanation of some sentiments and expressions in my printed letter. I finished it about a week or ten days ago; but it will not go until next Friday, on account of the difficulty of sending such things safely since the post has been declared inviolable. It is long and full; as full, at least, as the subject of his inquiry demanded. He seemed willing that it should be something which might be published. He has my leave to publish or to suppress it, as he thinks may be best for his cause. He, and gentlemen in his situation, are the only competent judges of what that *best* is . . .[36]

Two months later he wrote to another French correspondent, who had apparently got wind of the new letter:

I should be happy to send you a copy of the letter which I wrote to a person of distinction in Paris, in answer to one from him. But as I have my doubts whether what I wrote in the present temper of the times, and the present posture of affairs, might be useful in the publi-

36. *Idem*, pp. 193–194. The editors of *Correspondence* incline to think that this letter was addressed to Mme. d'Osmond; a reproduction of part of it which is now in the Morgan Library, New York, is evidence for its having been written to Mme. de Montrond.

cation, I left the matter to the gentleman's own discretion, promising not to disperse any copies without his leave. This, I hope, my dear sir, will plead my excuse to you. I did hear that a translation of that letter was preparing at Paris. If this be the case, you will see it very soon. It will, I am afraid, afford you no very great satisfaction. Some part of the letter was to exculpate myself (or rather perhaps to apologize) from some faults which the gentleman found in my pamphlet. The rest was to show, from the actual state of France, (as well as I was able to enter into its condition,) the utter impossibility of a counter-revolution from any internal cause.[37]

Apparently the Frenchman thought Burke's letter likely to help his cause; the French translation duly appeared, followed by the English edition published in the middle of May.[38]

The problem of the identity of the correspondent of November 17 has been allowed to appear more difficult than perhaps it really is. Burke's early biographers, hampered by their belief that the "very young man," the translator, and the Member of the Assembly had to be all one single person, became so entangled by contradictory rumors that they never gave the Member any name at all. Monsieur Mantoux, though he cut the Gordian knot by supposing three individuals, did not take full advantage of his own conjecture; he gave an excellent account of a Member of the Assembly by the name of de Menonville, saying no more than that it was "probable" that he was Burke's correspondent; the probability he argued very weakly.

Neither Monsieur Mantoux nor any of his predecessors seem to have paid attention to a phrase of Burke's own which bears directly upon this matter. In his second *Letter on a Regicide Peace*, published in 1796, Burke began one sentence: "When I wrote my letter in answer to M. de Menonville, in the beginning of January, 1791 . . ."[39] The context makes it certain that Burke is referring

---

37. *Idem*, pp. 202–203.
38. See advertisement in the *London Chronicle*, May 19–21, 1791.
39. Burke, *Works*, V, 370–371. Professors Ross Hoffman and Paul Levack call attention to this passage in a footnote of their excellent work, *Burke's Politics* (New York, 1949), p. 382. I had noticed the passage before reading their work. I am pleased to find that I agree with these two careful scholars that it settles the identity of the person addressed in Burke's *Letter*.

to his *Letter to a Member of the National Assembly*, which bears the date January 19, 1791. As we know that there was only one gentleman by the name of de Menonville elected to the first National Assembly, we can be reasonably sure of our man.

Monsieur Mantoux gives us the main facts about him:

François-Louis Thibault de Menonville, Seigneur of Sambroch, Major-General, Chevalier of Saint-Louis and of the Society of Cincinnatus, was sent to the Estates-General by the nobility of the constituency of Saint-Dié. In the Assembly, he sat on the Right: Dugour, in his *École de Politique*, cites him among the deputies "who were faithful in religion, to their country, and to their oaths." His political ideas were of a kind to bring him close to Burke . . . He was surely familiar with England, for when he mounted the Tribune of the Assembly, he spoke of English institutions as a man who had studied them . . . M. de Menonville's career is known to us. His promotions in rank, most honorable ones, are preserved at the Archives of War. He was, in January, 1756, Cadet-Royal of Poland, on April 12, 1757, Lieutenant at the School of La Fère, and on December 30, 1769, Captain in the Engineering Corps. He served in the Corsican campaign in 1769, took part in the Polish war in 1772, and the American expedition from 1780 to 1783. Field-Marshall since September 21, 1788, he was more than fifty years old at the time the *Reflections* appeared.

Several points in the account are suggestive. Monsieur de Menonville is clearly a man of "rank and consideration," who could address Burke as an equal, approving and correcting him as well as asking his political advice. He is a devoted adherent of the Right, whom others could praise in almost the same terms Burke applied to his correspondent. He takes enough interest in English institutions to make them the subject of a formal utterance. He has known something firsthand about the American Revolution. His position in the army would make it appropriate for him to think of counterrevolution in terms of a General Monk.

We should certainly like to know more about this gentleman, but such as it is Monsieur Mantoux's account agrees with what we learn elsewhere about Burke's third correspondent.

IV

In the great war of pamphlets which the *Reflections* provoked it is not surprising that once or twice attention was paid to the young man Burke mentioned in his preface. Though Burke would not reveal his name, rumors of his identity got abroad. Indeed, there is some evidence that Burke's first letter to him, that of October, 1789, may itself have got abroad—or at least have escaped from the strict secrecy Burke had tried to maintain.

Two ephemeral publications are the chief sources of this evidence. The first of these is a small pamphlet printed early in 1791 under the title *Answer to the Reflections of Edmund Burke. By M. Depont.*[40] It purports to be a personal letter from Burke's young Frenchman, protesting against the mistakes and excesses of the *Reflections*. It carries other marks besides the spelling "Depont" of being a hoax perpetrated by someone not familiar with the whole story of the correspondence. Nonetheless, the last paragraph of the introduction hints that the letter of October, 1789, is accessible to the pamphlet's editor:

Mr. Burke, from . . . regard to his correspondent, studiously concealed his name. Mr. Depont, however, has himself disclosed the secret, and has given leave for the publication of his answer. It is not improbable but from the same valuable source we may be honored with the first letter of Mr. Burke, for which we are sensible how much our readers would be indebted to us.

The other work is a set of verses entitled "Answer from M. Dupont to Mr. Burke, by Lord Camelford." Whether it was published as early as 1791 we do not know; Nichols, who printed it in his *Literary History of the Eighteenth Century* in 1831, does not say where he got it.[41] It is a livelier performance than the "Depont" pamphlet, but follows the same formula of answering Burke in the name of his correspondent. It begins:

My very good patron and friend Mr. Burke,
Give me leave to return you my thanks for the work,
Which in form of a letter to me you address . . .

40. Published in London, 1791. A copy is in the Yale University Library.
41. VI, 123–125.

Nichols supplies a note to the third line: "Letter to Mr. Dupont, a Member of the National Assembly." This sounds as if Nichols thought the verses an answer to *A Letter to a Member of the National Assembly,* but it is at least equally probable that they were intended to be an answer to the *Reflections.* The concluding lines refer to Monsieur Dupont's intention of paying a visit to England in the spring—which is reminiscent of the opening passage of Burke's letter of October, 1789:

> Though I fear we no longer are birds of a feather,
> I trust we may still drink a bottle together.
> Your wine's always good; I'll come over in Spring,
> And I'll pledge any toast—but the Church and the King.

When Tom Paine returned to England in the spring of 1790, he talked with several of Burke's friends about his plan of answering the *Reflections* as soon as it appeared. One of his remarks in a conversation with Sir George Staunton is rather suggestive: "I told him of a letter I saw from Mr. B(urke) to a gentleman at Paris, the contents of which surprised me." [42] Sir George too had knowledge of a letter "from a gentleman at Paris to Mr. Burke." If either one of the letters belonged to the Dupont correspondence, we have a partial explanation of those rumors which Burke's early biographers recorded.

Only two of the biographers' rumors about "Monsieur Dupont" can still be said to present difficulties. We have no evidence that any of our three gentlemen was "a near relation and confidential friend of the Baron de Menou"; but this may be because we do not know enough about any of them to be well informed about his relations and friends. Second, we do not know that any of our three "afterwards filled the President's chair in the French Assembly"; Pierre-Samuel Du Pont, however, Victor's father, did fill the president's chair in 1790, and since we are dealing with rumors, his achievement may have been mistakenly attributed to his son. If the latter is the case, the mistake is paralleled by still another rumor, though not one supplied by Burke's biographers. It is

42. Paine, *Writings* (ed. Foner), II, 1301.

found in a paragraph in a London periodical, *The Gazeteer*, under the date January 19, 1791:

Mr. Burke's letter, though it has so much the air of a declamation, is said to have been really sent in a series of communications to a gentleman in Paris, who is considered by all companies as the correspondent of the defender of monarchy. His name is Du Pont, and is [*sic*] a member of the Club of 1789.[43]

Pierre-Samuel Du Pont was one of the leading members of the conservative group—for a time a rival of the Jacobin Club—which called itself the Club of 1789.

It is now obvious what kind of harmony of all other rumors the present study proposes. We have reached the point of adopting Monsieur Mantoux's hypothesis as our own conclusion: three gentlemen did combine to make up "Monsieur Dupont." One was a Member of the National Assembly, one was an "advocate formerly of Paris," one was a "very young gentleman at Paris" who had previously visited Burke in England. All might be described as "of the reasonable class of well-wishers to freedom," or as men of "talents and connections." If one was Monsieur du Pont, another Monsieur de Menonville, and a third able to give his name as Monsieur Du Pont de Mignonville, a confusion of their names is not excessively hard to explain. The mistakes and contradictions of Prior, of the editors of *Correspondence*, and of other scholars before and since, can be reconciled in our account.

43. There is a copy of this issue of *The Gazeteer* in the Yale University Library.

APPENDIX A

M'CORMICK'S QUOTATIONS FROM THE LETTER OF OCTOBER, 1789

It has already been pointed out that it was not Prior but the earlier and less reputable biographer, Charles M'Cormick who first printed passages from Burke's important letter of October, 1789. We did not pause to answer an obvious question concerning this publication, namely, how M'Cormick ever happened to have a copy of the letter from which to print. No authorized text was published until the appearance of Burke's *Correspondence* in 1844. M'Cormick certainly did not have the confidence of Burke's literary executors; on the contrary, he was recognized as a crudely abusive political opponent of Burke's, whose biography was undertaken chiefly for the purpose of vilifying its subject. Then by what chance, we ask, was he in a position to publish portions of this letter?

The question may not allow of a conclusive answer, but there are a few of the facts we have noticed which suggest a plausible theory as to what happened. We have seen that there are reasons for suspecting that the secret of the October letter was not perfectly kept. Lord Camelford seemed to be familiar with part of the contents as early as the first months of 1791. The editor of the mysterious *Answer to the Reflections of Edmund Burke. By M. Depont* thought he could procure the letter itself to print in pamphlet form. Tom Paine in Paris read a letter of Burke's, "the contents of which surprised" him, in the winter of 1789-90. All three facts point to the same possibility, namely, that young Monsieur Dupont was at the start not much impressed by the dangers of being the letter's recipient, and showed it around more or less indiscreetly among his friends in Paris. It would not be too much to suppose that he even allowed a part of it to be copied and to get out of his hands.

It is worth examining M'Cormick's passages with exactly this possibility in mind. He published his biography in 1797—anywhere from six to eight years after the letter may have "got out." But in so controversial a period as the 1790's there is no reason to doubt that if Burke's antagonists ever got a copy of the letter, they would have held onto it indefinitely for a future use. M'Cormick was certainly in touch with some of Burke's antagonists, and could have got his copy from one of them.

If we place side by side the passages which M'Cormick printed, totaling about three pages in all, and the text of the letter as it was finally published in 1844, we can be fairly certain that M'Cormick had access to the opening pages of the letter substantially as it survives. He did not quote every word of those pages, but the parts he omitted were either of no general interest or were the allowances and qualifications by which Burke made his argument more reasonable than M'Cormick wished it to appear. The fact that M'Cormick's quotations are all from the earlier portion makes it a pretty strong probability that he did not have the entire letter. Almost certainly he would have used it all if he had. M'Cormick had no nice theories about keeping his narrative in proportion; when he had full letters he printed them at length; he had far too few as it was to give his biography a proper look of authority.

Only about the first third of the letter as it is printed in *Correspondence* needs to be quoted here to afford a comparison with M'Cormick's passages.

Burke, *Correspondence*

THE RIGHT HON. EDMUND
BURKE TO MONS. DUPONT.
October, 1789.

Dear Sir,

We are extremely happy in your giving us leave to promise ourselves a renewal of the pleasure we formerly had in your company at Beconsfield and in London. It was too lively to be speedily forgotten on our part; and we are highly flattered to find that you keep so exactly in your memory all the particulars of the few attentions which you were so good to accept from us during your stay in England. We indulge ourselves in the hope that you will be able to execute what you intend in our favour; and that we shall be more fortunate in the coming spring, than we were in the last.

You have reason to imagine that I have not been as early as I ought, in acquainting you with my thankful acceptance of the correspondence you have been pleased to offer. Do not think me insensible to the honour you have done me. I confess I did hesitate for a time, on a doubt, whether it would be prudent to yield to my earnest desire of such a correspondence.

M'Cormick, *Memoirs of Edmund Burke*

A near relation and confidential friend of the baron DE MENOU, who afterwards filled the president's chair in the French assembly, had lately opened a correspondence with MR. BURKE, whose opinions upon what was then doing at Paris were eagerly requested by the young statesman. MR. BURKE's answer, which was written in October 1789, and which he then intended to publish, is a masterpiece of deception. Under the shew of the utmost delicacy and diffidence, he half discovers his sentiments, artfully blending them with such principles as no person could easily controvert, but from which he might afterwards draw sophistical inferences, to justify an open disavowal or recantation of his former tenets. With what an air of modesty does he begin this letter, a copy of which is now before us!

Your frank and ingenuous manner of writing would be ill answered by a cold, dry, and guarded reserve on my part. It would, indeed, be adverse to my habits and my nature, to make use of that sort of caution in my intercourse with any friend. Besides, as you are pleased to think that your splendid flame of liberty was first lighted up at my faint and glimmering taper, I thought you had a right to call upon me for my undisguised sentiments on whatever related to that subject. On the other hand, I was not without apprehension, that in this free mode of intercourse I might say something, not only disagreeable to your formed opinions upon points on which, of all others, we are most impatient of contradiction, but not pleasing to the power which should happen to be prevalent at the time of your receiving my letter. I was well aware that, in seasons of jealousy, suspicion is vigilant and active; that it is not extremely scrupulous in its means of inquiry; not perfectly equitable in its judgments; and not altogether deliberate in its resolutions. In the ill-connected and inconclusive logic of the passions, whatever may appear blameable is easily transferred from the guilty writer to the innocent receiver. It is an awkward as well as unpleasant accident; but it is one that has sometimes happened. A man may be made

"As you are pleased," he says to his correspondent, "to think that your splendid flame of liberty was first lighted up at my faint and glimmering taper, you have a right to call upon me for my sentiments on whatever relates to that subject." He then makes an apology for past delay, and goes on thus:

a martyr to tenets the most opposite to his own. At length a friend of mine, lately come from Paris, informed me that heats are beginning to abate, and that intercourse is thought to be more safe. This has given me some courage; and the reflection that the sentiments of a person of no more consideration than I am, either abroad or at home, could be of little consequence to the success of any cause or any party, has at length decided me to accept of the honour you are willing to confer upon me.

You may easily believe, that I have had my eyes turned, with great curiosity, to the astonishing scene now displayed in France. It has certainly given rise in my mind to many reflections, and to some emotions. These are natural and unavoidable; but it would ill become me to be too ready in forming a positive opinion upon matters transacted in a country, with the correct political map of which I must be very imperfectly acquainted. Things, indeed, have already happened so much beyond the scope of all speculation, that persons of infinitely more sagacity than I am, ought to be ashamed of any thing like confidence in their reasoning upon the operation of any principle, or the effect of any measure. It would become me, least of all, to be so confident, who ought, at my time of life, to have

"You may easily believe, that I have had my eyes turned with great curiosity, and no small concernment, to the astonishing scene now displayed in France. It has certainly given rise in my mind to many reflexions, and to some emotions. These are natural and unavoidable; but it would ill become me to be too ready in forming a positive opinion upon matters transacted in a country, with the correct political map of which I must be very imperfectly acquainted. Things, indeed, have already happened so much beyond the scope of all speculation, that persons of infinitely more sagacity than I am, ought to be ashamed of any thing like confidence in reasoning upon the operation of any principle, or the effect of any measure. It would become me least of all to be so confident, who ought, at my time of life, to have well

well learned the important lesson of self-distrust,—a lesson of no small value in company with the best information, but which alone can make any sort of amends for our not having learned other lessons so well as it was our business to learn them. I beg you, once for all, to apply this corrective of the diffidence I have, on my own judgment, to whatever I may happen to say with more positiveness than suits my knowledge and situation. If I should seem any where to express myself in the language of disapprobation, be so good as to consider it as no more than the expression of doubt.

You hope, sir, that I think the French deserving of liberty. I certainly do. I certainly think that all men who desire it, deserve it. It is not the reward of our merit, or the acquisition of our industry. It is our inheritance. It is the birthright of our species. We cannot forfeit our right to it, but by what forfeits our title to the privileges of our kind. I mean the abuse, or oblivion, of our rational faculties, and a ferocious indocility which makes us prompt to wrong and violence, destroys our social nature, and transforms us into something little better than the description of wild beasts. To men so degraded, a state of strong constraint is a sort of necessary substitute for freedom; since, bad as it is, it may deliver them in some measure from the worst of all slavery,—that

learned the important lesson of self-distrust,—a lesson of no small value in company with the best information,—but which, alone, can make any sort of amends for our not having learned other lessons so well as it was our business to learn them. I beg you, once for all, to apply this corrective of diffidence in my own judgment to whatever I may happen to say with more positiveness than suits my knowledge and situation. Never suppose that any appearance that I may shew of disapprobation to what is now transacted is meant to express more than a doubt. We have but one advantage over you in France—we are nearer to the character of cool byestanders."

This introduction is perfectly of a piece with the fallacious principles that follow. We call them *fallacious*, because they may be twisted and turned to any side of the question which a subtle reasoner might find it his interest to adopt. "You hope, sir," continues Mr. Burke, "that I think the French deserving of liberty. I certainly do. I certainly think that all men who desire it, deserve it. It is not the reward of our merit, or the acquisition of our industry. It is our inheritance. It is the birthright of our species. We cannot forfeit our right to it, but by what forfeits our title to the privileges of our kind, I mean the abuse or oblivion of our national faculties; and a ferocious is, the despotism of their own blind and brutal passions.

You have kindly said, that you began to love freedom from your intercourse with me. Permit me then to continue our conversation, and to tell you what the freedom is that I love, and that to which I think all men entitled. This is the more necessary, because, of all the loose terms in the world, liberty is the most indefinite. It is not solitary, unconnected, individual, selfish liberty, as if every man was to regulate the whole of his conduct by his own will. The liberty I mean is *social* freedom. It is that state of things in which liberty is secured by the equality of restraint. A constitution of things in which the liberty of no one man, and no body of men, and no number of men, can find means to trespass on the liberty of any person, or any description of persons, in the society. This kind of liberty is, indeed, but another name for justice; ascertained by wise laws, and secured by well-constructed institutions. I am sure that liberty, so incorporated, and in a manner identified with justice, must be infinitely dear to every one who is capable of conceiving what it is. But whenever a separation is made between liberty and justice, neither is, in my opinion, safe. I do not believe that men ever did submit, certain I am that they

indocility, which makes us prompt to wrong and violence, destroys our social nature, and transforms us into something little better than the description of wild beasts. To men so degraded, a state of strong constraint is a sort of necessary substitute for freedom; since, bad as it is, it may deliver them, in some measure, from the worst of all slavery, that is the despotism of their own blind and brutal passions. You have kindly said, that you began to love freedom from your intercourse with me. Permit me then to continue our conversation, and to tell you what the freedom is that I love. It is not solitary, unconnected, individual, selfish liberty. It is social freedom. It is that state of things, in which the liberty of no man and no body of men is in a condition to trespass on the liberty of any person, or any description of persons in society. This kind of liberty is, indeed, but another name for justice, ascertained by wise laws, and secured by well-constructed institutions. I am sure that liberty, so incorporated, and in a manner identified with justice, must be infinitely dear to every man who is capable of conceiving what it is. But whenever a separation is made between liberty and justice, neither is, in my opinion, safe. I do not believe, that men ever did submit, certain I am that they never

never ought to have submitted, to the arbitrary pleasure of one man; but, under circumstances in which the arbitrary pleasure of many persons in the community pressed with an intolerable hardship upon the just and equal rights of their fellows, such a choice might be made, as among evils. The moment *will* is set above reason and justice, in any community, a great question may arise in sober minds, in what part or portion of the community that dangerous dominion of *will* may be the least mischievously placed.

If I think all men who cultivate justice, entitled to liberty, and, when joined in states, entitled to a constitution framed to perpetuate and secure it, you may be assured, sir, that I think your countrymen eminently worthy of a blessing which is peculiarly adapted to noble, generous, and humane natures. Such I found the French, when, more than fifteen years ago, I had the happiness, though but for too short a time, of visiting your country; and I trust their character is not altered since that period.

I have nothing to check my wishes towards the establishment of a solid and rational scheme of liberty in France. On the subject of the relative power of nations, I may have my prejudices; but I envy internal freedom, security, and good order,

ought to have submitted, to the arbitrary pleasure of one man, but under circumstances, in which the arbitrary pleasure of many persons in the community pressed with an intolerable hardship upon the just and equal rights of their fellows. Such a choice might be made as among evils. The moment *will* is set above reason and justice in any community, a great question may arise in sober minds, in what part or portion of the community that dangerous dominion of *will* may be the least mischievously placed."

Let us now see how cautiously he applies his general principle to the particular case of the French. "If," says he, "I think all men who cultivate justice entitled to liberty, and, when joined in states, entitled to a constitution framed to perpetuate and secure it; you may be assured, sir, that I think your countrymen eminently worthy of a blessing, which, good as it is for all, is peculiarly adapted to noble, generous, and humane natures. Such I found the French, when, more than fifteen years ago, I had the happiness, though but for a short time, of visiting your country; and I trust their character is not altered since I had the means of observing it more nearly than I am able to do at present. I have nothing to check my wishes towards the establishment of a solid to none. When, therefore, I shall learn that, in France, the citizen, by whatever description he is qualified, is in a perfect state of legal security, with regard to his life,—to his property,—to the uncontrolled disposal of his person,—to the free use of his industry and his faculties:—When I hear that he is protected in the beneficial enjoyment of the estates to which, by the course of settled law, he was born, or is provided with a fair compensation for them; —that he is maintained in the full fruition of the advantages belonging to the state and condition of life in which he had lawfully engaged himself, or is supplied with a substantial, equitable, equivalent:—When I am assured that a simple citizen may decently express his sentiments upon public affairs, without hazard to his life or safety, even though against a predominant and fashionable opinion:—When I know all this of France, I shall be as well pleased as every one must be, who has not forgot the general communion of mankind, nor lost his natural sympathy, in local and accidental connexions.

and rational scheme of liberty in France. On the subject of the relative power of nations I may have prejudices; but I envy internal freedom, security, and good order to none. When, therefore, I shall learn, that in France, the citizen, by whatever description he is qualified, is in a perfect state of legal security, with regard to his life, to his property, to the uncontrolled disposal of his person, to the free use of his industry and his faculties;—when I hear, that he is protected in the beneficial enjoyment of the estates, to which by the course of settled law he was born, or is provided with a fair compensation for them; that he is maintained in the full fruition of the advantages belonging to the state and condition of life, in which he had lawfully engaged himself, or is supplied with an equitable equivalent;—when I am assured that a simple citizen may decently express his sentiments upon public affairs, without hazard to his life or safety, even though against a predominant and fashionable opinion;—when I know all this of France, I shall be as well pleased as every one must be, who has not forgot the general communion of mankind, nor lost his natural sympathy in local and accidental connexions."

APPENDIX B

M'CORMICK'S QUOTATIONS FROM A SECOND LETTER OF BURKE'S

M'Cormick immediately followed his first set of excerpts, from the letter of October, 1789, by excerpts from another letter which he said was addressed to the "same correspondent." This letter has never been printed entire, so that M'Cormick's excerpts are our only proof of its existence. Style and content leave virtually no doubt that it is genuinely by Burke. Indeed it is one of his important compositions. Passages in it anticipate the famous assault on Rousseau in the *Letter to a Member of the National Assembly*, as well as the famous tribute to Montesquieu in the *Appeal from the New to the Old Whigs*.

One can only guess at the date of this letter. Its contents make it clear that it was written after the so-called Insurrection of Women on October 5–6, 1789, which brought Louis XVI and Marie Antoinette from Versailles to Paris. One or two phrases suggest that that insurrection was still a recent event at the time the letter was written. Burke says: "Were the King to escape from his palace, where he is now, in reality, a prisoner with his wife and almost his whole family . . ." He refers to "those horrid deeds, which surely have not been misrepresented to us." Both phrases make it sound as if he were speaking of fairly fresh news.

If we can conclude from such hints that the letter was written as early as late October or early November, we might fairly assume it to be the "short letter" mentioned in the preface of the *Reflections*. That "short letter" was written, the preface says, at the time Burke first felt it safe to forward the longer letter he wrote in October. It is naturally of some significance that M'Cormick, who had access to at least the early pages of the letter of October also had access to this letter to the "same correspondent."

"The best comment on all this canting, the best elucidation of Mr. BURKE's real design in laying down such doctrines, appears in a second letter addressed to the same correspondent, but intended, as well as the former, for the people of England. We shall soon be able to trace the cause of their not having been printed; but let us first insert a few extracts from the latter. After some compliments on the taste, judgment, and genius of his young friend, he throws off a great part of the reserve and disguise, which he had before thought necessary; and says, 'With regard to the state of things in France, I am afraid that, as matters appear to me at present, I cannot at all agree with you, until at least my information is as good as yours. I hope you do not think me weak enough to form my opinion of what is doing there upon the representations in newspapers, much less upon those of the newspapers of a country in which the true spirit of the several transactions cannot be generally known. English newspapers, however, do not, I believe, lead the opinions of people here; but, as I conceive, rather follow the current of the notions most prevalent. As for me, I have read, and with some attention, the authorised, or rather the equally authentic documents on this subject, from the first instructions to the representatives of the several orders down to this time. What else I have read has been for the greater part on the side of those who have a considerable share in the formation and conduct of public measures. A great many of the most decisive events, I conceive, are not disputed as facts, though, as usual, there is some dispute about their causes, and their tendency. On comparing the whole of fact, of public document, and of what can be discerned of the general temper of the French people, I perfectly agree with you that there is very little likelihood of the old government's regaining its former authority. Were the king to escape from his palace where he is now in reality a prisoner with his wife and almost his whole family, to what place could he fly? Every town in France is a Paris. I see no way, by which a second revolution can be accomplished. The only chance seems to consist in the extreme instability of every species of power, and the uncertainty of every kind of speculation. In this I agree with you; in most other particulars I can by no means go so far. That a police is established at Paris, I can readily believe. They have an army, as I hear, of six thousand men, apparently under their command. They have some militia too in pretty constant service; and this militia may be augmented to almost any given number for any exigency. They have the means of preserving quiet; and since they have completely obtained their ends, they must have the disposition. A total anarchy is a self-destructive thing. But if the same ends should hereafter require the same courses, which have been already pursued, there is no doubt but the same ferocious delight in murder and the same savage cruelty will be again renewed. If any of those horrid deeds, which surely have not been misrepresented to us, were the acts of the rulers, what are we to think of an armed people under such rulers? Or if, (which possibly may be the case) there is in reality and substance no ruler, and that the chiefs are driven before the people rather than lead them; and if the armed corps are composed of men who have no fixed principle of obedience, and are embodied only by the prevalence of some general inclination; who can repute himself safe among a people so furious and senseless? As to the destruction of the *Bastile*, of which you speak, we both know it was a thing in itself of no consequence whatever. The *Bastile* was at first intended as a citadel undoubtedly; and when it was built, it might serve the purposes of a citadel. Of late, in that view, it was ridiculous. It could not contain any garrison sufficient to awe such a city as Paris. As a prison, it was of as little importance. Give despotism, and the prisons of despotism will not be wanting, any more than lamp-irons will be wanting to democratic fury.' Mr. Burke, and his correspondent, and every man of the least capacity in Europe, must have been convinced, that the destruction of the *Bastile* was an event of the greatest consequence. That fortress of despotism had been deemed impregnable; and when the report of its being taken reached Versailles, it was universally discredited by all the poor, cowardly, debilitated *reptiles that burrowed under the throne,* and had no idea of the giant powers of *freemen.* But when the intelligence was confirmed, they fled in despair, and abandoned to his fate the weak monarch who had been the dupe of their pernicious counsels. Even marshal Broglio turned pale as death, and gave up every thing for lost, when he saw the flag of liberty displayed over the ruins of those dungeons contrived by despotism to gratify its capricious cruelty, and to extinguish in their first glow all the vital sparks of public spirit.

"But Mr. Burke's strongest objection to the great arch of national freedom, which the French were then erecting, was, he confesses, its not being fashioned upon any *old model,* but partly upon *establishments lately made,* and partly upon the *rights of man.* 'In all appearance,' he tells his friend, 'the new system is a most bungling, and unworkmanlike performance. I confess I see no principle of coherence, co-operation, or just subordination of parts in this whole project, nor any the least aptitude to the condition and wants of the state to which it is applied, nor any thing well imagined for the formation, provision, or direction of a common force. The direct contrary appears to me. *I think it carries evident marks of the incurable ignorance of this most unenlightened age, the least qualified for legislation that perhaps has been since the first formation of civil society.*' Yet TOM PAINE thinks this to be *the age of reason;* but what is the opinion of PAINE or of the rest of the world, when opposed to that of a man, who mounting the tribunal of superlative conceit and arrogance, passes sentence upon all his contemporaries of the human race, and consigns them to incurable ignorance and stupidity!

"There was one principle of nature, however, which Mr. BURKE says, the French legislators could not entirely overthrow. 'Man is a gregarious animal. He will by degrees provide some convenience suitable to this his natural disposition; and this strange thing may, some time or other, assume a more habitable form. The fish will at length make a shell which will fit him. I beg pardon for dwelling so long and employing so much thought upon a subject, on which its contrivers have evidently employed so little. I cannot,' he adds, 'think with you, that the assembly have done much. They have, indeed, *undone* a great deal, and so completely broken up their country as a state, that I assure you, there are few here such *antigallicans* as not to feel some pity on the deplorable view of the wreck of France.' [Was there any *malice in this compassion?*] 'I confess to you that, till I saw it, I could not conceive that any men in public could have shewn so little mercy to their country. You say, my dear sir, that they read MONTESQUIEU—I believe not. If they do, they do not understand him.' [How should Frenchmen, convicted of *incurable ignorance,* understand a book, though written in their own language, without the aid of Mr. BURKE's preternatural light?] 'He is often obscure; sometimes misled by system; but, on the whole, a learned, and ingenious writer, and sometimes a most profound thinker. Sure it is, that they have not followed him in any one thing·they have done. Had he lived at this time, he would certainly be among the fugitives from France. With regard to the other writers you speak of, I do believe the directors of the present system to be influenced by them. Such masters, such scholars. Who ever dreamt of VOLTAIRE and

ROUSSEAU as legislators? The first has the merit of writing agreeably; and nobody has ever united blasphemy and obscenity so happily together. The other was not a little deranged in his intellects, to my almost certain knowledge.' [Mr. BURKE had studied insanity, till he himself became almost insane, and looked upon every body as a fool, or a madman, who happened to differ from him in opinion.] 'But he [ROUSSEAU] saw things in bold and uncommon lights, and he was very eloquent—But as to the rest!—I have read long since the *Contrat Social.* It has left very few traces upon my mind. I thought it a performance of little or no merit; and little did I conceive, that it could ever make revolutions, and give law to nations. But so it is. I see some people here are willing that we should become their scholars too, and reform our state on the French model. They have begun; and it is high time for those who wish to preserve *morem majorum,* to look about them.' Mr. BURKE *did look about him;* but it was for a specious opportunity of deserting his old friends, and publishing to the world his deceitful opinions. It was not long before such an opportunity presented itself. . . ."

APPENDIX C

THE TWO VERSIONS OF BURKE'S LETTER TO HIS TRANSLATOR

The authorized edition of Burke's *Correspondence* published in 1844 included a letter of Burke's to "Mons. Dupont," whom the editors identified as the translator of the *Reflections.* The letter was dated October 28, 1790, that is, three days before the *Reflections* was published. It is a letter of considerable interest, recording a difference of opinion between Burke and the translator. Apparently Monsieur Dupont, though he was enough in sympathy with Burke's purposes to undertake the task of translation, had a mind of his own and was not to be wholly swept away by the force of impassioned argument. On one point in particular he thought Burke in the wrong. Burke had treated the character of Henry IV of France with far less reverence than most Frenchmen were then taught to expect. Actually he had said nothing altogether defamatory; he had only pointed out that besides being a humane and benevolent prince, Henry had been attentive to the preservation of his own power, and had not hesitated to shed the blood of his subjects in defense of what he regarded as his own rights. This struck Monsieur Dupont as too cold-blooded a judgment to pass upon one of the chief idols of prerevolutionary France. He wrote to Burke protesting against the harshness of certain of the expressions used. The letter of October 28 was Burke's reply.

So much of the story can be derived from the simple text of the letter as it appears in the *Correspondence* of 1844. There is, however, a little more to be told. In the first edition of Prior's *Life of Burke,* published in 1824, Burke's letter to his translator was also printed, prefaced by the statement: "The following letter by Mr. Burke, which does not appear in his Works, or in any other volumes connected with him, was addressed to M. Dupont . . ." When we examine the text of Prior's letter, however, we discover that though in all its main outlines it resembles the text as printed in *Correspondence,* there are many small changes in the language, as well as several small omissions and some insertions. We note too that Prior's version is not dated October 28, 1790, but rather January 2, 1791.

The two dates rather strongly suggest a reason for the two versions of the letter, namely, that one is the original, as Burke wrote and sent it, and the other a revision for publication. Purely in terms of chronology such a hypothetical explanation can be made fairly plausible. If Burke wrote and sent the letter first on October 28—not at all unlikely—he could easily have kept a copy with an eye to eventual publication. The great rush of activity which began for him with the appearance and instantaneous success of the *Reflections* at the beginning of November would be an explanation of the fact that he did not arrange publication at once. Parliament convened on November 25, and between claims upon him as an active statesman and other claims as the author of a best seller his time was fairly well disposed of. It was only with the Christmas recess of Parliament that Burke had any time to return to his unfinished French affairs. This he tells us himself. At the end of the *Letter to a Member of the National Assembly,* which bears the date of January 19, 1791, he apologizes to his correspondent for having neglected to answer his letter of November 17: "I have been somewhat occupied since I was honored with your letter; and I should not have been able to answer it at all, but for the holidays, which have given me means of enjoying the leisure of the country." Burke's conception of the "leisure of the country" would astonish many people. The *Letter to a Member of the National Assembly* is not so much a letter as a good-sized pamphlet; in Burke's *Works* it runs to fifty-three pages. We also know of two other important letters to French correspondents which were composed in this period; together they run to ten pages in Burke's *Correspondence*.

It would appear, then, that it was in a period dedicated chiefly to French affairs that Burke returned to his letter of October 28. Probably he not only revised it but got it into print at this time, in a newspaper or other periodical; when many months later it appeared in a pamphlet, together with another letter of Burke's, the publisher's advertisement declared that both letters had "been in some of the daily prints."

Probably Prior encountered this one there. His version, dated "Beaconsfield, January 2d, 1791," gives us a fair guess at the date of the first publication. January 2 was a Sunday; Burke must have sent his revision off to be printed in the papers of the following week.

This recital of events, though confessedly based on inference, is strongly supported by what we observe when we study the two versions of the letter side by side. The version of October 28, besides bearing the earlier date, bears several signs of having been intended for a private rather than a public audience. It contains references to Burke's expectation of sending the letter by the hand of his son; these are absent from the version of January 2. It contains sharp, perhaps too unguarded, expressions, such as "blanc mange" to describe the routine flatteries with which Henry IV treated his nobles; these are banished from the other version, sometimes at a sacrifice of vigor. The changes of emphasis from one version to the other seem to be made systematically, and always on considerations which make the letter of January 2 more appropriate to public use.

Seeing the two versions side by side may do more, however, than convince us that one of them is an alteration of the other. There is a value in being reminded that Burke waged his antirevolutionary campaign with more deliberation than at first appears. As we read the *Reflections*, the *Letter to a Member of the National Assembly*, or indeed almost any of Burke's writings on France, it is easy to catch the tone of anger and alarm which they all have, and conclude that they were written and published in a white heat of excitement. A qualification should be made. It is altogether likely that while Burke was working upon these tracts he was often in a state of passionate excitement. It does not follow, however, that the publication of the tracts was ill considered or even hasty. Probably the exact opposite was true. By the time the French letters were written Burke had made up his own mind how he felt about the principles of the French Revolution and the dangers with which they threatened the order of society. He wanted those principles publicly discussed. The *Reflections* and the letters and tracts he wrote early in 1791 were not merely angry denunciations of the principles of the Revolution; they were intended as challenges and provocations. Burke was waving red flags to lure the proponents of revolution out into the arena.

It is in the light of such a reading of Burke's purposes that one should analyse the two versions of the letter to his translator. They are a small part of a large controversy. Burke had published the *Reflections* two months before January 2, when we think the letter to his translator was printed. Then it was time to add more fuel to the fires! What he had to say about Henry IV was obviously provocative, especially to Frenchmen. It was intended to be; it would bring a few more people into the controversy. When the excitement might have died down again, the *Letter to a Member of the National Assembly* was on hand as a fresh challenge. By the time that had spent its force the *Appeal from the New to the Old Whigs* (a 150-page pamphlet) was coming out. The whole series, from the *Reflections* to the *Appeal*, was published within a period of about nine months, during which the controversy Burke had initiated gradually developed into the greatest ideological struggle ever carried on in England.

Burke, *Correspondence*

Prior, *Life of Burke*

[The following letter by Mr. Burke, which does not appear in his Works, or in any other volumes connected with him, was addressed to M. Dupont, who complained that the character given of this great monarch in the "Reflections," was somewhat harsh. The passage in question runs thus: "Henry of Navarre was a politic and active prince. He possessed indeed great humanity and mildness; but an humanity and mildness that never stood in the way of his interests. He never sought to be loved without first putting himself in a way to be feared. He used soft language with determined conduct. He asserted and maintained his humanity in the gross, and distributed his acts of concession only in the detail. He spent the income of his prerogative nobly, but he took care not to break in upon the capital; never abandoning for a moment any of the claims which he made under the fundamental laws, nor sparing to shed the blood of those who opposed him, often in the field, sometimes upon the scaffold."]

THE RIGHT HON. EDMUND
BURKE TO MONS. DUPONT.
October 28, 1790.

MY DEAR SIR,
I have just now received your kind letter of yesterday. I send my answer by my son, who is going to town, and will have the happiness of seeing you and thanking you, in all our names, for your goodness towards us.

You wish me to reconsider the words I have used concerning Henry the Fourth of France, in page 208 of my letter, "never abandoning for a moment any of the claims which he made under the fundamental laws, nor sparing to shed the blood of those who opposed him, often in the field, sometimes on the scaffold." The austerity of this description you wish a little softened. I am not surprised at your request. From your

"SIR,
"Yesterday I had the honour of receiving your letter, in which you desire that I may revise and soften the expressions which I have made use of concerning Henry IV. King of France. I am not at all surprised

infancy you have seen nothing brought forward in the portrait of that prince, but his mildness and be-nignity. His character of vigilance and vigour, which he displayed at least equally, and without which he had ill-deserved the name of Great, is thrown entirely into the shade, and in a manner disappears. The policy of this proceeding is evident enough. The name of Henry the Fourth was deservedly popular. The kings of France were proud of their descent from that hero. It was upon his example they were to form them-selves. The conspirators against them, and against all law, religion, and order, endeavoured, under the sanction of that venerated name, to persuade their king to abandon all the precautions of power against the designs of ambition; and having thus persuaded him to disarm him-self, they were resolved to deliver him, as well as his nobility, his clergy, and his magistrates, the natu-ral supports of his throne, into the hands of robbers and assassins. The general plot was laid long ago. It was to be pursued according to cir-cumstances; and this method of hanging out the picture of Henry the Fourth in profile, was one of the instruments in that truly traitor-ous design, of laying traps for men, and baiting them with their virtues.

at your request, for, since your childhood, you have heard every one talk of the pleasing manners and mild temper of that prince. Those qualities have shaded, and al-most obliterated, that vigilance and vigour without which he would never have either merited or en-joyed the title of Great. The inten-tion of this is self-evident. The name of Henry IV. recalls the idea of his popularity; the Sovereigns of France are proud to have descended from this hero, and are taught to look up to him as to a model. It is under the shelter of his venerable name that all the conspirators against the laws, against religion, and against good order, have dared to persuade their King that he ought to abandon all the precautions of power to the designs of ambition. After having thus disarmed, they have resolved to deliver their Sovereign, his no-bility, and his magistrates (the natu-ral supporters of his throne), into the hands of thieves and of assassins. It is a long time since this plot was first formed. It was resolved to put it into execution according to cir-cumstances; and the mode adopted of everywhere suspending the por-traits of Henry IV., was one of the means employed for the success of the design—a means truly perfidious, as it holds out snares to the unwary, and catches mankind by the bait of their own virtues.

Whenever that politic prince made any of his flattering speeches, as he often did, he took care that they should not be construed too literally. It was, I think, at some sort of assembly of notables, that he talked of resigning himself entirely into their hands; but when he served them with this, and the rest of his *blanc-mange*, of which he was sufficiently liberal, he attended at the table, as he expressed himself, with his hand upon his sword. Men whose power is envied, and against whose very being desperate factions exist, cannot be safely good upon any other terms. Trajan, Marcus Aurelius, every man in that situation who could dare to be virtuous, enjoyed that arduous and critical prerogative, by religiously securing the means of supporting the consideration and authority, by which alone he was able to display his beneficence. In that position a prince may, with great security, and often with as great wisdom as glory, divide his authority with his people; because he has an authority to divide at his discretion, and not merely to surrender. Otherwise, in an arrangement and distribution of power, he will not be able to reserve any thing; and he can have no merit in his concessions. But whatever the honour of such a voluntary partition may be, or whatever the policy of making it a sacrifice to circumstances, Henry

"Every time that this politic Prince had occasion to deliver one of his insinuating harangues (which was very often), he took particular care not to be too literal in his expressions. It was, I suppose, to a kind of assembly of notables that he spoke of his design to free himself entirely from their restraint. But when he employed these courtly threats, of which by the bye he was very liberal, he advanced his right foot, and, as he himself says, 'always clapped his hand upon the hilt of his sword.' Those men whose power is envied, and against whom violent factions are formed, cannot with safety be good in any other manner. Trajan, Marcus Aurelius, and all others in similar situations, who have dared to be virtuous, could never have enjoyed this arduous and critical pre-eminence but by inviolably pursuing all the means in their power of attracting respect, and of sustaining their authority. Without this, they could not have exercised their benevolence. In such a situation a Prince may with safety, and with as much sagacity as glory, divide his authority with his people, because then he has the power to divide it at his discretion, and is not forced to abandon it.

"Whatever may be the honour annexed to such a voluntary division, whatever may be the political motive that can induce a Sovereign to the Fourth did neither the one nor the other. He never made any partition whatsoever of his power. What I have said of him is strictly true. Did he abandon, to any judgment of the people of Paris, his claim, by the fundamental constitution of the kingdom, to be their master and their sovereign lord? Did he ever come to any compromise with them, relative to his title? Which, in the long catalogue of the unbounded prerogatives exercised by the kings of France, justly or unjustly claimed, did he surrender, or abridge, or even submit to define? He would have been still more glorious, if, after his conquest and his purchase of his kingdom, he had done this, and made himself the founder of a regular constitution. But whether he was in a condition to entitle himself to this true glory, or whether he could have taken any steps towards it at that time, with more safety than has been attempted lately, is what, upon the face of historical facts, I am not able to determine to my own satisfaction. But is it most probable that he never thought of any such thing; and if you read the memoirs of Sully attentively, and will suppose that the sentiments of the minister were not greatly at variance with those of his master, you will soon observe how much they were both of them royalists, in a very large sense of the word;

make such a sacrifice in certain cases, Henry IV. neither did the one nor the other; he never in any manner whatever parted with an atom of his authority. Did he ever leave it to the judgment of the citizens of Paris to determine the right which the laws of the kingdom gave him, of being their King and their Sovereign? Did they ever enter into any treaty with him concerning his title to the throne? Where is there in the long catalogue of the unlimited prerogatives of the King of France (be they just or unjust) an article which he ever abandoned, limited, or even submitted to inquiry? He would have been still more illustrious, if after having purchased and conquered his kingdom he had done this, and if he had become the founder of a regular constitution. Historical facts have not furnished me with the means of deciding in a proper manner, if ever he found himself in a situation to acquire this glory, or if he then could have made any attempts of that kind, with a greater degree of safety than has been done on a recent occasion. But it is very probable that he never had any of this kind. If you read the Memoirs of Sully with attention (and I suppose that the opinions of the Minister differed little from those of his master), you will easily perceive that they were both royalists in all the extent of and how little partial to any other mode of government.

As to his shedding blood;—not one drop, to be sure, beyond what was necessary for the support of that title which he never would submit to any sort of popular decision; but every drop which that necessity demanded, he did shed. How many bloody battles did he fight against the far greater majority of the people of France? How many towns did he sack and plunder? Was his minister and favourite ashamed to take the share of pillage that had fallen into his hands? It is true that he winked at the relief which a set of poor famished wretches gave to themselves, by gathering, at the hazard of their lives, a few ears of corn beneath the walls of his capital, whilst he held it under a strict blockade. I approve of this, but I look upon it with no enthusiastic admiration. He had been almost a monster in cruelty, as well as a driveller in policy, if he had done otherwise than he did.

But if he was thus indulgent to a few dozens of starving people, it cannot be forgotten that it was he who starved them by hundreds of thousands, before he could be in a condition to bestow this scanty mercy to a few of the miserable individuals. He certainly, in starving Paris, availed himself of the law of war, fairly, but he availed himself

the expression, and, with some few exceptions, they constantly maintained that species of government.

"As to the blood that Henry shed, he never spilt one drop more than was necessary for the maintenance of his *right*, which he on no occasion would submit to any species of popular decision; he however could *kill* when it was necessary. How many bloody battles did he not fight against the majority of the French nation? How many cities did he not sack and pillage? Was his Minister ashamed of sharing the booty that fell into his hands? It is true, that while closely besieging his own capital, he relieved and protected the unfortunate families who, at the peril of their lives, sallied forth to gather a scanty harvest under the walls of this very capital. I approve this conduct, but it does not inspire me with an enthusiastic admiration. He would have almost been a monster in cruelty, and an idiot in politics, had he done otherwise. But while he was so compassionate to a few wretches dying of hunger, one cannot forget that it was he himself who famished them by hundreds and by thousands, before he was in a situation to treat thus compassionately a few isolated individuals. It is true, indeed, that in starving Paris he did nothing but what was conformable to the right of war; but that was a right which he enforced in all its of that law to the full. The act of mercy was his temper and his policy; the famine he caused was his necessity. But can you bear the panegyrics of Henry the Fourth, relative to the siege of Paris, when you consider the late scarcity, and all the transactions in consequence of it? But on this I say nothing more; though I think it must fill every honest heart with indignation and horror.

plenitude. He followed the dictates of his heart and of his policy in the acts of compassion attributed to him; as to the famine which he occasioned, it was in consequence of the position of his army. But can you support the panegyrists of Henry IV. in regard to this very siege of Paris, when you recollect the late deplorable scarcity, and, above all, what has been done in consequence of that unhappy epoch? Of the occurrences that followed I shall not speak at present, although I think that that ought to be done to inspire every honest heart with horror and indignation.

As to the "scaffold;"—whether Henry the Fourth could have saved the Mareschal Biron with prudence, instead of beheading, in the Bastile, a man to whom and to whose father he owed pretty serious obligations, it is impossible at this day to settle. That prince was less distinguished for gratitude than clemency, but he never did shed blood without great cause. I suppose he acted as was best for his people and his throne. But we must agree, that if he had saved that rash, impetuous man, he could not be much censured for such an act of mercy. However, if he thought that M. de Biron was capable of bringing on such scenes as we have lately beheld, and of producing the same anarchy, confusion, and distress in his kingdom,

"As to the 'scaffold,' it is impossible to decide at this moment whether it would not have been more prudent for Henry IV. to have saved the Marechal de Biron, instead of cutting off his head within the walls of the Bastille. He was under great obligations to this Marechal of France, as well as to his father; but Henry was less remarkable for his gratitude than his clemency. As he never shed blood but for just reasons, I suppose that he thought himself obliged to do it then, on account of the good of his people and the security of his throne. It must be allowed, however, that if he had pardoned this rash and impetuous man, he would never have been reproached with this act of commiseration. If he imagined that the as preliminary to the establishment of that humiliating as well as vexatious tyranny, we now see on the point of being settled, under the name of a constitution, in France, he did well,—very well,—to cut him off in the crude and immature infancy of his treasons.

He would not have deserved the crown which he wore, and wore with so much glory, if he had scrupled, by all the preventive mercy of rigorous law, to punish those traitors and enemies of their country and of mankind. For, believe me, there is no virtue where there is no wisdom. A great, enlarged, protecting, and preserving benevolence has it, not in its accidents and circumstances, but in its very essence, to exterminate vice, and disorder, and oppression from the world. Goodness spares infirmity. Nothing but weakness is tender of the crimes that connect themselves with power, in the destruction of the religion, laws, polity, morals, industry, liberty, and prosperity of your country. Henry the Fourth, if he had had such men as his subjects, would have done his duty, I doubt not. The present king is in the place of the victim, not of the avenger, of these

Marechal de Biron was capable of some of those scenes which we have lately seen exhibited in your kingdom; if he supposed that he might produce the same anarchy, the same confusion, and the same distress, as the preliminaries to a humiliating and vexatious tyranny, which we are on the point of beholding in France under the name of a Constitution; it was right, very right, to cut, on its very formation, the very first thread of so many treasons!

"He would never have merited the crown that he acquired, and which he wore with so much glory, if, interposing his compassion to defeat the preservative effects of a severe execution, he had scrupled to punish those traitors and enemies of their country, and of the human race; for, believe me, there can be no virtue where there is no wisdom. Weakness only, that is to say, the parent and ally of crimes, would have allowed itself to be affected by misdeeds, which have a connexion with power, and which aim at the usurpation of a certain degree of authority. To pardon such enemies, is to do the same thing as those who attempt the destruction of religion, of the laws, of policy, of morality, of industry, of liberty, and of the prosperity of your country. If Henry IV. had such subjects as those who rule France at this very moment, he would do nothing more crimes. That he did not prevent them with the early vigour, activity, and foresight of an Henry the Fourth, is rather his misfortune than his offence. He has, I hear and believe, a good natural understanding, as well as a mild and benevolent heart, and these are the rudiments of virtue. But he was born in purple, and of course was not made to a situation which would have tried a virtue most fully perfected. By what steps, by what men, by what means, on what pretexts, through what projects, by what series of mistakes, and miscalculations of all kinds, he has been brought to the state in which he is obliged to appear as a sort of instrument in the ruin of his country, is a subject for history.

This is what I have been led to trouble you with, in consequence of your letter. My son, whom I intended as the bearer of this, was obliged to go off immediately after breakfast; so I send this by the post. You may print it, as an appendix to your translation, or in any way you please; or keep it only for your private satisfaction, as you like.

Most truly, my dear sir,
Your obliged and obedient humble servant,

EDM. BURKE

than his duty in punishing them. The present Sovereign is in the situation of a victim, and not the avenger of rebellion. It is rather a misfortune than a crime, that he has not prevented this revolution with that vigorous precaution, that activity, and that momentary decision, which characterized Henry IV. Louis XVI., according to what I hear and believe, has received from nature as perfect an understanding, and a heart as soft and humane, as his illustrious ancestor. These are, indeed, the elements of virtue; but he was born under the canopy of a throne, and was not prepared by adversity for a situation, the trials of which the most perfect and the most absolute virtue could have scarce resisted.

"As to the men, the means, the pretexts, the projects, the consequences arising from false plans and false calculations of every nature and every species, which have reduced this Sovereign to appear in no better light than an instrument for the ruin of his country—these are circumstances to be recorded and commented on by the historian. —These remarks, Sir, have been occasioned by reading your letter; you may print them as an appendix to your work, or in whatever manner you please; or you may keep them for your own private satisfac-

tion. I leave it entirely to your discretion.

"I am, Sir,

   "Your very humble servant,
      "E. BURKE.

"Beaconsfield, January 2d, 1791."

INDEX

ST. MARY'S COLLEGE OF MARYLAND
ST. MARY'S CITY, MARYLAND

41064